Scripture and Song in Nineteenth-Century Britain

Scripture and Song in Nineteenth-Century Britain

Edited by
James Grande and Brian H. Murray

BLOOMSBURY ACADEMIC
NEW YORK • LONDON • OXFORD • NEW DELHI • SYDNEY

BLOOMSBURY ACADEMIC
Bloomsbury Publishing Inc, 1385 Broadway, New York, NY 10018, USA
Bloomsbury Publishing Plc, 50 Bedford Square, London, WC1B 3DP, UK
Bloomsbury Publishing Ireland, 29 Earlsfort Terrace, Dublin 2, D02 AY28, Ireland

BLOOMSBURY, BLOOMSBURY ACADEMIC and the Diana
logo are trademarks of Bloomsbury Publishing Plc

First published in the United States of America 2024
This paperback edition published 2025

Copyright © James Grande and Brian H. Murray, 2024
Each chapter copyright © by the contributor, 2024

For legal purposes the Acknowledgements on p. vii constitute
an extension of this copyright page.

Cover design: Louise Dugdale
Cover image: Hosannah!, After Simeon Solomon (British, London
1840–1905 London), Anonymous Gift, 1926, Met Museum.

All rights reserved. No part of this publication may be: i) reproduced or
transmitted in any form, electronic or mechanical, including photocopying,
recording or by means of any information storage or retrieval system without
prior permission in writing from the publishers; or ii) used or reproduced
in any way for the training, development or operation of artificial intelligence
(AI) technologies, including generative AI technologies. The rights holders
expressly reserve this publication from the text and data mining exception
as per Article 4(3) of the Digital Single Market Directive (EU) 2019/790.

Bloomsbury Publishing Inc does not have any control over, or responsibility for,
any third-party websites referred to or in this book. All internet addresses given
in this book were correct at the time of going to press. The author and publisher
regret any inconvenience caused if addresses have changed or sites have
ceased to exist, but can accept no responsibility for any such changes.

Whilst every effort has been made to locate copyright holders the publishers
would be grateful to hear from any person(s) not here acknowledged.

A catalog record for this book is available from the Library of Congress.

ISBN: HB: 978-1-5013-7637-5
PB: 978-1-5013-7641-2
ePDF: 978-1-5013-7639-9
eBook: 978-1-5013-7638-2

Typeset by Deanta Global Publishing Services, Chennai, India

For product safety related questions contact productsafety@bloomsbury.com.

To find out more about our authors and books visit www.bloomsbury.com
and sign up for our newsletters.

Contents

List of illustrations   vi
Acknowledgements   vii
List of contributors   viii

1. Introduction   *James Grande and Brian H. Murray*   1
2. The Ballad and the Bible   *Oskar Cox Jensen*   29
3. The Movements of the Old Hundredth Psalm Tune   *Jonathan Hicks*   49
4. 'The Son of God goes forth to war': The Imperial Martyr's Hymnbook   *Brian H. Murray*   73
5. The Song of Zion in Nineteenth-Century Europe: Sacred Choral Music, Emancipation and Modernity in Jewish Liturgy   *Rachel Adelstein*   95
6. A Temperament of 'ideal cast, lofty tone, sacrificial flame and haughty purity': Jenny Lind's Faith and Her Career   *Matildie Wium*   117
7. Urban Hymns: The Sacred Harmonic Society and Exeter Hall   *James Grande*   133
8. Singing, Playing, Seeing: Scripture and the Multi-Sensorial Gothic Revival in Late Victorian Church Interiors   *Ayla Lepine*   155
9. Secularizing the Sacred, Sanctifying the Commercial: Tonic Sol-fa and the Professionalization of Evangelical Hymnody   *Erin Johnson-Williams*   175
10. Antisemitism and Hebrew Music in Carl Engel's *The Music of the Most Ancient Nations* (1864)   *Bennett Zon*   201

Bibliography   223
Index   230

Illustrations

2.1	John Flaxman, 'Charity'	30
5.1	First line of a setting of *Mah Tovu* by Abraham Saqui (1824–1893) of Liverpool in the Blue Book, *Kol Rinnah V'Todah*, with tonic sol-fa notion of the soprano and alto lines	103
5.2	First page of Lewandowski's setting of *Mah Tovu* from *Todah W'Simrah*	107
7.1	John Brandard, the Handel Festival at the Crystal Palace ('Israel in Egypt')	134
7.2	View of Exeter Hall on the Strand	140
7.3	The orchestra at Exeter Hall, during the meeting of the Sacred Harmonic Society	143
8.1	Ninian Comper, organ case, St Sepulchre Chapel, St Mary Magdalene, Paddington, London, 1895	157
8.2	A. W. N. Pugin, organ case, Jesus College Chapel, Cambridge, 1849	162
8.3	Ninian Comper, plainsong scroll, St Sepulchre Chapel, 1895	164
8.4	Ninian Comper, altar canopy, St Sepulchre Chapel, 1895	167
8.5	Ninian Comper, organ case, All Saints, St Ives, Cambridgeshire, 1894–9	172
9.1	John Knox Bokwe, *Amaculo Ase Lovedale*, 2nd edn (Lovedale: Lovedale Mission Station, 1894), 1	189
9.2	William Macgavin, *The Tonic Sol-fa School Song Wreath: A Collection of Songs Arranged for Two Trebles and Bass* (Edinburgh: Gall & Inglis, 1877), 1	190
9.3	Wolfgang Amadeus Mozart, ed. W. G. McNaught, *The Requiem Mass: Translated into Tonic Sol-fa Notation* (London: Novello, Ewer and Co., 1896), 3	191
9.4	Arthur Roby, *At Home Aboard: A Comic Opera in Two Acts* (London: J. Curwen & Sons, 1899), 1	192

Acknowledgements

Scripture and Song began life as a workshop, 'Hebrew Melodies: Music and the Bible in Nineteenth-Century Europe', co-hosted by two European Research Council–funded interdisciplinary research projects: 'The Bible and Antiquity in Nineteenth-Century Culture' (CRASSH, University of Cambridge) and 'Music in London 1800–1851' (King's College London). This event was kindly supported by the Centre for Research in the Arts, Social Sciences and Humanities (CRASSH) and King's College London. Along with the contributors to this volume, the editors wish to thank all those who participated in the initial workshop, including Nicole Grimes, Alana Harris, Theodor Dunkelgrün, Gareth Atkins, Michael Ledger-Lomas, Ceri Owen, Shinjini Das, Kate Nichols, Alison Knight, Jocelyn Betts, Ruth Jackson Ravenscroft, Roger Parker and Simon Goldhill.

'The Bible and Antiquity in Nineteenth-Century Culture' project was funded by the European Union's Seventh Framework Programme (FP7/2007–2013) (ERC grant no. 295463). The 'Music in London 1800-1851' project was also funded by the European Research Council (RCN 106939). The research leading to several chapters in this volume, and the editing of the volume as a whole, has benefitted from the support of these generous grants.

The editors are extremely grateful for the diligence and patience of our publishing team at Bloomsbury, especially Leah Babb-Rosenfeld and Rachel Moore.

Contributors

Rachel Adelstein is an ethnomusicologist, and the ritual coordinator at Congregation Beth El-Keser Israel in New Haven, Connecticut, USA. She received her PhD from the University of Chicago, USA, in 2013, with a dissertation entitled 'Braided Voices: Women Cantors in Non-Orthodox Judaism.' Between 2014 and 2017, she was the Gaylord and Dorothy Donnelley Junior Research Fellow at Corpus Christi College, University of Cambridge. Her published and forthcoming work addresses women's music and agency in Jewish sacred spaces; the music of British Reform, Liberal and Masorti synagogues; and the history and meaning of congregational melodies in Jewish life.

James Grande is Senior Lecturer in Eighteenth-Century Literature and Culture at King's College London, UK. He is the author of *William Cobbett, the Press and Rural England: Radicalism and the Fourth Estate* (2014) and co-editor of *The Opinions of William Cobbett* (2013), *William Cobbett, Romanticism and the Enlightenment* (2015) and *William Hazlitt: The Spirit of Controversy and Other Essays* (2021). He was a postdoctoral research fellow on the ERC project 'Music in London, 1800–1851' and is completing a monograph entitled *Articulate Sounds: Music, Dissent, and Literary Culture, 1789-1840*. He is a trustee of Keats-Shelley House, Rome and edits the *Keats-Shelley Review*.

Jonathan Hicks is Lecturer in Music at the University of Aberdeen, UK, having previously held research fellowships at Lincoln College Oxford (UK), King's College London (UK) and Newcastle University (UK). His work is principally concerned with the criss-crossing of musical and urban histories in the long nineteenth century. He co-edited *The Melodramatic Moment: Musical and Theatrical Culture, 1790-1820* with Katherine Hambridge and has published in journals including *Nineteenth-Century Music*, *Journal of Musicology* and *Cambridge Opera Journal*.

Oskar Cox Jensen is NUAcT Fellow in Music at Newcastle University, UK. His current project is 'The Invention of Pop Music: Mainstream Song, Class, and Culture, 1520–2020'. Oskar is part of oursubversivevoice.com and the Romantic

National Song Network. He is the author of *Vagabonds: Life on the Streets of Nineteenth-Century London* (2022), *The Ballad-Singer in Georgian and Victorian London* (2021) and *Napoleon and British Song, 1797–1822* (2015); and co-editor of *Charles Dibdin and Late Georgian Culture* (2018) and a special forum of *Journal of British Studies*: Music and Politics in Britain (2021). Oskar is also a BBC New Generation Thinker and novelist.

Erin Johnson-Williams is Lecturer in Music Education and Social Justice at the University of Southampton, UK. Her research focuses on decolonizing the nineteenth century; the imperial history of music education; trauma studies; and the intersections between music, sound and maternity. Erin is co-editor of *Intersectional Encounters in the Nineteenth-Century Archive* (2022), and the forthcoming volumes *Hymns and Constructions of Race: Mobility, Agency, De/Coloniality* and the *Oxford Handbook of Music Colonialism*. She has also co-edited special issues of the journals *Women and Music* and the *Yale Journal of Music and Religion*.

Ayla Lepine is an art historian and theologian whose research focuses on Christianity in modern Britain. Following her PhD in art history at the Courtauld Institute of Art, UK, she held postdoctoral fellowships at the Courtauld and Yale, USA, and was Lecturer and Fellow in Art History at the University of Essex, UK. Her publications include articles in *British Art Studies, Architectural History* and the *Journal of Sexuality and Theology*, and she curated the National Gallery exhibition *Fruits of the Spirit: Art from the Heart* in 2022. She is Associate Rector at St James's Church, Piccadilly in London and a Trustee of Art and Christianity.

Brian H. Murray is Senior Lecturer in Nineteenth-Century Literature at King's College London, UK. His publications include articles on travel writing, exploration, the Victorian reception of Classical and biblical antiquity and nineteenth-century Ireland. He is co-editor of *Travel Writing, Visual Culture and Form, 1760–1900* (2015), *Commodities and Culture in the Colonial World* (2017) and *Chosen Peoples: The Bible, Race and Empire in the Long Nineteenth Century* (2020). Brian is director and co-founder of The Bear Yard Press, a historical print workshop at King's.

Matildie Wium teaches musicology and music theory in the Odeion School of Music at the University of the Free State in Bloemfontein, South Africa. Since completing her doctorate on the music of Arnold van Wyk (1916–1983), she has maintained her research interest in twentieth-century South African art music and has broadened her focus to include the musical practices and experiences of female opera singers in mid-nineteenth-century London. She has contributed to multiple edited volumes and has published in the *Journal of the Royal Musical Association* as well as several South African journals, including *South African Music Studies* (SAMUS), which she currently co-edits.

Bennett Zon is a professor of Music at Durham University, UK, and Director of its Centre for Nineteenth-Century Studies. He is General Editor of *Nineteenth-Century Music Review* and the Music in Nineteenth-Century Britain book series, and an editor of the *Yale Journal of Music and Religion*, the Congregational Music Studies book series and *Nineteenth-Century Contexts*. He was recently elected as inaugural President of the International Nineteenth-Century Studies Association. Zon researches the relationship of music, religion and science in the long nineteenth-century. Recent books include *Evolution and Victorian Musical Culture* (2017) and the co-edited volume *Victorian Culture and the Origin of Disciplines* (2020).

1

Introduction

James Grande and Brian H. Murray

The idea that nineteenth-century composers and performers drew inspiration from the Bible is uncontroversial. Yet insufficient attention has been paid to the relationship between contemporary transformations in religion, music, history, archaeology and biblical scholarship. While new historical sciences called into question the historicity of the Bible, controversies raged over the performance, publication and censorship of new and old musical forms. From oratorio to opera, from parlour song to pantomime and from hymn to broadside, nineteenth-century Europeans encountered elements of the biblical past in musical form. Music, both elite and popular, played an important role in the formation, regulation and contestation of religious and cultural identity and became a way of addressing questions of class, nation and race. Nineteenth-century developments in music, literature and intellectual enquiry, including the beginnings of ethnomusicology, were often underpinned by a sense of biblical and musical history.

Sacred and secular songs were an important, yet often overlooked, channel for the transmission of biblical narratives, themes and ideas. The chapters in this volume explore the Bible as source, as liturgy, as mythological quarry and as font of spiritual and philosophical inspiration. In so doing, we seek to analyse both points of contact and sites of conflict between media and disciplines; moments of intercourse but also sparks of tension between the concert hall and the chapel, between the secular and the sacred. While there is already a wealth of scholarship on sacred and church music, and the engagement of individual composers and songwriters with biblical themes, few critical texts have attempted to grapple with the broader relationship between the Bible and song in the period. How did musical developments in performance and composition transform the ways in which people read (or listened) to the Bible? Did breakthroughs in biblical and historical scholarship effect the ways in which composers, performers and choirs approached biblical themes and texts?

Significantly, these questions were *not* overlooked by nineteenth-century scholars. Countless studies and dissertations – the work of pious amateurs and professional scholars alike – were devoted to the music of the Bible and the Bible as music. In his monograph *Music of the Bible* (1864), Enoch Hutchinson presented his topic as the subject of inquiry for almost every discipline of modern scholarship and the key to unlocking a treasure house of ancient arts and sciences:

> In ancient times the signification of the term music was far more comprehensive than it is at present. It included dancing, gesture, poetry, and sometimes the aggregate of all the sciences. Hence philosophers were accustomed to speak of music human, divine, terrestrial, celestial, active, contemplative, enunciative, intellectual, and oratorical.[1]

As song collectors, folklorists and poets sought cultural authenticity and the roots of national culture in uncontaminated ballads of the peasantry, ethnologists, historians and philologists began to interpret the Bible as the product of a primitive oral culture grounded in the specificities of place and race. As Walter Scott explained in his 1830 preface to *Minstrelsy of the Scottish Border*, the germ of great textual traditions – and the poetic genius of every nation – was to be found in 'primitive' and 'savage' rituals of music, dance and song.

> [All] must admit, the general taste and propensity of nations in their early state, to cultivate some species of rude poetry.... The savage, after proving the activity of his limbs in the chase or the battle, trains them to more measured movements, to dance at the festivals of his tribe, or to perform obeisance before the altars of his deity. From the same impulse, he is disposed to refine the ordinary speech which forms the vehicle of social communication betwixt him and his brethren, until, by a more ornate diction, modulated by certain rules of rhythm, cadence, assonance of termination, or recurrence of sound or letter, he obtains a dialect more solemn in expression.... The investigation of the early poetry of every nation, even the rudest, carries with it an object of curiosity and interest. It is a chapter in the history of the childhood of society.[2]

---

[1] Enoch Hutchinson, *Music of the Bible, or Explanatory Notes Upon Those Passages in the Sacred Scriptures Which Relate to Music* (Boston: Gould and Lincoln, 1864), 15.

[2] Walter Scott, 'Introductory Remarks on Popular Poetry' [1830], in *The Minstrelsy of the Scottish Border* (Edinburgh: Robert Cadell, 1849), vol. 1, 5–6, 13–14.

Although Scott hypothesized a balladic root for the Homeric epics, he avoided speculation on the origins of scriptural poetry and song. Yet by the beginning of the nineteenth century, criticism had already reduced the Bible's unitary authority to something more like 'a plurality of competing voices'.[3] Sacred texts could no longer be insulated from the investigations of folklorists, philologists and critics. The Psalms of David, for example, had been a familiar part of British devotional life for centuries, but in the nineteenth century, scholars began to interpret such texts as characteristic 'survivals' of remote oral and musical traditions. The popular Tractarian poet John Keble was not known for his embrace of radical criticism. But in his lectures as Oxford Professor of Poetry (delivered in Latin), Keble invited students to compare the 'primitive poetry' of Jeremiah, the authors of the psalms and even passages from Genesis with 'such remains of song among savage races as survive to us' and the 'lays so common among Northern peoples'.[4] By the mid-nineteenth century then, the musical and poetic cultures recorded in scripture could be simultaneously familiar and remotely *other* to modern Britons.

Studies of nineteenth-century religion and biblical reception have, understandably, tended to privilege literature and textual analysis at the expense of other forms of evidence and other methodological approaches. As Timothy Larsen, Kirstie Blair and others have demonstrated, the Bible was central to Victorian everyday life, even for doubters and non-believers.[5] Yet this emphasis on the Bible as ubiquitous text risks eliding the fact that the lived social experience of scripture was often mediated by song. The architectural historian, William Whyte, argues that the 'auditory church' of the eighteenth century – with a focus on the voice of the preacher – gave way to a 'visual church' in the nineteenth century as the Gothic Revival revolutionized liturgical performance and ecclesiological taste.[6] Yet Whyte also demonstrates that this architectural and ritual transformation opened the door to new sounds: choirs and organs were reconfigured to meet the demands of new spaces and old forms of sacred music

---

[3] Stephen Prickett, *Origins of Narrative: The Romantic Appropriation of the Bible* (Cambridge: Cambridge University Press, 1996), 108.
[4] John Keble, *Keble's Lectures on Poetry, 1832–1841*, trans. Edward Kershaw Francis (Oxford: Clarendon Press, 1912), Lecture IV, 63.
[5] Timothy Larsen, *A People of One Book: The Bible and the Victorians* (Oxford: Oxford University Press, 2011); Kirstie Blair, *Form and Faith in Victorian Poetry and Religion* (Oxford: Oxford University Press, 2012).
[6] William Whyte, *Unlocking the Church: The Lost Secrets of Victorian Sacred Space* (Oxford: Oxford University Press, 2017), 63.

were revived to fill vaulted ceilings and Gothic chancels.[7] As with the warring parties who debated liturgy, ritual, architecture and the meaning of scripture, Bennett Zon reminds us that nineteenth-century arguments about church music also relied on 'notion[s] of authority through antiquity and tradition'. Advocates for the revival of Gregorian plainchant in the Church of England echoed and intersected with theological arguments made by the Oxford Movement and ecclesiological principles of the Cambridge Camden Society.[8] From 1843, the journal of the Camden Society, the *Ecclesiologist*, included essays on early church music, while Tractarians like Frederick Oakeley saw the resurgence of Gregorian plainchant as a complement to the Gothic Revival in architecture, the 'aesthetic realization of high churchmanship'.[9] As Zon has shown, the 'plainchant revival' in England began with Roman Catholics in the mid-eighteenth century. With the gradual easing of penal laws, English Catholics began to reassert their identity through conserved and revived practices of ritual, devotion and music.[10] As with the Established Church, fashions in Roman Catholic architecture, liturgy and music were closely intertwined. The Gothic architect and Catholic convert, A. W. N. Pugin published *An Earnest Appeal for the Revival of the Ancient Plain Song* in 1850.[11] The Catholic mass had long integrated scriptural passages set to music into its liturgy. Originating in Germany in the 1860s, the Cecilian Movement promoted a return to plainchant and renaissance polyphony as the most appropriate forms for sung liturgy. Like the Nazarenes in the visual arts, Austrian and German enthusiasts for plainchant and renaissance polyphony sought to reinvigorate moribund tradition through the emulation of neglected 'old masters', most importantly Palestrina.[12] As Thomas Muir has shown, the 'universal Roman liturgy, especially one using Latin only, allowed Catholic church music to cross borders'. Cecilian Societies subsequently flourished in British and Irish cities, preserving an 'evolving continuity of tradition' well into the twentieth century.[13] Thus transformations in Roman Catholic Church music

---

[7] Whyte, *Unlocking the Church*, 86–7.
[8] Bennett Zon, *The English Plainchant Revival* (Oxford: Oxford University Press, 1999), 1.
[9] Zon, *English Plainchant*, 251–3.
[10] Zon, *English Plainchant*, 7.
[11] Zon, *English Plainchant*, 167.
[12] Siegfried Gmeinwieser, 'Cecilian Movement', *Grove Music Online* (Oxford: Oxford University Press, 2001), https://www.oxfordmusiconline.com/grovemusic/view/10.1093/gmo/9781561592630.001.0001/omo-9781561592630-e-0000005245, accessed 5 January 2022.
[13] T. E. Muir, 'Sacred Sound for a Holy Space: Dogma, Worship and Music at Solemn Mass during the Victorian Era, 1829–1903', in *Music and Theology in Nineteenth-Century Britain*, ed. Martin V. Clarke (Farnham: Ashgate, 2012), 37–60 (49–51). On the Cecilian movement in Britain, see Thomas E. Muir, *Roman Catholic Church Music in England, 1791–1914: A Handmaid of the Liturgy?* (Aldershot: Ashgate, 2008), 105–6, 113–33 and Paul Collins, ed., *Renewal and Resistance: Catholic*

strongly reflected Continental trends, while Roman Catholics in Britain and Ireland simultaneously constructed identities amidst and against the Established Churches.

By concentrating on the musical dissemination and mediation of scripture, we aim to investigate sacred song as an expression of communal and confessional solidarity but also enthusiastic Dissent. The forms of affective communal engagement fostered by congregational singing charged the sacred text with powerful new resonances. Yet the musical setting of the biblical text also created problems, particularly for those deeply invested in the sanctity and authority of scripture. Is a line from the Bible still 'scripture' when communicated through music or song? Is every book of the Bible a legitimate quarry for musicians and composers? What happens to the authority of the text once it is disseminated through the human voice – or the collective voices of a choir or congregation? Or conversely, might the words of scripture become less important – or even irrelevant – once they are repackaged as mere lyrics or libretti? As J. Cheryl Exum, a scholar of biblical interpretation and adaptation, has argued, each musical setting of scripture is 'an interpretation of the text', shedding light on the complexities and nuances of a scriptural source.[14] Helen Leneman likens opera libretti and orchestrations to a form of 'midrash' or 'creative re-telling', revealing new meanings in the original.[15] Likewise, in a discussion of Handel's *Messiah*, Andrew Davies suggests that both music and libretti constitute powerful examples of popular 'exegesis'.[16] But if the 'setting' of scripture to music has exegetical value, it is also a potentially dangerous practice, leaving the composer or performer open to charges of heretical distortion and overzealous interpretation.

Anxieties about the potential of music to distort or obscure scriptural meaning were often expressed by Dissenting and Nonconformist Protestants – perhaps unsurprisingly, given their absolute commitment to the sacred text. After the Baptist Jane Attwater attended a performance of Handel's *Messiah* in Salisbury Cathedral in 1775, she wrote in her diary that 'the musick was noble

Church Music from the 1850s to Vatican II (Oxford: Peter Lang, 2010). For Ireland, see Kieran Daly, *Catholic Church Music in Ireland 1878–1903: The Cecilian Reform Movement* (Dublin: Four Courts, 1995).

[14] J. Cheryl Exum, *Retellings: The Bible in Literature, Music, Art and Film: Reprinted from Biblical Interpretation* (Leiden: Brill, 2007).

[15] Helen Leneman, 'Re-visioning a Biblical Story through Libretto and Music: *Debora e Jaele* by Ildebrando Pizzetti', in *Retellings*, ed. Exum (Leiden: Brill), 78–113 (79).

[16] Andrew Davies, 'Oratorio as Exegesis: The Use of the Book of Isaiah in Handel's *Messiah*', in *Retellings*, ed. Exum (Leiden: Brill), 114–34.

& the words more so & if the hearts of the musicians & their auditors were rightly engaged in it 'twas a noble performance'.[17] The searching equivocation of Attwater's response admits the possibility that the hearts of musicians and listeners may *not* have been rightly engaged and maintains a clear, hierarchical separation between text and music. While the first London performances of *Messiah* in the 1740s aroused hostility by taking a sacred text into the profane space of the theatre, Handel's oratorio ultimately overcame suspicions about its musical setting and theatrical performance to achieve an exalted position in nineteenth-century culture, becoming the mainstay of choral societies and oratorio concerts. Another unlikely alliance between sacred text and theatrical song is evident in the popularity of Methodist hymn-singing, which in the second half of the eighteenth century transformed the hymn from an object of silent devotion into a truly popular musical form. As Peter Mandler writes, 'Calvinists' preference for a toneless psalmody gave way to a glorious burst of Methodist hymnody, probably Britain's greatest accession of musical culture before the age of the electronic mass media'.[18] The legendary origins for Methodist hymnody lay in a 1735 voyage to Savannah, Georgia, when John Wesley observed a group of psalm-singing Moravian missionaries during a violent storm. 'A dreadful screaming was heard among the English', but the Moravians 'calmly sung on'.[19] Having previously regarded hymns as textual aids to personal meditation and prayer, the Wesleys were converted to a belief in the possibilities of collective song and Charles Wesley went on to write over six thousand hymns. In doing so, he freely adapted tunes from theatres, tavern songs and street ballads, famously refusing to let the devil keep all the best tunes. As Misty Anderson argues, 'the bricolage of theatrical and ballad tunes made the Methodist hymn, at least to outsiders, a species of holy ballad opera'.[20]

By 1800, the Methodist revival had placed the affective experience of hymn-singing at the centre of a reformed 'religion of the heart'. As Nicholas Temperley has argued, 'the Wesleys brought a new degree of emotional fervour into religious singing', with hymn-singing among a range of somatic practices (including fainting, weeping and love feasts) that were viewed with deep suspicion by

---

[17] Diary of Jane Attwater Blatch (1753–1843), 5 October 1775, in *Nonconformist Women Writers, 1720–1840*, gen. ed. Timothy Whelan, 8 vols (London: Pickering & Chatto, 2011), vol. 8, 218–19.
[18] Peter Mandler, 'Afterword: Liberalism in the Round', in *Music and Victorian Liberalism: Composing the Liberal Subject*, ed. Sarah Collins (Cambridge: Cambridge University Press, 2019), 222.
[19] Robert Southey, *The Life of Wesley; and the Rise and Progress of Methodism*, 2 vols (London: Longman, Hurst, Rees, Orme, and Brown, 1820), vol. 1, 81.
[20] Misty G. Anderson, *Imagining Methodism in Eighteenth-Century Britain: Enthusiasm, Belief & the Borders of the Self* (Baltimore: Johns Hopkins University Press, 2012), 171–2.

conservative Anglicans. Critics of hymn-singing believed that sacred texts might be undermined or obscured by their musical setting. Moreover, the affective power of music aligned it with the more enthusiastic strains of Protestant Nonconformity, rendering it an object of suspicion for Anglicans and Rational Dissenters. Such suspicions could run in both directions, however, as we can see in the work of the radical enthusiast William Blake. Blake's work is imbued with the contemporary culture of sacred song, but also subjects it to rigorous critique, alert to the full range of functions that song can serve. In the 'Holy Thursday' poems of *Songs of Innocence and Experience* (1794), Blake describes the Ascension Day procession of thousands of orphans from the city's charity schools through the streets of London to St Paul's Cathedral, to hear a sermon and sing psalms before their benefactors. This spectacle was among the most impressive rituals of musical life in the city, provoking pious responses from visiting composers such as Joseph Haydn in 1791 ('No music ever moved me so deeply in my whole life as this devotional and innocent') and Hector Berlioz in 1851 ('incomparably the most impressive, the most Babylonian ceremony ... a part of my dreams come true and a proof that the power of musical masses is still absolutely unknown').[21] The sublime pathos of this spectacle lay in the way it united the richest and poorest inhabitants of the city, defined through reciprocal relations of charity and gratitude, in the sacred space of St Paul's. In *Songs of Innocence*, the scene is one of divine purity: 'The children walking two & two in red & blue & green / Grey headed beadles walkd before with wands as white as snow / Till into the high dome of Pauls they like Thames waters flow.'[22] The biblical images associate song with joy and charity, an outpouring of faith as natural and irresistible as 'Thames waters' and as powerful as the 'mighty wind' that precedes the 'still small voice' of the divine (1 Kgs 19:11-12). The radiant 'flowers of London town' combine to send up a single 'voice of song', delivering an ostensibly simple, even self-congratulatory, moral message to their auditors, the 'aged men wise guardians of the poor': 'cherish pity, lest you drive an angel from your door'.[23] In the corresponding lyric from *Songs of Experience*, however, the spectacle fails to mask the misery and poverty of the children. The

---

[21] H. C. Robbins Landon, *The Collected Correspondence and London Notebooks of Joseph Haydn* (London: Barrie and Rockliff, 1959), 261; A. W. Ganz, *Berlioz in London* (London: Quality Press, 1950), 98.

[22] *The Complete Poetry & Prose of William Blake*, ed. David V. Erdman, with a commentary by Harold Bloom (rev. edn, New York: Anchor Books, 1988), 13. Subsequent references to this edition will be given in parentheses.

[23] As W. H. Stevenson has shown, the music for the Ascension Day service at St Paul's included the 100th Psalm, in the metrical version by William Kethe, sung to the traditional tune of the 'Old

complacent assertions of the 'Innocence' poem are challenged by the speaker's insistent questioning, which reveal a desolate allegorical landscape: the 'eternal winter' of 'a land of poverty' (19). The 'song of joy' is exposed as a 'trembling cry', and the characteristically Blakean dialectic suggests that while song is often associated with faith and joy, it can also serve as an instrument of discipline and control. Read together, the poems show how song can function as a form of false consciousness, concealing the true conditions of musical production. In doing so, they recall Blake's chimney sweeper in *Songs of Experience*, whose parents 'taught me to sing the notes of woe' and now choose to interpret their child's song as evidence of his well-being:

> And because I am happy, & dance & sing,
> They think they have done me no injury:
> And are gone to praise God & his Priest & King
> Who make up a heaven of our misery. (23)

Parental and religious authority are here united against the interests of the child, a form of false consciousness mediated by song.

Questions about which tunes and lyrics should be used, *who* could sing sacred songs and *how* they should be sung were fiercely contested. Congregational hymn-singing was an integral part of collective worship for Dissenters and Methodists, a key part of their popular appeal and a contributing factor to their success in recruiting worshippers. As Jon Mee argues, the injunction of 2 Cor. 3:6, 'the letter killeth but the spirit giveth life', was central to the culture of religious enthusiasm. In musical terms, this approach to animating the text inspired musical practices such as the improvisatory hymn-singing of the Moravian Church, a spontaneous expression of religious feeling, based on a shared repertoire of hymns that had been memorized and internalized.[24] If singing could function as a form of discipline, it could also serve as the vehicle of visionary enthusiasm: a channelling of direct inspiration that exceeded both the semantic capacities of language and the dead letter of the musical text. By contrast, the Church of England effectively banned hymn-singing until 1820, restricting sacred song to the chanting of psalms by the congregation and performance

---

Hundredth', and prose psalms chanted to a tune by the St Paul's organist John Jones (1728–96). See 'The Sound of "Holy Thursday"', *Blake/An Illustrated Quarterly* 36, no. 4 (2003): 137–40.

[24] Jon Mee, *Dangerous Enthusiasm: William Blake and the Culture of Radicalism in the 1790s* (Oxford: Clarendon Press, 1992), 71; Sarah Eyerly, 'The Sensual Theology of the Eighteenth-Century Moravian Church', in *Christian Congregational Music: Performance, Identity and Experience*, eds. Monique Ingalls, Carolyn Landau, and Tom Wagner (Farnham: Ashgate, 2013), 155–68.

of anthems and chorales by church and cathedral choirs. This prohibition on hymn-singing was only lifted in 1820 after a case was brought against Thomas Cotterill, a Sheffield clergyman, and the poet James Montgomery, for publishing *A Selection of Psalms and Hymns for Public and Private Use, Adapted to the Services of the Church of England* (Sheffield, 1819). The decision of the Ecclesiastical Court at York to allow the publication was interpreted as finally sanctioning congregational hymn-singing within the Church of England and led to an outpouring of new hymnals. The decision to allow hymns in Anglican worship reflected the popularity of Methodist and Dissenting hymn-singing and served as a tacit admission that the Church of England needed to allow congregational singing in order to stem the flow of worshippers away from the Established Church. As late as 1838, the Roman Catholic hierarchy in England ruled against the use of English hymns and psalms in services.[25] Yet the embrace of hymnody across the confessional spectrum ultimately proved impossible to suppress.[26] The popularity of congregational singing, its role in attracting worshippers to church or chapel, would remain important later in the century as increasing numbers began to turn away from Christian worship altogether.

Tracing the impact of these early nineteenth-century debates and controversies, the remainder of our introduction calls for renewed attention to the intertwined histories of music and biblical reception in nineteenth-century Britain. We begin with two indicative case studies. First, we examine the popular anthology *Hebrew Melodies* (1815), a collaboration of the poet Lord Byron and the composer Isaac Nathan. Second, we examine the career of the novelist George Eliot, from her early wish that 'the only music heard in our land were that of strict worship', to the musical cosmopolitanism exemplified by her searching exploration of race, religion, art and nationalism in her final novel *Daniel Deronda* (1876).

To sweep the harp of David

As we have shown, the folkloric search for the musical origins of nations and peoples informed Romantic understandings of both scripture and song. One

---

[25] Muir, 'Sacred Sound for a Holy Space', 37–60 (49).
[26] Though significantly, many of the most successful English Catholic hymnodists – including Frederick William Faber and John Henry Newman – were converts from Anglicanism. Faber's *Hymnbook of the Oratory of St. Philip Neri* (London: Burns, 1850), for example, includes some of the most popular and enduring Catholic hymns in English.

popular manifestation of this was the new genre of 'national songs'. The initial taste was for airs and ballads from the Celtic fringe. The genre was inaugurated by Robert Burns and George Thomson's *Original Scottish Airs* (1793) and arguably peaked with Thomas Moore and John Stevenson's *Irish Melodies* (from 1808). As Celeste Langan has shown, in the context of popular antiquarianism and Romantic nationalism, folk and national songs were exotic print commodities 'imported from the periphery' to the metropolitan parlour.[27] The implicit nationalism (and Jacobitism) of many of these songs was tolerated 'so long as sentimental longing did not give way to militant pride'.[28] Moore's nostalgic Irish nationalism, for example, was sufficiently defanged to ensure his melodies could be enjoyed by those who remained unmoved by claims for Irish Home Rule or the rights of Roman Catholics. While ostensibly routed in authentic 'peasant' cultures, the national song's focus on the melancholy plight of oppressed peoples and conquered nations owed much to the poetics of the Hebrew Bible. As we suggested above, nineteenth-century Christians had begun to interpret the poetic books of the Hebrew Bible (especially the psalms) as both a universal 'Christian' inheritance and a peculiar product of the Jewish nation and race.

Hebrew Melodies (1815) was a timely collaboration between the English Jewish composer, Isaac Nathan and the most celebrated poet of the era, Lord Byron. The son of Menehem (or Menachem) Mona, a cantor at a synagogue in Canterbury, Nathan had studied at an Anglo-Jewish boarding school in Cambridge before taking up music under the mentorship of Domenico Corri. A student of Haydn's master Nicola Porpora, Corri was an early exponent of the national song craze, publishing *A Select Collection of Forty Scotch Songs* in 1780. An influential figure in London's West End, Corri had arranged material for the celebrated Jewish tenor John Braham. Through Corri's influence, Nathan was appointed singing master to Princess Charlotte and music librarian to her father, the Prince Regent.[29] Nathan's initial pitch for *Hebrew Melodies* appeared in the *Gentleman's Magazine* in May 1813. The composer promised a book of melodies 'all of them upwards of 1000 years old and some of them performed

---

[27] Celeste Langan, 'Scotch Drink & Irish Harps: Mediations of the National Air', in *The Figure of Music in Nineteenth-Century British Poetry*, ed. Phyllis Weliver (Aldershot: Ashgate, 2005), 25–49 (30).
[28] Thomas L. Ashton, *Byron's Hebrew Melodies* (London: Routledge & Kegan Paul, 1972), 4.
[29] Ashton, *Byron's Hebrew Melodies*, 7. Frederick Burwick and Paul Douglass, 'Introduction: The Creation of *Hebrew Melodies*', in *A Selection of Hebrew Melodies, Ancient and Modern, by Isaac Nathan and Lord Byron* (Tuscaloosa: University of Alabama Press, 1988), 1–36 (1–4); Sheila A. Spector, 'The Liturgical Context of the Byron-Nathan "Hebrew Melodies"', *Studies in Romanticism* 47, no. 3 (2008): 393–412 (395).

by the Antient [sic] Hebrews before the destruction of the temple'.[30] After an unsuccessful attempt to persuade Walter Scott to provide lyrics, Nathan wrote repeatedly to Byron, stressing the 'undoubted antiquity' of his tunes and his desire 'that the Poetry for them should be written by the first Poet of the present age'.[31] With the aid of Douglass Kinnaird, a banker involved in the management of the Theatre Royal, Drury Lane, Nathan eventually secured the participation of Byron and persuaded John Braham to lend his name as co-composer on the title page of the song book. Braham also performed the songs at Drury Lane.[32] Although initially reluctant, Byron eventually became Nathan's enthusiastic and committed collaborator and friend.[33] Nathan's claims of antiquity clearly caught the poet's imagination and in correspondence Byron expressed excitement at Nathan's rediscovery of 'the real old undisputed Hebrew melodies, which are beautiful & to which David & the prophets actually sang the "songs of Zion"'.[34]

Nathan undoubtedly exaggerated the antiquity of his sources, but subsequent critics have recognized the *Melodies* as a genuine effort to introduce Jewish sacred music to a wider audience. Whether or not Nathan believed the music of the ancient Hebrews was preserved in contemporary synagogues, there is 'enough evidence to be sure that he did seriously intend to preserve what he was hearing in London and Canterbury synagogues'.[35] Musicologists have traced Jewish (mostly Ashkenazi) liturgical origins for nine of twelve songs in the first volume of *Hebrew Melodies*.[36] Some of Nathan's settings, which adapted the cantillations (a system of notation for liturgical chanting) from the Masoretic text of the Hebrew Bible, bore an intimate relationship to scripture, albeit refracted through a lens of Purcell and Handel, classical Italian ornamentation and contemporary German *lieder*.[37] The published preface to the first edition (ascribed to Nathan and Braham but likely overseen by Kinnaird) dropped the extravagant claim of antiquity and admitted the 'age and originality' of the tunes 'still sung in religious Ceremonies of the Jews . . . must be left to conjecture'. Rather than claim an uncorrupted and archaeological antiquity, the subtitle to the first edition (*Ancient and Modern*) emphasized a complex play between

---

[30] Burwick and Douglass, 'Introduction', 7.
[31] Burwick and Douglass, 'Introduction', 5. Nathan to Byron, 30 June 1814. Quoted by Ashton, *Byron's Hebrew Melodies*, 9–10.
[32] Ashton, *Byron's Hebrew Melodies*, 14–15.
[33] Ashton, *Byron's Hebrew Melodies*, 17.
[34] Byron to Arabella Millbanke (24 October 1814). Qtd. in Burwick and Douglass, 'Introduction', 15.
[35] Burwick and Douglass, 'Introduction', 11.
[36] Spector, 'The Liturgical Context', 397.
[37] Burwick and Douglass, 'Introduction', 12, 32.

ancient origins and the accretions of tradition. As the preface argued, the 'latitude given to the taste and genius of their performers has been the means of engrafting on the original Melodies a certain wildness and pathos, which have at length become the chief characteristic of the Sacred Songs of the Jews'.[38] In a similar vein, Byron's lyrics ranged from balladic adaptations of biblical narratives to more abstract lyrics, exploring themes of melancholy, persecution and exile, suitably ornamented with Levantine imagery.

Although *Hebrew Melodies* was a commercial success, the hostility of contemporary reviews betrays a revealing combination of antisemitism and offended Christian piety. The Tory High-Church *British Critic* scoffed at Byron's new vocation as 'poet laureat [*sic*] to the synagogue' and suggested London audiences had been duped by the (fictional) 'Society for the Propagation of Judaism among Christians'.[39] Yet the same reviewer also points to deeper problems with the adaptation of scripture as song. The use of Hebrew psalms in Christian liturgy has long encouraged congregations to enter 'into the sorrows of those who formed so large a link in the dispensation of redeeming mercy; by partaking in their humiliation'. Yet this spiritual exercise is, we are told, 'perfectly foreign to the minds of those, to whom we are indebted for these Hebrew Melodies'.[40] The objection is not so much to the setting of scripture as song – the same reviewer praises the metrical psalm settings of Tate and Brady – but the sincerity and earnestness of the singer. Sacred song can never be a matter of mere musical or literary skill:

> That simplicity, that purity, and that pathos, which are essential to such compositions can exclusively arise from no taste however cultivated, from no fancy however vivid, from no feelings however warm ... to these must be added a pure and chastened heart, a soul impressed with dignity and the awe of its holy task, and affections consecrated to God.[41]

Much of the criticism was more moderate but still expressed an unease with such a worldly lyricist adapting Holy Writ for the fashionable parlour. The liberal

---

[38] I. Braham, I. Nathan, and Lord Byron, *A Selection of Hebrew Melodies: Ancient and Modern* (London: I. Nathan, 1815), unpag.

[39] Rev. of *Hebrew Melodies*, *British Critic*, 2nd Series, III (June 1815), 602–11 (603–4). Collected in Donald H. Reiman, ed., *The Romantics Reviewed: Contemporary Reviews of British Romantic Writers*. Part B, vol. 1 (New York: Garland, 1972), 257–61. Byron's own support for British Jews was wavering and inconsistent. On Byron's later antisemitic poem, *The Age of Bronze* (1823), see Michael Scrivener, '"Zion Alone Is Forbidden": Historicizing Antisemitism in Byron's "The Age of Bronze"', *Keats-Shelley Journal* 43 (1994): 75–97.

[40] *British Critic*, 604–5.

[41] *British Critic*, 609–10.

congregationalist Josiah Conder reckoned the *Melodies* stood 'a fair chance of rivalling in popularity the compositions of his friend Moore, of which indeed they often remind us'. But Conder was uneasy with the *Melodies*' attempt 'to accommodate subjects selected from the Hebrew Scripture to the light measures of love song'. Conder himself would later became a prolific composer of hymns, but the setting of scripture to song was a delicate task, best left to earnest believers. The *Hebrew Melodies*, by contrast, offered:

> Fresh proof . . . that the Scriptures are not honoured by the attempts of mere artists or poets to illustrate them; – that something besides genius is necessary in order to secure success; that devotional feeling and religious knowledge are no less indispensable requisites; that in order to sweep the harp of David, a man needs be not only pre-eminently a poet, but emphatically a Christian.[42]

Several reviews compared the *Melodies* unfavourably to the metrical psalm settings of Tate and Brady and Sternhold and Hopkins, implying that metrical and musical adaptation of scripture was not in itself the issue. But reviewers consistently found Byron and Nathan wanting in sincerity and sensitivity. The *Critical Review* took issue with some of the jaunty and 'vulgar' metres chosen by Byron, which amounted to 'a sort of poetical profanation of Holy Writ' and reduced the 'dreadful solemnity' of the books of the prophets to mere 'Burlesque'. Byron's adaption of Ps. 137 ('By the rivers of Babylon') likewise betrayed a 'modern sentimental air and other affectations, which quite destroy the beautiful pathos of the original'. Nathan's music similarly was 'too much Italianated' when 'more simplicity of accompaniment would have better suited'.[43] Another liberal evangelical, William Roberts, writing in the *British Review*, insisted that a genuine author of Hebrew melodies should 'come out of the schools of the prophets. He should know his Bible, believe his Bible, and love his Bible, to write with true feeling upon the subjects of the Bible'.[44]

Much of the controversy in Britain focused on the potential offence to Christianity. But as Sheila Spector has shown, for listeners familiar with the liturgical significance of Nathan's Ashkenazi themes, the juxtaposition with Byron's lyrics would have suggested new and provocative interpretations. In several of the *Melodies*, for example, the 'Byronic skepticism of the lyrics' plays 'counterpoint to liturgical religiosity' of the music, mirroring arguments over

---

[42] Josiah Conder, rev. of *Hebrew Melodies*, *Eclectic Review* 4 (July 1815), 94–6.
[43] Rev. of *Hebrew Melodies*, Second Series. *Critical Review* 3.4 (April 1816), 357–66.
[44] *British Critic*, 611.

faith and reason at the heart of the Jewish Enlightenment (or *Haskalah*).[45] We know that scripture and the psalms were as household words to Georgian and Victorian Britons. But the critical response to *Hebrew Melodies* reveals how easily these texts could be made uncomfortably exotic and disruptive with the addition of the right (or wrong) music. The Irish or Hungarian national song was a satisfyingly exotic museum piece, but the notion that scripture might belong to the national songbook of another nation, and another race, was more challenging for British audiences.

'To make undying music in the world'

The importance of the Bible as a model of divinely inspired song and a source for song lyrics continued to occupy Victorian writers. We can trace the intertwined histories of scripture and song, and the bearing that they had on ideas about voice, gender, race and religious identity, through George Eliot's shifting attitudes to music. Eliot grew up as Mary Anne Evans within a middle-of-the-road Anglican family but her early beliefs were influenced by evangelical and Nonconformist teachers at her schools in Nuneaton and Coventry, reflecting the strength of evangelicalism and Dissent in the English midlands during the 1820s and 1830s. Eliot later described herself as having been 'a strong Calvinist' in her youth and this determined her rejection of the luxury and ornament of musical performance.[46] After attending an oratorio concert at the age of eighteen, where she had heard singers including John Braham, she wrote to a school friend that she had 'said farewell to all such expenditures of time and money. I think nothing can justify the using of an intensely interesting and solemn passage of Scripture, as a rope-dancer uses her rope', wishing that 'the only music heard in our land were that of strict worship'. The musical setting here becomes a corruption of the biblical text and the pleasures of musical performance a distraction from the serious business of scriptural understanding: 'I ask myself can it be desirable, and would it be consistent with millennial holiness for a human being to devote the time and energies that are barely sufficient for real exigencies on acquiring expertness in trills cadences, etc.?'[47] Eliot's austere Calvinism was, however,

---

[45] Spector, 'Liturgical Context', 398–405. For more interpretations in the Jewish liturgical context, see Jeremy Hugh Baron, 'Byron's Passovers and Nathan's Melodies', *Judaism* 51 (2002): 19–29.
[46] Rosemary Ashton, *George Eliot: A Life* (London: Hamish Hamilton, 1996), 25.
[47] George Eliot to Martha Jackson, Griff, 4 September 1838, in *The George Eliot Letters*, ed. Gordon S. Haight, 9 vols (New Haven: Yale University Press, 1954–78), vol. 1, 9.

short-lived and by 1841 she had abandoned Christianity altogether in favour of a secular humanism. This loss of faith came about partly as the result of her friendship with Charles and Cara Bray, manufacturers, philanthropists and freethinking Unitarians. For Eliot – as for many others in the period – liberal Dissent formed the intellectual high road to atheism.

Despite her rejection of Christian belief, Eliot's early religious fervour continued to influence her later philosophy in a variety of ways. Moreover, the liberal heresies of Unitarianism, with its denial of the Trinity and the divinity of Jesus Christ, remained the form of Christianity that Eliot felt closest to and she occasionally attended Unitarian services. The persistence of evangelical and Nonconformist ideas and attitudes is rarely acknowledged within discussions of Eliot and music. The relationship between scripture and song continues to operate, however, as a powerful residual category within Eliot's treatment of music and can help to explain some of the complexities of music as it appears both in her journalism and fiction.

Eliot's writings on music were informed by her own study, her piano playing, frequent concert and opera attendance in London and contact with some of the leading composers and performers of the day. In 1854, she and George Henry Lewes spent several months in Weimar, meeting such musical luminaries as Franz Liszt, Anton Rubinstein and Clara Schumann, and the following year they encountered Richard Wagner during his visit to London. Eliot's essay 'Liszt, Wagner and Weimar', published in *Fraser's Magazine* in July 1855, has been claimed as the 'earliest appreciative account of [Wagner's] art to be published in the British press'.[48] Her response, however, is at best equivocal, recognizing Wagnerian opera as an important development in the 'lyric drama' while regretting the absence of easily discernible melodies:

> As to melody – who knows? It is just possible that melody, as we conceive it, is only a transitory phase of music.... We are but in 'the morning of the times', and must learn to think of ourselves as tadpoles unprescient of the future frog. Still the tadpole is limited to tadpole pleasures; and so, in our state of development, we are swayed by melody.

Listening to a Beethoven quartet after Wagner's *Lohengrin* is – in recognizably Wordsworthian idiom – 'like returning to the pregnant speech of men

---

[48] Delia da Sousa Correa, *George Eliot, Music and Victorian Culture* (Basingstoke: Palgrave Macmillan, 2003), 4.

after a sojourn among glums and gowries'.⁴⁹ This privileging of melody and comparison to speech that is filled with meaning might be traced back to the hermeneutic habits of Dissent, from Calvinist belief in the primacy of scripture and importance of self-scrutiny to the rational universe of Unitarian thought. An alternative set of contexts is supplied, however, by Eliot's reading of post-Hegelian philosophy and, in particular, the writings of Ludwig Feuerbach. In *The Essence of Christianity*, which Eliot translated into English, Feuerbach associated melody with affect, asking, '[w]ho has not experienced the overwhelming power of melody? And what else is the power of melody but the power of feeling? Music is the language of feeling; melody is audible feeling – feeling communicating itself'.⁵⁰ But Feuerbach was also profoundly suspicious about the place of hearing within the religious sensorium, writing that '[t]he only fearful, mystical, and pious sense is that of hearing'.⁵¹

These apparently contradictory contexts, of Protestant Nonconformity and post-Hegelian philosophy, are closely connected within Eliot's work; as Tim Dolin has argued, 'the values, practices, and ways of being that were central to her evangelical upbringing . . . remained central to her fiction because they were central to her atheism. At the heart of Calvinist self-examination . . . the Feuerbachian Eliot finds the humanistic quality of moral self-consciousness'.⁵² To this account of the continuities in Eliot's moral imagination, we might add a simultaneous and equally sincere enthusiasm and anxiety about the power of song, shaped by both her early religious education and the new forms of German philosophy and Austro-German music she went on to encounter, and for which her writings formed an important conduit for British readers.

These contradictions inform Eliot's final and most densely musical novel, *Daniel Deronda* (1876). In writing this follow-up to *Middlemarch: A Study of Provincial Life* (1871), Eliot told her publisher, John Blackwood, that she wanted to 'widen the English vision a little . . . and let in a little conscience and refinement'.⁵³ While *Daniel Deronda* does offer a broader, more cosmopolitan vision, readers have long struggled to reconcile the 'English' and 'Jewish' sections of the novel: F. R. Leavis notoriously suggested that the Jewish sections

---

⁴⁹ George Eliot, 'Liszt, Wagner, and Weimar', *Fraser's Magazine* (July 1855), 48–62 (50–1).
⁵⁰ Ludwig Feuerbach, *The Essence of Christianity*, trans. Marian Evans [George Eliot] (London: John Chapman, 1854), 3.
⁵¹ Quoted in Leigh Eric Schmidt, *Hearing Things: Religion, Illusion, and the American Enlightenment* (Cambridge, MA: Harvard University Press, 2000), 250.
⁵² Tim Dolin, *George Eliot* (Oxford: Oxford University Press, 2005), 176.
⁵³ George Eliot to John Blackwood, London, 3 November 1876, in *George Eliot Letters*, ed. Haight, vol. 6, 304.

should be removed altogether, leaving a country house romance, to be retitled 'Gwendolen Harleth'.⁵⁴ Other, more sympathetic critics have argued for the essential relationship between the two halves of the novel. In particular, Isobel Armstrong has argued that 'the "broken" halves of the novel that have disturbed commentators so much, from Henry James onward, are the result of a deliberate attempt to move between the visual and the aural'.⁵⁵ For Armstrong, Gwendolen's narrative – realist, detailed and primarily visual in mode – exists in dialectical relationship with the Mordecai narrative, which is messianic, generalized and aural: 'in the Jewish parts of the novel Eliot attempts writing as music, intends it to *be* music'.⁵⁶ If such a reading risks idealizing musical forms of communication, it at least does so in a way that is true to Eliot's own ideas about (to borrow Wordsworth's phrase) the power of sound.

Both the Princess Halm-Eberstein, the woman revealed to be Deronda's mother, previously known on stage as Alcharisi (the self-described 'greatest lyric actress of Europe'), and Mirah, Deronda's destined wife, are professional singers (538). Moreover, both, in different ways, show the challenges that female singers faced in light of contemporary ideas about female respectability.⁵⁷ Gwendolen's 'voice was a moderately powerful soprano (some one had told her it was like Jenny Lind's), her ear good, and she was able to keep in tune', and when her family are suddenly impoverished she too considers a career as a professional singer (38). However, her musical limitations are made clear early on, when her performance of 'a favourite aria of Bellini's' is condemned by Herr Klesmer, the novel's surrogate for the New German School of Liszt and Wagner, as 'a form of melody which expresses a puerile state of culture . . . the passion and thought of people without any breadth of horizon. There is a sort of self-satisfied folly about every phrase of such melody: no cries of deep, mysterious passion – no conflict – no sense of the universal. It makes men small as they listen to it' (38–9). Klesmer's role exposes not just Gwendolen's limitations ('even more galling was the hint that she could only be accepted on the stage as a beauty who hoped to get a husband', 221) but the 'lack of idealism in English politics' (202). However, his own music is treated with irony; the piano fantasia he performs

---

⁵⁴ F. R. Leavis, *The Great Tradition* (London: Chatto & Windus, 1948), 79–125.
⁵⁵ Isobel Armstrong, *Novel Politics: Democratic Imaginations in Nineteenth-Century Fiction* (Oxford: Oxford University Press, 2016), 247.
⁵⁶ Armstrong, *Novel Politics*, 249.
⁵⁷ George Eliot, *Daniel Deronda*, ed. Graham Handley, with an introduction by K. M. Newton (Oxford: Oxford University Press, 2014), 538. Subsequent references will be given in parentheses in the main text.

after Gwendolen is described as 'an extensive commentary on some melodic ideas not too grossly evident' (40). Moreover, there is, of course, a glaring contradiction in Eliot's incorporation of Wagner, already by this time notorious for his antisemitism, within a novel that gives such a sympathetic account of Jewish history and identity. Ruth Solie has suggestively described the novel as 'a commentary on its author's ambivalence toward "the music of the future" – which is to say, toward Wagner. . . . Like the contemporary debate about Jewish identity, the conversation about music's future imagines a decision to be made between the preservation of a cultural past and the embrace of a cosmopolitan future'.[58]

The brother and sister Mordecai and Mirah are representatives of this cultural past and of religious enthusiasm more broadly: Mordecai is described as having a 'consumptive voice, originally a strong high baritone, with its variously mingling hoarseness, like a haze amidst illuminations', intoning Hebrew verses with 'absorbing enthusiasm' (403–4). Even the practical Mrs Meyrick describes Mirah's voice as 'just perfect: not loud and strong, but searching and melting, like the thoughts of what has been' (302). Mirah's earliest memories are of her mother's voice, fusing maternal affection with Hebrew hymnody:

> I think my life began with waking up and loving my mother's face: it was so near to me, and her arms were round me, and she sang to me. One hymn she sang so often, so often: and then she taught me to sing it with her: it was the first I ever sang. They were always Hebrew hymns she sang; and because I never knew the meaning of the words they seemed full of nothing but our love and happiness. (175)

This idea of sung or chanted words that are powerful despite – perhaps because – they are incompletely understood is invoked again when Deronda visits a synagogue in Frankfurt, and 'having looked enough at the German translation of the Hebrew in the book before him to know that he was chiefly hearing Psalms and Old Testament passages or phrases, gave himself up to that strongest effect of chanted liturgies which is independent of detailed verbal meaning – like the effect of an Allegri's *Miserere* or a Palestrina's *Magnificat*' (307). This effect is one that can only be gestured towards within the representational terms of nineteenth-century realist fiction. Furthermore, the novel ultimately leaves open the question of whether it is capable of reviving the arrested state of English culture,

---

[58] Ruth A. Solie, *Music in Other Words* (Berkeley and Los Angeles: University of California Press, 2004), 159–60.

embodied in the Gwendolen narrative. In leaving this question unresolved, Eliot reflects not only her response to the political debates of the day but also a much older set of concerns surrounding the role of song in religious life.

The final invocation of the Hebrew Bible in the novel comes after Deronda reveals to Gwendolen his new mission and vocation: 'I am going to the East to become better acquainted with the condition of my race in various countries. . . . The idea that I am possessed with is that of restoring a political existence to my people, making them a nation again' (676–7). His words carry a devastating effect for Gwendolen:

> There was a long silence between them. The world seemed getting larger round poor Gwendolen, and she more solitary and helpless in the midst. . . . There comes a terrible moment to many souls when the great movements of the world, the larger destinies of mankind, which have lain aloof in newspapers and other neglected reading, enter like an earthquake into their own lives. . . . Then it is as if the Invisible Power that has been the object of lip-worship and lip-resignation became visible, according to the imagery of the Hebrew poet, making the flames his chariot and riding on the wings of the wind, till the mountains smoke and the plains shudder under the rolling, fiery visitation. (677)

The language of divine power from Ps. 104 ('who maketh the clouds his chariot: who walketh upon the wings of the wind: Who maketh his angels spirits; his ministers a flaming fire', Ps. 104.3–4) is used here to chastening effect. The manifestation of the 'Invisible Power', however, also finds unlikely echo in Eliot's poem, 'O May I Join the Choir Invisible' (1874), with its wish to live on through others and achieve a type of secular immortality:

> O may I join the choir invisible
> Of those immortal dead who live again
> In minds made better by their presence . . .
> In thoughts sublime that pierce the night like stars,
> And with their mild persistence urge man's search
> To vaster issues.
>   So to live is heaven:
> To make undying music in the world.[59]

---

[59] George Eliot, 'O May I Join the Choir Invisible', in *The Legend of Jubal and Other Poems* (Edinburgh and London: Blackwood, 1874), 240–2 (240–1).

This became one of Eliot's most popular and well-known poems: the Liberal Churchman Llewellyn Davies claimed to find in it the 'germ of a new Hymnology' and the second and third lines are inscribed on Eliot's gravestone in Highgate Cemetery.[60] After her death, 'The Choir Invisible' would be set to music on at least seven occasions and used as a choral anthem in English Positivist meetings. With this poem-song, we seem to come circle from Eliot's early wish that 'the only music heard in our land were that of strict worship' to a new kind of secular, empirical, even scientific, song of faith, without the sanction of scriptural authority.

* * *

The chapters in this volume push against two deeply entrenched, interrelated narratives about religion and music in the nineteenth century: firstly, that this was a period of secularization, driven primarily by discoveries in geology and evolutionary science, and secondly, that art – and music above all – replaced religion as a new object of secular devotion. The first of these narratives privileges elite intellectual and literary discourse – from Tennyson's 'honest doubt' to Matthew Arnold's withdrawing 'sea of faith' – while ignoring contemporary religious revivals and a documented surge in religious participation and church-building in mid-Victorian Britain.[61] More recently, critics have also nuanced the literary-intellectual 'crisis of faith', demonstrating that many doubters embraced more flexible forms of belief. Victorian artists and intellectuals didn't simply reject the authority and veracity of scripture, they engaged robustly with a 'changing Bible' in an age of criticism and scientific discovery.[62] The second narrative, of the emergence of art as a new kind of religion, is often associated with the elevation of instrumental music through the claims of German Idealist philosophers and the music of Beethoven. In a reversal of eighteenth-century hierarchies, instrumental music was now seen as eloquent precisely because it was non-specific, liberated from language into an autonomous realm of pure

---

[60] Martha S. Vogeler, 'The Choir Invisible: The Poetics of Humanist Piety', in *George Eliot: A Centenary Tribute*, eds. Gordon S. Haight and Rosemary T. VanArsdel (London: Macmillan, 1982), 64–81 (76).

[61] Callum Brown, *The Death of Christian Britain: Understanding Secularization, 1800–2000* (London: Routledge, 2001); Doreen Rosman, *The Evolution of English Churches, 1500–2000* (Cambridge: Cambridge University Press, 2003).

[62] Charles LaPorte, *Victorian Poets and the Changing Bible* (Charlottesville: University of Virginia Press, 2011); Charles Taylor, *A Secular Age* (Cambridge, MA: Harvard University Press, 2007), Ch. 11.

meaning.⁶³ Textless forms such as the symphony and string quartet were now positioned at the apex of art and helped to produce new regimes of silent, devotional listening.⁶⁴ Genres of vocal music, too, from lieder to opera, bathed in the aura of music's new-found cultural prestige. This narrative has proven remarkably persistent and has never lacked advocates, from E. T. A. Hoffmann and Walter Pater through to modern champions of secular modernity and the triumph of art.⁶⁵ It undoubtedly holds a great deal of truth, but also carries with it a series of omissions and occlusions. It is, once again, a story that is most true of nineteenth-century elites; by contrast, religion continued to occupy a central position in the lives of the overwhelming majority of the population, and religious song remained one of the most ubiquitous cultural forms, both within and beyond the rarefied surroundings of the concert hall.⁶⁶

Our focus on places and sites at different levels of granularity (metropolis, empire, meeting halls, streets, churches and synagogues) allows us to interrogate the lack of attention paid to music in local and global accounts of nineteenth-century religion, culture and modernity. Our focus on 'song' necessarily excludes the important field of biblically inspired instrumental programme music. And while several chapters here consider the important influence of Classical and Romantic orchestral composers, we concentrate on popular vocal composition and communal performance. This is not to diminish the importance of instrumental music to religious experience in the period but rather to foreground the neglected role of song as a medium for transmission of the biblical text and a key site of both popular and scholarly exegesis.

In recent years, scholars of music and sound have moved beyond traditional studies of composers, schools, movements and institutions to think about the production and consumption of music from a variety of methodological perspectives and within different aesthetic and historical contexts. The

---

⁶³ See Carl Dahlhaus, *The Idea of Absolute Music*, trans. Roger Lustig (Chicago: University of Chicago Press, 1989): 'Music that is "dissolved" from verbal and functional constraints "sublimates" or "exalts" itself above the boundedness of the finite to an intimation of the infinite' (60). See also Lydia Goehr, *The Imaginary Museum of Musical Works: An Essay in the Philosophy of Music* (Oxford: Clarendon Press, 1992); Daniel K. L. Chua, *Absolute Music and the Construction of Meaning* (Cambridge: Cambridge University Press, 1999) and Mark Evan Bonds, *Absolute Music: The History of an Idea* (New York: Oxford University Press, 2014).
⁶⁴ James H. Johnson, *Listening in Paris: A Cultural History* (Berkeley: University of California Press, 1995).
⁶⁵ For one version of this story, see Tim Blanning, *The Triumph of Music: Composers, Musicians and their Audiences, 1700 to Present* (London: Penguin, 2009).
⁶⁶ On the tensions between music history and the history of religion in this period, see David Kennerley, *Sounding Feminine: Women's Voices in British Musical Culture, 1780–1850* (Oxford: Oxford University Press, 2020), 19–20.

development of interdisciplinary sound studies has prompted provocative new studies emphasizing the centrality of music and song to political, social and aesthetic developments and transformation in nineteenth-century Britain and the Anglo-World.[67] One recent focus of musicology has been work on music and the city, which has emphasized the diversity of musical practices and the place of music in the urban sensorium.[68] At the same time, scholars have argued for the importance of popular culture in both forging and contesting national, imperial and ethnic identities.[69] Our interdisciplinary approach allows exploration of unacknowledged or overlooked moments of convergence and intersection between different branches of knowledge and art. Bennett Zon argues that nineteenth-century scholarship on biblical music was responsive to the revolutionary ideas of evolutionary biologists, while Ayla Lepine draws our attention to the intimate relationship between the musical and decorative arts, as Gothic Revival churches became venues for the reinvention of sacred music.

Over the last two decades there has been a renewed attention to the relationship between music and religion in the nineteenth century. A comprehensive exploration of nineteenth-century musical interpretations of the Bible is perhaps impossible, though several recent works have provided methodological and conceptual inspiration for this collection. Martin Clarke's interdisciplinary edited collection on *Music and Theology in Nineteenth-Century Britain* (2012) offers case studies of intersections between religious belief and music in nineteenth-century Britain and the empire, exploring 'the interaction of music and theology as a way of understanding aspects of religious, cultural and social life in nineteenth-century Britain'.[70] Although we share Clarke's interest in the 'experiential aspects of music and spirituality', our emphasis on the biblical text – rather than theology as a discipline – provides a much-needed focus on the relationship between text

---

[67] John M. Picker, *Victorian Soundscapes* (Oxford: Oxford University Press, 2003); Collins, ed., *Music and Victorian Liberalism* (Cambridge: Cambridge University Press, 2019); Robin Ganev, *Songs of Protest, Songs of Love: Popular Ballads in Eighteenth-Century Britain* (Manchester: Manchester University Press, 2009); Charles McGuire, *Music and Victorian Philanthropy: The Tonic Sol-fa Movement* (Cambridge: Cambridge University Press, 2009); Sean Shesgreen, *Images of the Outcast: The Urban Poor in the Cries of London* (Manchester: Manchester University Press, 2002); Oskar Cox Jensen, *Napoleon and British Song, 1797–1822* (London: Palgrave, 2015); Weliver, ed., *The Figure of Music*.

[68] Roger Parker and Susan Rutherford, ed., *London Voices, 1820–1840: Performers, Practices, Histories* (Chicago: University of Chicago Press, 2019).

[69] Kate Bowan and Paul Pickering, *Sounds of Liberty: Music, Radicalism and Reform in the Anglophone World, 1790–1914* (Manchester: Manchester University Press, 2017); Jeffrey Richards, *Imperialism and Music: Britain, 1876–1953* (Manchester: Manchester University Press, 2001).

[70] Martin V. Clarke, ed., *Music and Theology in Nineteenth-Century Britain* (Farnham: Ashgate, 2012), 3.

and voice.[71] *Scripture and Song* seeks to develop important modes of enquiry begun by Clarke, Zon and other scholars of religion and music while continuing to demonstrate the potential for fine-grained interdisciplinary investigations of religious and musical cultures and subcultures.

Of the various musical genres interrogated in *Scripture and Song*, hymnody has received the most sustained critical attention.[72] Wide-ranging studies of Victorian hymnody by J. R. Watson and Ian Bradley provide an excellent overview.[73] However, the scale of such surveys necessarily disallows the kind of detailed case studies offered by our own contributors. Even the most searching and innovative studies of hymns and congregational and liturgical music have tended to offer arguments limited to discrete confessional or national traditions (e.g. studies of Methodist, Baptist or African American hymns). As the 'production of a hymnal was a key part in establishing a religious identity' for new and established sects, this is understandable.[74] However, the contributors to *Scripture and Song* are more concerned with tracing musical innovations and artefacts across sectarian and national divides. The chapters by Hicks and Murray, for example, demonstrate that individual hymns made extraordinary journeys across the imagined barriers and literal oceans that divided faith communities. As Rachel Adelstein demonstrates in her chapter on Jewish liturgical music, narrowly focused studies of hymnody have underplayed the impact of Christian musical innovations on non-Christian communities. We are not, however, suggesting an unproblematic celebration of the hymn as a universal or ecumenical form. As the chapters by Johnson-Williams and Grande illustrate, congregational singing could also become a tool to divide classes, races and genders in both the domestic and the imperial setting.[75] Moreover,

---

[71] Clarke, ed., *Music and Theology*, 1.
[72] Isabel Rivers and David Wykes, ed., *Dissenting Praise: Religious Dissent and the Hymn in England and Wales* (Oxford: Oxford University Press, 2011); Jon Michael Spencer, *Black Hymnody: A Hymnological History of the African-American Church* (Knoxville: University of Tennessee Press, 1992); Richard J. Mouw and Mark A. Noll, eds., *Wonderful Words of Life: Hymns in American Protestant History and Theology* (Grand Rapids: Eerdmans, 2004); David W. Music and Paul Richardson, eds., *'I Will Sing the Wondrous Story': A History of Baptist Hymnody in North America* (Macon: Mercer University Press, 2008); Alisa Clapp-Itnyre, *British Hymn Books for Children, 1800–1900: Re-Tuning the History of Childhood* (Farnham: Ashgate, 2016); Martin Clarke, *British Methodist Hymnody: Theology, Heritage, and Experience* (London: Routledge, 2017).
[73] Ian Bradley, *Abide with Me: The World of Victorian Hymns* (London: SCM Press, 1997); J. R. Watson, *The English Hymn: A Critical and Historical Study* (Oxford: Clarendon Press, 1997).
[74] Martin V. Clarke, '"Meet and Right it is to Sing": Nineteenth-Century Hymnals and the Reasons for Singing', in *Music and Theology*, ed. Clarke (Farnham: Ashgate, 2012), 21–36 (21).
[75] For a powerful illustration of the role of music (and histories of music) in fostering racist myths, see, for example, Ruth HaCohen, *The Music Libel Against the Jews* (New Haven: Yale University Press, 2012).

this collection will move well beyond histories of hymns and liturgical music by seeking out the Bible in unexpected genres (like the ballad), which often blurred the line between piety and irreverence.

Although the following chapters focus on musical and religious diversity within the British world, we also attend to imperial and transatlantic exchange and networks, and interrogate the politics and poetics of scriptural song through two related lenses. First, a bio-political focus on music as, on the one hand, a technology of educational and ideological discipline and, on the other, as a collective and congregational experience of great importance to both establishment and Dissenting communities. Second, we examine the embedding of scriptural-song traditions in imperial settings. In these colonial contexts, the Bible, as a record of the cultures and stories of past empires and imperial subjects, becomes a medium for thinking through strategies of imperial power and the global missionary project.[76] In the imperial context, the communitarian power of sacred music and song could serve both universalizing and exclusionary ends. Yet as with earlier cultures of sectarian non-conformity, sacred song often served as a channel for articulating resistance unspeakable through other media (as histories of African American hymnody have powerfully demonstrated).

The methodological approaches of our chapters are necessarily diverse, reflecting the broad range of disciplines the volume draws on and the sources the authors are working with. The case studies in our opening chapters examine the neglected influence of the Bible on some of the most popular genres and tunes of the nineteenth century. In Chapter 2, Oskar Cox Jensen explores the neglected and often strained relationship between 'the Ballad and the Bible'. The London ballad-singer was attacked by evangelicals and the Established Church alike as a token of all that was pernicious in secular culture: blasphemy, obscenity, disloyalty to Church and state. Yet Jensen demonstrates that these two cultures were mingled in myriad ways. His chapter explores shared tunes, lyrics and themes alongside the individual performers who navigated – and transgressed – the line between scared and profane. In an age of reform and Dissent, the two cultures were deeply linked, almost to the point of symbiosis. In Chapter 3, Jonathan Hicks surveys the various uses of one of the most popular tunes in the nineteenth-century English-speaking world: the 'Old Hundredth'

---

[76] On popular music and empire, see Richards, *Imperialism and Music*. For an exemplary study of the dissemination of religious texts and traditions through a variety of imperial contexts, see Isabel Hofmeyr, *The Portable Bunyan: A Transnational History of The Pilgrim's Progress* (Princeton: Princeton University Press, 2004).

Psalm Tune. As a case study in diffusion, the Old Hundredth reminds us of the seamlessness of sacred and secular culture in the Victorian age. At the same time, as an object of musicological enquiry, the psalm tune became bound up in attempts to regulate present practice by 'restoring' older traditions. By insisting on the works' popular status, Hicks reopens the question of what this music meant to those who sang or heard it, while reclaiming its central place in the audition of the Bible in Victorian Britain. In Chapter 4, Brian H. Murray follows the life cycle of a single hymn – the 'The Son of God goes forth to War' by Reginald Heber – through a variety of devotional and performance contexts in Britain and beyond. At the beginning of the nineteenth century, hymnody was still controversial and almost exclusively associated with Protestant Dissent. Yet Murray explains how High-Church Anglicans came to embrace the hymn book and utilize its devotional and liturgical power. The chapter argues that Anglican hymn writers engaged with much earlier literary form – martyrology – to craft modern hymns that looked simultaneously back to the origins of an episcopal tradition and forward to the global missionary project.

Moving on from these musical case studies, the following chapters interrogate sacred and scriptural song within specific religious communities, organizations and institutions. In Chapter 5, Rachel Adelstein discusses the practice of choral singing in nineteenth-century synagogues in Britain and Germany. Her chapter on 'Sacred Choral Music, Emancipation and Modernity in Jewish Liturgy' explores the ways in which Jewish communities adopted and adapted nineteenth-century cultural trends in music pedagogy, liturgical music and approaches to the music of the past. Adelstein's focus on choral singing reveals how Jewish communities combined biblical texts with modern musical styles to establish a group identity that was both European and Jewish. In Chapter 6, Matildie Wium explores the career of the evangelical Swedish opera singer Jenny Lind. Protestant piety and a concomitant embodiment of the values of female domesticity and charity were central components of Lind's celebrity image. Her commitment to her faith informed her decision to leave the stage at twenty-nine and her successful second career as an oratorio and concert singer. This chapter investigates the rationale of Lind's career choices – including her successful collaboration with the American impresario, P. T. Barnum – as compelling examples of the intersection and exchange between nineteenth-century Christian piety and commercial music practice. In Chapter 7, James Grande explores the early history of London's Sacred Harmonic Society, founded in 1832. The chapter places particular emphasis on the recently completed Exeter Hall, which soon became synonymous with amateur choral singing and formed a new focus for London's Dissenting community. The oratorio concerts here were seen to represent the ascendancy of the amateur chorus over virtuosic soloists, and artisans over aristocrats, signalling the growing acceptance of Dissenters in the mainstream of cultural life and (conversely) of music in Dissenting communities.

In Chapter 8, Ayla Lepine explores the materialization of musical and religious ideas in another London case study: the Gothic Revival organ cases of John Ninian Comper and his mentor, G. F. Bodley, which often featured painted inscriptions drawn from biblical sources. Focusing on Comper's elaborate memorial chapel in the crypt of St Mary Magdalene, Paddington, Lepine argues that biblical inscription and musical culture were crucial to such Gothic Revival interiors. Visual representations of music in late Victorian Gothic churches and chapels signalled an important double temporal move. These holy resonating chambers simultaneously looked forward to new uses of music in Anglican worship on the brink of the twentieth century and back to scriptural sources with stimulating results. In Chapter 9, Erin Johnson-Williams extends our exploration of scripture and song in the imperial world, exploring the development and expansion of the tonic sol-fa singing movement under the leadership of John Curwen. While the idea of non-denominational and 'classless' hymn-singing resonated with contemporary theories of universalism and British social process, the association of tonic sol-fa with missionary imperialism kept the movement largely separate from more elite strands of Victorian music education. While the tonic sol-fa movement navigated between theological and commercial concerns, it also brought unprecedented public attention to nationalistic definitions of the British hymn. Finally, Bennett Zon turns to the surprising cross-currents between ethnomusicology, sacred history and evolutionary science in his study of Carl Engel's influential treatise *The Music of the Most Ancient Nations* (1864). Engels viewed the development of music by ancient peoples, including the biblical Hebrews, from an evolutionary perspective. Yet despite what we might expect from an 'evolutionary' study of this period, Engel's method was explicitly non-Darwinian, drawing instead on the theories of Herbert Spencer and E. B. Tylor. As Zon demonstrates, Engel's unique fusion of ethnomusicology, ancient history and science ensured the persistence of non-Darwinian thinking in later nineteenth-century ethnomusicology.

The chapters in this volume combine to explore the presence of the Bible in everyday life and the rich diversity of sacred song in nineteenth-century Britain. *Scripture and Song* thus initiates an interdisciplinary discussion between scholars of music, cultural history, literature, theology and biblical studies, to reveal points of intersection and exchange between these disciplines and activities in the long nineteenth century. By interrogating the manifold musical adaptations, interpretations and mediations of scripture, we insist on the centrality of the Bible to Victorian music and the importance of song as a site of engagement with scripture in nineteenth-century Britain and beyond.

2

The Ballad and the Bible

Oskar Cox Jensen

Between Pontefract and Doncaster lies the village of Campsall. Its parish church, St Mary Magdalene, was for centuries a living in the gift of the Yarbrough family, and it was Thomas Yarbrough who, in 1803, commissioned the family memorial 'Charity' that may still be found in the chancel (see Figure 2.1). The artist was the noted sculptor, John Flaxman, R. A.[1] For an account of the monument's creation, we turn to a surprising source: an 1825 article on 'London Ballad Singers':

> By far the most elaborate and the most effective figure in the group . . . is that of a sailor [at left]. Will it be believed? Jack Stuart, our ballad-singer, our pseudo-sailor, stood to the sculptor for this figure. These artists, it seems, are constantly beating about for models. Flaxman, in one of his patrols, ran his head against Jack Stuart, as the poor fellow was maunding in the Borough. An appointment, succeeded by repeated visits, was the consequence; and to this accident was the ballad-singer indebted for his singular preservation from the common lot.[2]

That a sculptor should make use of cheaply hired layabouts with striking faces is no great surprise. The image itself, far from being incongruous, in fact sets up the power relations of our subject rather nicely, as 'charity' is dispensed from on high to the poor sailor-cum-singer, the latter aligned with other subaltern figures: women, the very old and the very young and even a dog. The journalist's incredulous amusement derives rather from the unlikely juxtaposition of a ballad-singer with a piece of devotional iconography. To educated contemporaries, ballad-singers were scoundrels, purveyors of filth, in league with pickpockets, beggarly corruptors of mass morality. The 'ballads' they sung were a medium rather than a musical genre: a disparate mix of songs with a wide range of origins. Some of the most celebrated ballads of the eighteenth century, which

---

[1] See *The Art Journal* 7 (1868): 2–3.
[2] *The Mirror of Literature* 6, no. 151 (16 July 1825): 53.

Figure 2.1 John Flaxman, 'Charity'. Impression from *The Art Journal*, 7 (1868): 3.

remained popular well into the nineteenth, were strikingly anticlerical, such as the obscene 'The Black Joke' and the cynical 'The Vicar of Bray', the former an attack (in part) on priests' sexual continence, the latter on the strength of their theological principles.[3] As late as 1847, ballads were written and sung to attack the clergy and circulated and posted in public places.[4] The Church was hardly toothless in the face of such assaults, however. The Society for Promoting Christian Knowledge (SPCK) distributed tracts warning readers against sinking

---

[3] See, respectively, Paul Dennant, 'The "barbarous old English jig": The "Black Joke" in the Eighteenth and Nineteenth Centuries', *Folk Music Journal* 10, no. 3 (2013): 298–318, and Bodleian Douce Ballads 4(49).

[4] Christopher Thomson, *The Autobiography of an Artisan* (London: John Chapman, 1847), 206.

to the level of a ballad-singer, using the moral example of Will Foster: 'At last he took to singing ballads in the street, and selling them, and was all his life a most shabby fellow, without a coat to his back, or a shoe to his foot, fit to be seen.'[5] James Plumptre, vicar of Hinxton near Cambridge, took a more direct approach:

> I met an old Sailor, begging his way to London. I asked him if he had not any thing to sell? 'He had a few *Godly Books*.' I desired to see them. He took them out. Some Ballads were on the outside of them, which he tried to put away, as if conscious they were bad. I took them away from him, but they were only stupid. He said he seldom sold Ballads, for he did not think them quite the thing[.][6]

It is significant that Plumptre's conduct was seen as both appropriate and legitimate, both by himself, as he published the account, and by the sailor, whose property was after all annexed and his livelihood impaired – the key factor being Plumptre's unquestioned moral authority as a man of the cloth.

This propensity to interfere directly in the songs sung in the street even became the subject of literary satire, in the Irish novelist Charles Johnstone's *Chrysal*. The work features the appropriately named 'Momus the ballad-singer',[7] who complains:

> The clerk of the parish sent me word yesterday, that understanding I sung my ballad to a psalm-tune, he let me know, that I must change my note directly, or he would order the beadles to whip me out of the parish, if ever I presumed to sing there again[.][8]

Given the parochial organization of both poor relief and the apprehending of vagrants, such threats were far from idle.

It was not only the Established Church that could wage holy war on ballads. In 1808, the *Satirist* reported an incident involving a London cobbler and the non-conformist pastor Rowland Hill. The latter finding the former singing a scurrilous song at work, Hill allegedly convinced the shoemaker to employ psalms as worksong, by a combination of argument and bribery. When Hill

---

[5] *Religious Tracts, Dispersed by the Society for Promoting Christian Knowledge*, 12 vols (London: F. & C. Rivington, 1800), vol. 12, 28.
[6] James Plumptre, *A Collection of Songs Moral, Sentimental, Instructive, and Amusing* (London: F.C. & J. Rivington, n.d.), 3–4 *fn*.
[7] It is worth observing that ballad lyrics themselves – both those penned by street hacks and those pirated from the pleasure gardens and theatres – often lifted names from classical paganism, Phoebus, Apollo and Diana appearing with great frequency, a tendency that troubled some Church authorities.
[8] Charles Johnstone, *Chrysal: Or, The Adventures of a Guinea*, 3 vols (London: Cooke, 1797 edn), vol. 2, 7, 12.

returned some days later he was met with the strains of 'The Black Joke', and the cobbler's own reproof, as relayed third hand by the journalist:

> 'Twould have ruined me shortly. Would your Honour believe it? though I got up an hour sooner, I was three whole days mending two pairs of shoes to 'All-peo-ple-tha à-àt-on-yearth-dò-dò-dwell': whereas, with *Morgan Rattler*, or *The Black Joke*, or any of them there quick sort of tunes, do you see, I knocks them off cleverly in a couple of hours.[9]

The truth of the encounter is impossible to determine – yet it was plausible enough to report, exemplifying the perceived divide between ballad and Bible. The two realms, secular and sacred, are portrayed both as antagonistic and as inhabiting discrete spheres – hence the absurdity of substituting sacred song for secular in a mundane, working context: the slow and stately tune will not aid the mending of shoes.

Such was the story on the surface: two ubiquitous cultural practices – religious observance and ballad-singing – locked in opposition, the one backed by state and ecclesiastical authority, financial heft and customs of social deference, the other by popular tradition and the desire for irreverent entertainment at work and at rest. Yet ballad and Bible (and here 'Bible' stands for wider forms of Christian activity, especially musical) had more in common than simply the Song of Songs. In the case of Rowland Hill and the shoemaker, for example, the pastor's suggested psalm is the Old Hundredth from Sternhold and Hopkins, whose Tudor collection gave rise to the term 'ballad metre', with the Old Hundredth itself playing a central, entangled role in encounters between the two spheres – a relationship studied quite superbly by Kate Horgan.[10] In what follows, I will pursue these connections more broadly: from attempts to co-opt ballad culture in the service of religion; to essential similarities of musical form, history, performance, education and function; to exploring why such connections were more dangerous than were differences; to accounts of balladry in Dissenting conversion narratives. This exploration will end where it began – not in Campsall chancel, but in the curious juxtaposition of the holy and profane. In treading that circle, I will enrich the mutual understanding of two areas rarely considered together historically after the Restoration.

[9] *Satirist*, 8 (May 1808): 244.
[10] Kate Horgan, *The Politics of Songs in Eighteenth-Century Britain, 1723–1795* (London: Pickering & Chatto, 2014), esp. 61–92.

Sheep in wolves' clothing: Infiltrations of ballad culture

> The power of music is but too well known by fatal experience, when it is misapplied – applied to cherish and call forth the evil that lies concealed in the corrupt heart of fallen man; to recommend and excite in him all the follies of levity and dissipation, of intemperance and wantonness. What are we to do in this case? Are we to renounce and disclaim music? No; let us employ music against music.[11]

Bishop Horne's influential eighteenth-century sermon on 'The Antiquity, Use, and Excellence of Church Music' contained this rallying cry to those concerned with the moral education of the general populace. In the wake of the French Revolution, renewed attention to popular culture centred on the ballad as both problem and potential solution. Thus wrote Hannah More, the leading activist of the decade:

> Some respectable clergy who are here, assure me that . . . the most indecent songs and papers are posted up in the cottages [of the poor]. Now it has occurred to me to write a variety of things somewhere between vicious papers and hymns, for it is in vain to write what people will not read[.][12]

Over the course of the Napoleonic Wars, a loose alliance of clerics, bluestockings and loyalists attempted to flood the popular print market with their own compositions, hoping that, if the poor must sing ballads, then they might sing better ones. These songs were backed up with pamphlets and tracts outlining what was proper to sing, and where and when to sing it, in the form of exemplary dialogues.[13]

Reverend Plumptre, encountered above, is of especial interest here, his significance lying less in his own compositions, which he himself admitted to be failures, than in his partnership with John Pitts, England's leading ballad printer, in producing the *Vocal Repository* series of song pamphlets, 1809–10, sold at well under the market price 'By all Booksellers, Newsmen, and Hawkers, in Town and Country. *Great Allowance made to Shopkeepers and Hawkers.* Price One

---

[11] George Horne, *Sixteen Sermons on Various Subjects and Occasions*, 2nd edn (Oxford: J. Cooke et al, 1795), 314–15.
[12] Hannah More to Mrs Bouverie, Bath, 24 Jan 1795, in George Chatterton, ed., *Memorials, Personal and Historical of Admiral Lord Gambier, G.C.B.*, 2 vols (London: Hurst and Blackett, 1861), vol. 1, 274–5.
[13] For example, Hannah More, *The Two Shoemakers. In Six Parts* (London: John Marshall, 1797) or Sarah Trimmer, *The Two Farmers* (London: T. Longman et al, 1787).

Penny'.[14] These were concerned with ostensibly secular subjects, from sailors to harvests, yet Plumptre's work was shaped by the context of his parish:

> The church singers in a parish are generally the singers also at the convivial meetings. With these the Clergyman has naturally some influence, and one copy given away amongst them, handed from one to another, with the songs best suited to the circumstances of the place, and to the talents of the singers, pointed out to them, would go very far towards furnishing a parish with excellent songs.[15]

Chief among his concerns was sobriety, a frequent topic of his sermons.[16] Plumptre fretted about what his Sunday congregation would get up to on Monday, traditionally known as 'Saint Monday', a day of revels:

> [I]f the song, the following evening, aided by liquor and company, were to be 'True joy is drinking,' or 'All get drunk if you wish to be happy,' it would, I fear, go far, very far, to do away any good impressions which the sermon might have left.[17]

Plumptre never underestimated his adversary, here putting the persuasiveness of a drinking song on a par with his preaching. Yet this equating of song with sermon was in another sense the movement's greatest failing.

Both More, whom he admired, and Plumptre himself, paid lip service to the generic conventions of the ballad, and the need to entertain if a song was to succeed. More tried 'to make them a little amusing in the manner, as well as ornamental in the appearance'.[18] Plumptre appreciated that actual psalms could not replace ballads:

> Desirable as I should think it to have our Sheep-shearings and Harvest-homes conducted in such a way, as that a psalm might be sung at them without profanation, yet, from what I have myself seen of such meetings, I should scarcely think it desirable or practicable. The introducing [of] cheerful proper

---

[14] Collected in the British Library volume of ballads 1078.e.6. Original emphasis. I have discussed Plumptre elsewhere, yet not with regard to his character as a churchman: see Oskar Cox Jensen, *Napoleon and British Song, 1797–1822* (Basingstoke: Palgrave Macmillan, 2015), 56, 67, and Oskar Cox Jensen, 'True Courage: A Song in History', in *Charles Dibdin and Late Georgian Culture*, eds. Oskar Cox Jensen, David Kennerley, and Ian Newman (Oxford: Oxford University Press, 2018), 115–36, 129–30.

[15] Plumptre, *A Collection of Songs*, 19.

[16] Song and drunkenness were often seen as codependent at this time, as a glance through the Old Bailey trials will attest. The fact that some ballads were drinking songs hardly helped their reputation.

[17] Plumptre, *A Collection of Songs*, 4.

[18] More to Bouverie, in Chatterton, 275. See also an earlier letter to the same (14 November 1793) where she writes: 'I known human nature rather too well to expect that my poor [school]girls should withstand the sound of a fiddle' – ibid., vol. 1, 231.

songs seems to be a middle step, and might be the means of purifying singing, and in time lead to so desirable an end.[19]

Yet in practice, neither was capable of keeping the sermon out of the song. More went so far as to include footnotes in her song texts to edify readers: her tone was that of a lecturer, not a narrator.[20] Plumptre found his scruples an obstacle to ballad composition – 'I shall object to all *derry downs*, and *toll de rolls*, as unmeaning impertinence . . . merely an apology for noise and riot' – and his volume met with little success, causing him to appeal to popular secular songwriters, in particular Charles Dibdin the Elder.[21] Dibdin was clearer on the difference between song and sermon, their similarities notwithstanding:

> A sermon and a song, even a comic song, may have the same drift, and produce the same effect. The song, written to please, may be so managed as to instruct; and the sermon, written professedly to instruct, will attract more attention if it be so managed as to please[.][22]

For a commercial songwriter, keen to fashion himself as an upholder of morality, to liken a ballad to a sermon, is perhaps unsurprising. It is more remarkable that the headmaster and essayist Rev. Vicesimus Knox recommended Dibdin in person and writing as 'the only man he ever knew, who could convey a Sermon through the medium of a Comic Song'.[23] Given what has gone before, the readiness of clergymen to enter into business with men like Pitts and Dibdin, and dirty their hands with ballads, appears – in Plumptre's own phrase – *infra dignitatem*.[24] Yet the ballad and the Bible were better bedfellows than might be imagined.

Singing from the same hymn-sheet

A sermon could share sentiment with a song, but not form. Psalms and hymns, however, were song forms as ubiquitous and influential as the ballad. Their

---

[19] Plumptre, *A Collection of Songs*, 20 *fn*.
[20] Cox Jensen, *Napoleon*, 45–7, 55–6.
[21] Plumptre, *A Collection of Songs*, 12. By contrast, the tune most frequently given by More to her ballads was 'Derry Down'.
[22] Charles Dibdin, *The Professional Life of Mr. Dibdin, Written by Himself*, 4 vols (London: Charles Dibdin, 1803), vol. 1, xxiii.
[23] William Kitchiner, *The Sea Songs of Charles Dibdin* (London: Printed for G. and W. B. Whittaker, 1823), 10.
[24] Plumptre, *A Collection of Songs*, 18.

common features have not escaped critical attention.[25] Like a 'traditional' ballad, a psalm such as the 'Old Hundredth' could stand as a simple evocation of an early modern past to a typical Victorian sensibility.[26] Scholars have drawn attention to compositional similarities between the melodies of sacred and secular eighteenth- and nineteenth-century songs, producing unlikely pairings such as Mendelssohn's 'O rest in the lord' and 'Robin Adair', Henry Smart's 'Gloria' and (of all songs!) 'The Vicar of Bray', or Dyke's 'Vox Dilecti' and 'John Anderson, My Jo'.[27] Given the generic restrictions of the prevalent modes and customary melodic contours (especially for opening phrases and closing cadences), these pairings, taken individually, may be no more than coincidence. More tellingly, seventeen of the psalms in the leading Anglican repertory, 'Sternhold and Hopkins', were set to ballad metre.[28] This speaks to an affinity of musical practice, borne out by the identical nature of contrafactum as a regenerative technique for metrical sacred song and broadside ballad alike. In both forms, tunes were repeatedly overwritten with new text, often displaying awareness of and engagement with previous lyrics, fitting with varying degrees of aptitude to the musical metre.[29] In this fashion (and in contrast with the examples above), both traditions were to a large extent developed by those of no musical learning, and thus capable of regeneration from below.

Indeed, the popular, populist connotations of psalmody in particular saw it subjected to the same attacks as balladry, on simultaneously social and technical grounds. The vocabulary of criticism of psalm-singing – 'uncouth', 'unskilled', 'discordant'[30] – is immediately familiar to any historian of ballad culture: social elites, educated in a Continental musical tradition, policed the boundary between the aesthetically respectable (what we would now term classical), and what they claimed to be disreputable, vernacular musics. Charles Burney, an influential member of that elite, observing mass musical learning in Italy, drew a haughty conclusion: not that the masses should be taught to sing better in England, but 'that those without specialised musical training should not attempt

---

[25] See again Horgan, *The Politics of Songs*, 61–92.
[26] J. R. Watson, 'Ancient or Modern, "Ancient and Modern": The Victorian Hymn and the Nineteenth Century', *The Yearbook of English Studies* 36, no. 2 (2006): 2. See also M. Pauline Parker, 'The Hymn as a Literary Form', *Eighteenth-Century Studies* 8, no. 4 (1975): 417.
[27] Orlando A. Mansfield, 'What is Sacred Music?', *The Musical Quarterly* 13, no. 3 (1927): 463–4.
[28] Horgan, *The Politics of Songs*, 66.
[29] Frank L. Harrison, 'Music, Poetry and Polity in the Age of Swift', *Eighteenth-Century Ireland* 1 (1986): 51.
[30] See Sammie A. Wicks, 'A Belated Salute to the "Old Way" of "Snaking" the Voice on Its (ca) 345th Birthday', *Popular Music* 8, no. 1 (1989): 63.

to sing'.³¹ Psalm and ballad alike, rooted in a tradition of unaccompanied, modal monophony, pitched at the upper limit of singers' registers with a good deal of nasal head voice – a tradition sustained especially by many Dissenting congregations – were easy targets for a musical elite raised on scores written in major and minor keys, to be sung in the idiom of the drawing room.³²

The psalm at least had the assurance of scriptural authority and a context of worship. More extreme was the crossover between Christian practice and the ballad found in the Christmas carol. At a time when city corporations across England were laying off their waits – stipendiary musicians who would have sung carols in public – while ephemeral print culture fuelled by increasing literacy was booming, ballad-singers became largely responsible for the sale and street performance of carols. Christmas was a boom season for balladeers in the nineteenth century. Grub Street writers composed new carols to capitalize on the increased demand, which resulted in large part from the material properties of the broadside: a carol sheet, with its elaborate border, not only gave the lyrics, but provided festive decoration when pasted on a wall.³³ A carol sheet might sell for 1*d* uncoloured but 2*d* coloured – the 100 per cent markup such a crucial source of revenue that printers and their families spent their days painting away.³⁴ Some became 'collectibles' that sold for up to five shillings.³⁵ More usually, the poor quality of the paper combined with the exigencies of circulation and the desire for novelty meant that last year's carols always needed replacing.

Carols' childhood and festive associations should not obscure the heavy biblical didacticism of these nineteenth-century sheets, which focused on the Old Testament, saints and the Crucifixion as well as the Nativity – themes emphasized by daunting woodcut illustrations.³⁶ These early examples of capitalist Christmas had more fire and brimstone in them than their modern successors. Yet this did not prevent contemporaries from waxing nostalgic. Douglas Jerrold, in 1840, praised:

[31] Ibid., 64.
[32] Ibid., 61, 64. See also Christopher Marsh, *Music and Society in Early Modern England* (Cambridge: Cambridge University Press, 2010), 391–453, esp. 414–16, 432–4; Horgan, *The Politics of Song*, 68, 75–83, and Vic Gammon, 'Problems in the Performance and Historiography of English Popular Church Music', *Radical Musicology* 1 (2006): unpaginated, 73 paragraphs, para. 18.
[33] James Caulfield, *Blackguardiana; or, A Dictionary of Rogues* (London: Printed for J. Shepherd, c. 1793), 54.
[34] Chalres Hindley, *The History of the Catnach Press* (London: Charles Hindley, 1887), xvi.
[35] John Thomas Smith, *The Cries of London* (London: J.B. Nichols, 1839), 48.
[36] For example, Bodleian: Johnson Ballads 1365 is headed by a skeleton and angel of death, its third carol a warning against sin and featuring threatening swords and cut throats, while Bodleian: Harding B 7(78), from Thomas Taylor of Spitalfields, is dominated by a harrowing illustration of the Crucifixion.

> [T]he Christmas-carol; the homely burden sung two centuries ago: the self-same words, too, that Shakspere [sic] in his childhood may have lain and listened to – that in his later years may have rapt his spirit, bearing it away to Bethlehem! . . . And this sweet, though brief emotion, we may owe to the Ballad-Singer. The peevishness, the selfishness of earth is hushed, forgotten in the rich melodious thoughts born of his antique lay, begotten by the Christmas carol.[37]

An 1861 article went so far as to compare these carols favourably with hymns:

> Looking at these Christmas broad-sheets, it really would seem as if the poorest of our brethren claimed their right to higher nourishment than common for their minds and souls, as well as for their bodies, at the time of year when all Christendom should rejoice. . . . We have been unable to detect in them even a coarse expression; and of the hateful narrowness and intolerance, the namby-pamby, the meaningless cant, the flaccid familiarity with holy things, which makes us turn with a shudder from so many modern collections of hymns, there is simply nothing.[38]

The disreputable, corrupting ballad-singers could then, at least at Christmas, become the central agents in a well-respected appropriation of the secular musical realm by sacred song. Nor were they ill equipped for the task, when one considers that ballad-singers' rudimentary literacy and musical knowledge was almost necessarily the product of the Church, in the form of Sunday- or ragged-schooling, pious small books, congregational singing or tuition by choirmaster or organist.

This was of course also true of the general populace. An incident in the childhood of Thomas Cooper, a radical writer and Chartist leader raised in Gainsborough, epitomizes the crossover between religious learning, secular occasion and sacred music. Cooper's own musical training – he could play by ear only – came from a dulcimer player in his choir, and his literacy from a church school.[39] In 1814, aged nine, he and ten young friends sought to celebrate – and profit from – the declaration of peace with France by busking outside local worthies' houses, sporting national ribbons and flags. Not knowing any patriotic songs:

---

[37] Douglas Jerrold, 'The Ballad Singer', in *The Heads of the People*, 2 vols (London: Robert Tyas, 1840), vol. 2, 293.
[38] Anon., 'Street Ballads', *National Review* 13, no. 26 (October 1861): 417–18.
[39] Thomas Cooper, *The Life of Thomas Cooper. Written by Himself*, 3rd edn (London: Hodder & Stoughton, 1872), 16, 5.

[We] stood and sung 'Awake, my soul, and with the sun,' and 'Glory to Thee, my God, this night,' and other hymns we had learned at school, or in the church, gave three cheers, after shouting 'Peace and Plenty! God save the King!' as we had heard them shout on the procession-day; and then one of us held his cap for coppers, with a low bow. We were well received.[40]

Simultaneously in the capital, broadside printers were publishing victory ballads more appropriate to Cooper's activities. Yet the boys' experience proved that the sacred could stand in for the loyal, and even the topical, especially during the Napoleonic Wars – years which proved that the boundaries between Church, king and country were more easily bridged than the English Channel.

The perils of keeping your enemy close

In his 1861 account of daily London life, George Augustus Sala mused on the midnight entertainment on offer at Evans' supper rooms, where a group of boys sang songs:

> If you scrutinise the faces of these juvenile choristers somewhat narrowly, and happen yourself to be a tolerably regular attendant at the abbey church of St. Peter's, Westminster, it is not at all improbable that you may recognise one or two young gentlemen whom, arrayed in snowy surplices, you may have heard trilling forth in shrill notes. . . . I wonder if it is very wicked for them to be found at Evans's thus late.[41]

Sala's wry comment perhaps masked a deeper anxiety: that worldly temptation was leading astray choirboys and, by implication, profaning their Sunday singing. Evans' was hardly the streets, of course. But the concern was a common one: balladry might corrupt, not owing to its differences from sacred song, but by dint of its coincidences. One working-class Methodist's memoir sketched just such a narrative, in which the youth is equally susceptible to both sacred and secular song, the former's promise of salvation counteracted by the corrupting influence of the latter. Aged six, the boy has a musical epiphany in the Gosford Street chapel: in this case, the song in question is harmonized.

---

[40] Ibid., 24.
[41] George Augustus Sala, *Twice Round the Clock; or the Hours of the Day and Night in London* (London: R. Marsh, 1861), 368–9.

A short-metre hymn was given out, and the old joyful tune, 'Cranbrook' was raised. The tune was taken up in all its parts; and as the light treble notes soared on high, like silvery foam on the waves of the rolling bass, the boy thought he had never heard such delightful harmony. . . . A spark of Divine light fell into the native darkness of his mind. . . . It was never extinguished, but was overlaid for many years with a worse than Egyptian night.[42]

Alas, aged twelve, the boy, now working in a Clerkenwell taproom, is exposed to profane, beer-induced song.[43] Three years later, he frequents a 'cock and hen club' filled with 'simpering girls' and 'brazen hussies'. As 'the drink circulates', the clientele 'call for songs "with more devil in 'em"', and 'the loudest plaudits are given to . . . a ditty which might have been written by the devil himself, in mockery of everything that is holy'.[44] From such depths, it is a long (if predictable) road back for the fallen youth.

Joseph Mayett, a rural labourer educated on Methodist texts, experienced a similar journey. Aged twelve, he held severely that 'Singing was a sin unless it was psalms or hymns'. Yet he soon found himself corrupted by the local militia: 'I was much delighted to see them and to hear the Musick this was Congenial with my Carnal nature.' Even loyalist ballads proved pernicious, as 'Satan' led Mayett 'to sing a good war song telling me there Could be no harm in that and from that to a merry love song and from that to all the paltry and filthey [sic] songs that could be devised'.[45]

In a conversion memoir of this sort, the dangers of balladry are necessarily made manifest in service to the narrative – moral descent being a precondition of epiphany. More troubling to established morality was the creeping influence of both the ballad and, on occasion, its theatrical overtones, on congregational singing. Back in Gainsborough, Thomas Cooper observed 'a poetical war, about the propriety of singing a hymn to Arne's grand melody of "Rule[,] Britannia"', hotly contested by clergy and parishioners alike.[46] After all, if Cooper and his friends could employ hymns for loyalist celebration, then why should not the reverse obtain? And indeed, in 1803 one Volunteer regiment set verses on Emmanuel to 'Rule, Britannia', for use in their Sunday services, while Rowland Hill set a new text to the tune for his *Surrey Chapel Music* collection and the

---

[42] Robert Maguire, ed., *Scenes from My Life, by a Working Man* (London: Seeleys, 1858), 19.
[43] Ibid., 25.
[44] Ibid., 36, 38.
[45] Ann Kussmaul, ed., *The Autobiography of Joseph Mayett of Quainton (1783–1839)* (Aylesbury: Buckinghamshire Record Society, 1986), 1–2; 4; 23.
[46] Cooper, *The Life*, 46.

London Missionary Society in 1797.[47] Strictly speaking, of course, 'Rule, Britannia' was not a ballad – but it had become a ballad tune by this point. As Kate Horgan points out, 'the term "anthem" had yet to be secularised'. What we would now call 'anthems' ('God Save the King' is her example) were then imbricated in a 'straddling of secular and religious spaces' – sometimes used as Christian anthems, yet tainted with the air of stage and street.[48]

It is likely that few proposers of 'Rule, Britannia"s use were by then aware of its origins in an oppositional 1740 masque – though they would have heard it on the streets and in parades. Nor was Arne's the only secular tune thus introduced: in the early nineteenth century, both the Chorus of Fairies from Weber's *Oberon*, and an 1752 tune known as 'Rousseau's Dream', were used as hymn settings, not uncontroversially, while in 1831, Rev. Christian La Trobe railed against the use among Dissenters of 'Rule, Britannia', Purcell's 'Britons, Strike Home' and the aforementioned ballad 'Robin Adair'[49]. Such a spate of appropriation had not been known since the seventeenth century, when the newly translated metrical psalms were set to a variety of secular tunes. In 1630, Bishop Laud reproved a cleric, Dr Slatyer, for setting psalms to ballad tunes. The fledgling Anglican Church, in a bid for cultural legitimacy, eventually constructed 'a sturdy cultural wall between the two genres' – yet by the nineteenth century, a range of denominations was sounding distinctly secular trumpets at its base.[50]

Yet repertoire was easier to control than style. Dibdin, in a pedagogical work, lectured that 'the best music the world has produced is that which has been composed in honour of the Deity. . . . It has been simple because it has been sublime'. And yet he worried that this principle was being eroded:

> But when, sense and propriety left in the lurch,
> Theatrical singing gets into the Church;
> When the Anthem, sustained by a skill ammirabile,
> Contains all the taste of an opera cantabile;
> What wonder, if melted and touched by the air,
> We forget every purpose for which we came there,
> And while, stead of Religion, the singer we laud,
> The pews cry out bravo, the galleries applaud,

---

[47] Anon., 'The Celebrated Ode in Honour of Great Britain, Called Rule, Britannia', *The Musical Times and Singing Class Circular* 41, no. 686 (1900): 230; Mansfield, 'What is Sacred Music?', 460.
[48] Horgan, *The Politics of Songs*, 86.
[49] Mansfield, 'What is Sacred Music?', 454, 460.
[50] Marsh, *Music and Society*, 420; 421; 422. See also, Chapter 4 (75–7) of the current volume on the contested role of hymns in Anglican worship at this time.

And reserved for the sermon the usual nap,
The Chapel resound with a general clap.[51]

Dibdin was not alone in his concern. As one Winchester poet insisted, songs should stay in their proper place:

For various scenes are various strains;
Measure with matter meets;
Hymns best suit churches, past'rals plains,
Odes Courts – but ballads streets.[52]

The two authors spoke to the same purpose. Balladry and its associated affectations should be kept out of the church, lest all services should mirror the experience of one SPCK tract writer, who found that:

[S]ome of the girls that stood by her sung the praises of God just as if they had been ballads; and tossed their bonnets back, and let their cloaks hang about their shoulders as if they were ballad singers. It is a wonder that shame does not keep girls from doing such things![53]

William Cobbett, discussing Methodism, suspected that:

The *singing* makes a great part of what passes in these meeting-houses. A number of women and girls singing together make very *sweet sounds*. . . . The parson seemed to be fully aware of this part of the '*service*'. The subject of his hymn was something about *love* . . . in a singularly *soft* and *sighing* voice. . . . I am satisfied that the singing forms a great part of the *attraction*.[54]

References to 'bewitched' men and 'snowy bosoms' suggest that we should read Cobbett's account as cynical, reinforcing the connection between the sexualized street practices lamented by the SPCK and the Methodist groups he observed.

If the seedier aspects of street singing could infiltrate the church, then as seen with carols, street singers could appropriate aspects of Christian practice. As the pioneering and controversial ethnomusicologist Alan Lomax has noted, the Anglo-American, Protestant ballad-singer's 'association with his audience is, in sociological terms, one of exclusive authority', along the (burlesqued) lines of the

---

[51] Charles Dibdin, *The Musical Mentor, or, St. Cecilia at School* (London: C. Chapple, 1805), 48.
[52] Anon., *The Hampshire Repository; or, Historical, Economical, and Literary Miscellany* (Winchester: Robbins, *c.* 1800), 197.
[53] *Religious Tracts*, vol. 12, 29.
[54] William Cobbett in *Rural Rides*, cited in John M. Golby and A. W. Purdue, *The Civilisation of the Crowd: Popular Culture in England, 1750–1900* (London: Batsford, 1984), 59.

lawyer, doctor – or priest. That is, the singer's delivery and control of narrative is one of moral and authorial dominion over an audience.[55] Singers could amplify this moral authority by appeal to specific religious ideas. The ballad-singer in Johnstone's *Chrysal* becomes the novel's mouthpiece for the denunciation of clerical hypocrisy, shaming the fallen prelate with 'the irresistible force of [his] powers of ridicule'.[56] Johnstone's character reflects a wider belief in, and indeed a fear of, the singer's moral authority.[57] By the mid-century, singers' performances were said to include 'appeals to Heaven, to . . . Christians in general, and moral reflections' – and usually in good faith, as when a ballad turned to 'Church matters', they were said to be 'handled in the streets in a spirit of conservative Protestantism'.[58] Jerrold even deemed the ballad-singer 'a useful minister in rude society'.[59]

A degree of scepticism might be advisable here – our authors may (naively or otherwise) have failed to spot satirical inferences – yet there were strong motivations for singers to adopt a pious tone. Earlier in the century an observational comic, discussing street singers, reflected upon:

> [T]he *serious* singers, the grunting, bellowing, lame and blind *warblers*, who really merit pity and benevolence. Yet, sometimes, you cannot avoid smiling at the *pathetic* efforts of the latter, . . . chaunting and *hymnifying*
>
> Good [C]hristians all, pray pity me,
> For I am blind, and *cannot see!*[60]

The writer, an anonymous professional miserabilist with a jaundiced view of the world, may not have been moved to charity by such devout pleas: yet many of his contemporaries were.[61]

There was an essential difference between Christian charity as preached by a minister and by a ballad-singer: it profited the latter directly. Far from denying this simple truth, singers played upon it. A London ballad of the mid-century, 'Anything to Earn a Crust', contained these verses:

> Next teetotal spouter turned,
> The water-drinking crew I cheats;

---

[55] Alan Lomax, 'Song Structure and Social Structure', *Ethnology* 1, no. 4 (1962): 440.
[56] Johnstone, *Chrysal*, 8–11.
[57] Ibid. See also Oskar Cox Jensen, *The Ballad-Singer in Georgian and Victorian London* (Cambridge: Cambridge University Press, 2021), esp. 81–121.
[58] 'Street Ballads', 405, 414.
[59] Jerrold, 'The Ballad Singer', 293.
[60] Anon., *Metropolitan Grievances; or, a Serio-Comic Glance at Minor Mischiefs in London and its Vicinity* (London: Sherwood, Neely, and Jones, 1812), 105.
[61] Cox Jensen, *Napoleon*, 27, 30.

> Then the pious dodge I learned –
> Sarmonizing in the streets.
>
> Ranting, tanting, teaching, preaching,
> Till too stale the game did grow
> Next behold me ramping, stamping,
> Leading man at a travelling show.[62]

Effectively, the song's vocalist is eliding preaching with a host of disreputable professions and con tricks: organized religion was tainted by association. This had long been a concern, especially for Nonconformists, whose own preaching, often conducted in the open air and on tour, had to negotiate an uncomfortable similarity to theatrical, fairground and low musical entertainments. Simon Lewis' ongoing research explores these tensions, which help explain the vociferousness with which many evangelist preachers attacked what was, in effect, their secular competition.[63] Scholarly attempts to define sacred song have been both prompted and complicated by this uneasy crossover of purpose and place – a liminality in need of careful policing by those with a stake in the sacred.[64]

Working-class memoir: Ballad meets Bible

The anxieties implicit in this ballad–Bible nexus were not only felt by clerics and scholars. In 1838, John James Bezer was on the point of becoming a Chartist, out of work, with an ill wife and newborn child. Penniless, he took to the streets. 'While wandering along Whitechapel Road, the sudden idea struck me that I would sing a hymn or two for bread and wife, and child – but I couldn't just there, known as I was all about the district.'[65] Destitute as he was, Bezer did not regard himself as on a level with ballad-singers, and thus walked as far as Brixton before starting to sing:

> [H]ere goes – 'God moves' – begin again – 'God moves in a' – out with it, and so
> I did, almost choking,

---

[62] 'Anything to Earn a Crust' (anon, no pub.). Bodleian Harding B 20(5).
[63] Simon Lewis, 'Early Anti-Methodism as an Aspect of Theological Controversy in England, c.1738–c.1770' (Oxford University D.Phil. thesis, 2017).
[64] See, for example, Mansfield, 'What is Sacred Music?', *passim* and Stephen A. Marini, *Sacred Song in America: Religion, Music, and Public Culture* (Champaign, IL: University of Illinois Press, 2003), 4–8.
[65] John James Bezer, 'The Autobiography of One of the Chartist Rebels of 1848', excerpted in *Testaments of Radicalism: Memoirs of Working Class Politicians 1790–1885*, ed. David Vincent (London: Europa, 1977), 179.

> 'God moves in a mysterious way
> His wonders to perform.'
>
> Just before I had concluded singing the hymn, a penny piece was thrown out. . . . I went on again with energy to the tune of 'Church Street,' 'God moves in a mysterious way,' and then, hymn after hymn, and street after street, without flagging, while the coppers came rattling down like manna from heaven.⁶⁶

Despite his success, Bezer kept his occupation from his family, pretending that he 'had a place'. For several days he busked, employing a range of hymns, and reflecting at length on his sense of 'shame'. Then came Sunday:

> On that day I sang too, but then it was in the dark at S—es Street Chapel, Bethnal Green. The congregation little thought when I gave out, with a deep sigh,
>
> 'God moves in a mysterious way,'
>
> that I had sung it scores of times on the previous days in the streets! Ah! the heart only knoweth 'its *own* bitterness'[.]⁶⁷

Although Bezer never technically took to ballad-singing, as he sold a performance rather than copies of the songs, his chief shame lay in his debasement to an equivalent act and in the disrespect shown to the hymns by exploiting them for gain in the street. A devout man of low status, he was deeply conscious of the impropriety of mixing the two cultures.

Bezer's autobiography was first published in the *Christian Socialist*. It is a fitting conclusion to this article, to find that most of our first-hand knowledge of ballad-singing comes from explicitly religious publications, many of them conversion narratives. This is neither irony nor coincidence. The low, disreputable experience of the ballad-singer might have been vicariously thrilling enough, because grubby, to find an audience, but in the early nineteenth century, one would be hard put to persuade a circumspect publisher. A moral message on the other hand, particularly if denominationally specific, could lend such narratives the requisite respectability, readership and necessary financial security. Ex-singers, reborn or saved, could comfortably (and even unconsciously) conform to the generic expectations of their conversion memoirs by exaggerating and sensationalizing the sinfulness and exoticism of their past lives, in order to make their narratives more readable and thus commercially successful; to strengthen

---

⁶⁶ Ibid., 179–80.
⁶⁷ Ibid., 182.

the effect of the conversion described and thus inspire others to reform; and, by employing Christian rhetoric of forgiveness and charity, to call upon their readers and by extension both private organizations and the state to adopt a more benevolent attitude towards sinful singers.[68] Thus the memoir of the ballad-singer David Love, which includes a Methodist conversion in 1796 and examples of his own religious compositions, is also full of exhortations to treat singers well.[69] The memoir of Mary Saxby dwells in its earlier parts upon the sexual perils of ballad-singing as a young woman, charting a Hogarthian succession of shameful (and potentially titillating) encounters, before the spectacular rupture of her salvation.[70] John Magee's memoir, meanwhile, is a peculiar mix of demotic zealotry combined with pointed anticlericalism: at one point he is attacked on his travels by a minister's dog, only to find its owner more hostile and uncharitable still.[71]

With Magee we come full circle. Having begun with the incongruous face of a ballad-singer in Campsall chancel, we end with the incongruous spirit of a preacher in the person of a ballad-singer. Magee, unlike many of his contemporaries, was untroubled in combining in his performance and wares both secular ballads and religious tracts, reasoning that 'so very different is the taste of men'. Yet more often than not, his spiritual ardour was disappointed, the ballad proving more desirable than the Bible: 'As I carry with me in my travels a few pious books and sermons for sale, when I enter any house, and shew these articles, the common salutation I get is, We want no good books; for we have more good books than we have time to read.'[72]

Love, Saxby and Magee were all itinerants, embodying both piety and impropriety, wandering at will to disseminate virtue or vice, depending on the circumstance or one's perspective. As such, they are much like the music itself. The inherent porosity of music, easily able to carry different, even opposing signification, and its sonic dimension – sound, unlike image, is hard to shut out – was combined with the promiscuous nature of both the ballad and sacred

---

[68] The definitive account of the genre remains D. Bruce Hindmarsh, *The Evangelical Conversion Narrative: Spiritual Autobiography in Early Modern England* (Oxford: Oxford University Press, 2007).

[69] David Love, *The Life, Adventures, and Experience, of David Love. Written by Himself*, 3rd edn (Nottingham: Printed for the Author, 1823 (actually 1824)), *passim* and esp. 86–91.

[70] Mary Saxby, *Memoirs of a Female Vagrant, Written by Herself* (London and Dunstable: J. W. Morris, 1806), *passim* and esp. 1–20.

[71] John Magee, *Some Account of the Travels of John Magee, Pedlar and Flying Stationer, in North & South Britain, in the Years 1806 and 1808: With an Account of many Wonderful Instances of Divine Providence* (Paisley: G. Caldwell jun., 1826), *passim* and 10.

[72] Ibid., 18.

song as a medium deriving from many sources, caught between vernacular and elite aesthetics. The result was a potent, permissive practice that troubled state and Church authorities alike. The face of Jack Stuart could be set in stone, safely fixed in Campsall chancel. The songs he sang could not.

3

The Movements of the Old Hundredth Psalm Tune

Jonathan Hicks

I may safely presume, at the outset, that a very small proportion of my readers are in the unhappy position of a friend of mine, to whom I recently played the famous tune we are about to consider, and who surprised me with the remark, that he 'could not say he had heard it before.'[1]

Introduction

Suppose we could name the most popular tune in Victorian Britain – what should we make of it, and how might we write its history? In this chapter I take up these questions by pursuing the case of the Old Hundredth psalm tune, which was, if not *the* most popular tune of the era, then certainly among the most widely known and performed. One measure of its success is found in my epigraph, the opening line of an 1883 article in *The Quiver*, an illustrated London periodical aimed at a broadly middle-class readership, founded by the evangelist and temperance supporter, John Cassell (1817–1865). What brings significance to this anecdote is not the author, who remains nameless, but the fact that it was also printed the same year on the other side of the Atlantic, in a *Sunday Magazine* founded by the English-born engraver Frank Leslie (1821–1880).[2] As we shall see, the Old Hundredth was a truly international phenomenon. Its likely composer – a subject debated at some length in the nineteenth century – was the French music theorist and compiler of Calvinist hymns, Loys Bourgeois (*c.* 1510– *c.* 1560). Bourgeois's tune was initially used to set the 134th Psalm. However,

---

[1] Anon., 'The Old Hundredth Psalm Tune', *The Quiver* 18, no. 877 (January 1883): 193.
[2] Anon., 'The Old Hundredth Psalm Tune', *Frank Leslie's Sunday Magazine* 14 (1883): 253.

in the Anglophone world the melody came to be linked with a translation of the 100th Psalm by William Kethe (*d.* 1594), who worked on both the Geneva Bible (1560) and the Anglo-Genevan 'metrical' Psalter (1561), which contained settings of the Book of Psalms in rhyming vernacular poetry.

Given the time in which the tune has been in circulation it is hardly surprising that the Old Hundredth has accommodated various texts. One example is the 1674 doxology, or short hymn of praise by the Anglican clergyman and hymnologist Thomas Ken (1637–1711), beginning 'Praise God, from Whom all blessings flow'. In Nahum Tate and Nicholas Brady's *New Version of the Psalms of David* (1696), number 100 begins: 'With one consent let all the earth'. It was around this point, at the turn of the eighteenth century, that the words familiar from sixteenth-century Psalters, as well as the tune to which they had been attached, acquired the moniker of the *Old* Hundredth. And it seems that the distinction of age was no barrier to success, since it was Kethe's 'All people that on earth do dwell' that remained the line most associated with the increasingly popular tune.[3] Indeed, for one editor of the aforementioned *Sunday Magazine*, the earth was only the half of it: 'I remark, again', preached the Rev. Dr Thomas De Witt Talmage (1832–1902), a leading figure in both the Presbyterian Church and the Reformed Church of America, 'that all our departed Christian friends who, in this world, were passionately fond of music, are still regaling that taste in the world celestial'. Talmage's remark is followed by what probably sounded like a reasonable prediction: 'there must be millions of souls in heaven who know "Coronation," and "Antioch," and "Mount Pisgah," and "Old Hundred." The leader of the eternal orchestra need only once tap his baton, and all heaven will be ready for the hallelujah'.[4]

These sorts of comments, in which the Old Hundredth is casually listed among the commonest of congregational properties, are not hard to come by. Elsewhere we find even more explicit claims for the status of this psalm tune: in an 1885 issue of *Brainard's Musical Opinion & Music Trade Review*, for instance, between a reprinted article on the patriotic songs of Charles Dibdin (1745–1814) and a write-up of an organ recital in the London suburb of Camberwell, there is brief history of 'the most popular church tune now used in the Protestant churches of England and America'. As the writer observes: 'There has scarcely

---

[3] Other verses that continued to be associated with the tune include a paraphrase of Ps. 95, 'O Come, Loud Anthems Let Us Sing', found in the North American shape-note hymnbook, *The Sacred Harp*, first published in 1844.

[4] Anon., 'Employments of Heaven', *Frank Leslie's Sunday Magazine* (July–December 1887): 395–6.

been a hymn and tune book published in either of these two countries that did not contain this tune.'[5] To the best of my knowledge, the writer's claim is no exaggeration. The question for the present chapter is not *whether* the Old Hundredth held an exceptional place in nineteenth-century hymnody and hymnology – and, by extension, an exceptional place in the musical lives of most of the British population and many of those overseas who lived under British rule or influence – but *why* it came to such prominence, and *how* it was considered as both an object of historical enquiry and an agent of change. The *Brainard's* discussion is instructive on this point: '"Old Hundredth" is one of the few tunes of olden times that have survived the shock and use of centuries. It is a model of a church tune because of its stately character, and its freedom from strong rhythms.' We might also note how the Old Hundredth is contrasted with the 'new-fangled gospel tunes' and compared instead to 'an anchor . . . deeply grounded . . . like a rock it will for ever [*sic*] stand out prominently as a landmark to show what true church music once was and what eventually it will again be'. Of course, such promises of divine continuity and preordained renewal were the bread and butter of Protestant prose, but in this case they are routed through a particular sense of what music ought to be:

> What is grander than to hear a large congregation open its services with the L[ong]. M[easure]. Doxology: – 'Praise God from whom all blessings flow.' There is music and religion combined in that hymn and tune, and we hope the blessed day will not be far off when the church will purify her music by throwing off all the light, sensational stuff now so extensively used, and return again to a pure and devotional style of church music, a genuine specimen of which is 'Old Hundredth.'[6]

The issue of purity recurs again and again in the Victorian discourse on the Old Hundredth; it is manifest both in religious fervour and historicist pedantry. One subscriber to *Brainard's*, for example, felt moved to contact the editor after reading the piece quoted above: 'Long standing errors are hard to kill, and it is therefore the more necessary to indicate whenever they put in a fresh appearance.' The correspondent rebukes the writer in question who 'seems not to be aware of anything written since the publication of Havergal's book, thirty years ago. A reference to Grove's Dictionary of Music will give him full information about the Old Hundredth tune; and in the *Musical Times* (June to Nov., 1881) he will

---

[5] Anon., 'The "Old Hundredth"', *Brainard's Musical Opinion & Music Trade Review* 8, no. 96 (September 1885): 589.
[6] Ibid.

find the history of the Psalter in which it first appeared'. In case these citations were not enough, the sign-off includes one last learned observation: 'The Psalter preserved in the library of St. Paul's Cathedral is the Anglo-German of 1561. See an account of it in *Notes and Queries* for June 2nd, 1882. Yours faithfully, G.A.C.'[7] The details of the subscriber's objections are perhaps less important than their vintage, since the latest date to which G.A.C. refers is 1697. The only hint of more recent times comes in the form of a joke at the article-writer's expense: 'the name "Savoy" [sometimes used to refer to the tune of the Old Hundredth] has no more connection with Savoyards than with barrel organs and white mice. The Savoy meant is that in London, where a congregation of French protestants met in the time of Charles the Second'.[8]

The problem for this complainant – a problem shared by other commentators who preferred to view the Old Hundredth through the philological lens of book history and textual variance – is that popular tunes have a habit of inserting themselves into the messy business of human lives, well beyond the control of editorial intervention. In this instance, to assert that the name 'Savoy' bears no relation to Savoyards, barrel organs and white mice is to wilfully overlook the common Victorian practice of grinding out the tune on modern mechanical instruments. Nicholas Temperley, no stranger to research on the publication history of the Old Hundredth, records its inclusion on no fewer than sixty-six barrels, which places it right at the top of his chart for 'Tunes most frequently found on [English] church barrel organs (c.1790–1860)'.[9] Looking a little later in the century, *c*. 1860–90, John Ogasapian and N. Lee Orr have observed the importance of variation form in American organ music: 'Even the simplest workman delighted in the clearly followable elaborations on "Annie Laurie," "Home, Sweet Home," "Old Hundredth," "Vesper Hymn," "Hail! Columbia," "The Star-Spangled Banner," "The Last Rose of Summer," or the national anthems of Austria and Russia.'[10] By the early twentieth century, the Old Hundredth could be found midway between 'Abide with Me' and 'Yankee Doodle' in a collection of *Songs the Whole World Sings* published in New York in 1915 by D. Appleton. The title page promised its purchaser 'more than two hundred songs which are

---

[7] G.A.C., 'The Old Hundredth', *Brainard's Musical Opinion & Music Trade Review* 9, no. 97 (October 1885): 30. The 'Havergal's book' mentioned is an 1854 study discussed later in this essay.
[8] Ibid. For more on this matter, see *Proceedings of the Huguenot Society of London* 13 (1929): 64–76.
[9] Nicholas Temperley, *Music of the English Parish Church*, vol. 1 (Cambridge: Cambridge University Press, 1993), 236.
[10] John Ogasapian and N. Lee Orr, *Music of the Gilded Age* (Westport, CT: Greenwood Press, 2007), 97. One example from the early twentieth century is a 1909 'Festival Prelude and Fugue' on 'Old Hundredth' by the American organist Hiram Clarence Eddy.

dear to the hearts of young and old in every nation, arranged for use as songs or piano pieces'. These last examples are just two of the many arrangements of the psalm tune for flashy public display and private amateur performance – that is, arrangements designed for rendition outside the context of religious service.

In fact, the illustration in *The Quiver* article with which I began shows a woman seated at a domestic keyboard. And while this may have been a stock image bearing little connection to the piece in question, it is nevertheless telling that the print-setter deemed it fit for purpose. My research suggests that the first arrangements for the home market date from the 1840s, though there may well be earlier examples. Certainly by 1854 one reviewer for *The Musical World*, a self-styled bastion of aesthetic taste and decency, sought to discredit the work of a composer named Mr Wallace who dared meddle with the sacred music: 'why, in the name of Martin Luther [to whom the tune was sometimes attributed], take such a theme as the "Old Hundredth Psalm," Mr. Wallace? Would nothing serve for mincing up into demisemiquavers but this old fragment of Gothic melody, which, of all things in the world, people here associate with their church and their worship?' The reviewer goes on to state that: 'Frankly, we dislike the notion so much, the whole thing seems such a jumble of the absurd and irreverend [*sic*], that the technical cleverness manifested goes for nothing.'[11] Such protestations seem to mark the beginning of a losing battle. At any rate, we do not have to cast the net very far to catch a sense of the Old Hundredth's inclusion in a range of more or less 'irreverend' cultural products: the thirty-third chapter of *The Pickwick Papers* (1836), for example, sees the eponymous hero and his companions visit a temperance association in Brick Lane, East London, where they hear Dibdin's 'Waterman' adapted to the Old Hundredth.[12] In 'Pickwick Abroad', G. W. M. Reynolds' contemporary spin-off story, serialized in *The Monthly Magazine*, the same tune is name-checked as Mr Jopling suggests that Pickwick 'tip us a stave of the old hundredth psalm'.[13] Another nod to the tune in Dickensian fiction occurs in chapter eighteen of *Old Curiosity Shop* (1841), wherein a dog grinds the 'most mournful music' on a barrel organ while his master and company eat at the table: 'When the knives and forks rattled very much, or any of his fellows got an unusually large piece of fat, he accompanied the music with a short howl,

---

[11] '"The Old Hundredth Psalm", Transcribed for the Pianoforte by W. V. Wallace' [review], *The Musical World* 32, no. 39 (September 1854): 647.
[12] James T. Lightwood, *Charles Dickens and Music* (London: Charles H. Kelly, 1912).
[13] 'Pickwick Abroad', *The Monthly Magazine, or, British Register* 25 (1838): 359.

but he immediately checked it on his master looking round, and applied himself with increased diligence to the Old Hundredth.'

Before the decade was out the same tune would make a more respectable appearance as a quotation in the finale of Mendelssohn's Second Piano Trio (1845). Later generations of composers, especially in Britain and America, would continue the tradition of setting or quoting the Old Hundredth: Hubert Parry, Virgil Thomson and Benjamin Britten all deserve a mention, so does Ralph Vaughan Williams, whose arrangement for Queen Elizabeth's coronation in 1953 gave renewed exposure to a hymn that remains a fixture of the Anglican choral tradition to this day. To return to the nineteenth century, we might note more arrangements for amateur pianists, singers and church musicians, alongside further references in contemporary fiction: Thomas Hardy's eponymous *Fiddler of the Reels* (1893), for example, had 'never bowed a note of church music. . . . All were devil's tunes in his repertory'; the marker of his ungodliness was the fact that he could not play the 'Wold Hundredth' in time.[14] If we look to the burgeoning realm of popular sheet music, Derek Scott has noted how the early Tin Pan Alley hit, 'The Volunteer Organist', published in the same year as Hardy's *Fiddler*, included an allusion to the Old Hundredth.[15] Finally, it should come as no surprise that, with the advent of sound recording, the psalm tune in question was among the earliest entrants to the catalogue of London's Gramophone Company (formed 1898): one of the company's first engineers, Fred Gaisberg – once a chorister at St John's Episcopal Church in Washington, DC – captured the Old Hundredth on a set of chimes in 1902.[16]

Anytime, anywhere

So what are we to make of such a haul? And what is the significance of the tune's biblical associations? To be sure, the Old Hundredth is not unique; we might suggest other hymns, anthems, songs and operatic excerpts with equally wide cultural reach. Nevertheless, the life of the tune is remarkable, and any study ought to engage with the sheer variety of its forms and uses. Clearly, if the choice is between a book-bound search for origins (à la G.A.C.) and a worldly play

---

[14] Thomas Hardy, *The Fiddler of the Reels and Other Stories* (London: Dover Thrift Editions, 1997), 72.
[15] Derek B. Scott, 'The Musical Soirée: Rational Amusement in the Home', victorianweb.org/mt/parlorsongs/scott1.html.
[16] Gaisberg's recording is listed in the online discography of the Centre for the History and Analysis of Recorded Music, charm.rhul.ac.uk.

of practice and adaptation then the latter wins hands down. But that is only a starting point: What would we gain by typing a belated letter to an unidentified Victorian nit-picker, informing them of the consensus in current musicology and historiography? It cannot be enough to simply assert the presence of the Old Hundredth in popular culture at large; we are obliged, I think, to say something more meaningful about the nature of hymnal ubiquity in the nineteenth century, not least because the concept of ubiquity has typically been deployed in relation to music of much more recent vintage.

Anahid Kassabian's work on 'ubiquitous listening' and 'ubiquitous music', for example, concentrates on popular music of the present day and recent past.[17] This is no coincidence, since Kassabian draws explicitly on Mark Weiser's studies of 'ubiquitous computing' wherein the smallness of recent technology allows for increased portability and hence increased ubiquity. The same connection has been made, in relation to 'mobile music studies', by Sumanth Gopinath and Jason Stanyek: 'The terms "ubiquity" and [the] adjectival variant "ubiquitous" are symptomatic of a new media lifeworld in which space and time were transformed to an unprecedented degree.'[18] For Gopinath and Stanyek this lifeworld begins more or less where my introduction to the Old Hundredth ended: 'what would be the components', they ask, 'of a long history of mobile music, one extending from the dawn of sound recording in the nineteenth century to its digitized, networked variant in the early twenty-first century?'[19] Their first 'entry point' to this long history is 'the notion of "portability." Which then opens out into a range of key terms and phrases: "miniaturization," "ubiquity," "anytime, anywhere," and "on the go," among them'.[20] They also cite Paul Valéry's 'remarkably prescient' essay of 1929, 'La conquête de l'ubiquité' (The Conquest of Ubiquity), an extract of which, we are reminded, served as an epigraph to Walter Benjamin's essay on the 'Work of Art in the Age of its Technological Reproducibility'. What draws Gopinath and Stanyek to Valéry's ideas is the emphasis he places on the technicalities of sound's distribution. Specifically, Valéry mentions the new possibility of 'a piece of music [being] instantly audible at any point on the earth, regardless of where it is performed' and the ability to 'reproduce a piece of music

---

[17] Anahid Kassabian, *Ubiquitous Listening: Affect, Attention, and Distributed Subjectivities* (Berkeley: University of California Press, 2013) and Anahid Kassabian, Marta Garcia Quinones, and Elena Boschi, eds., *Ubiquitous Music* (London: Ashgate, 2013).
[18] Sumanth Gopinath and Jason Stanyek, 'Anytime, Anywhere? An Introduction to the Devices, Markets, and Theories of Mobile Music', in *The Oxford Handbook of Mobile Music Studies*, eds. Gopinath and Stanyek, vol. 1 (Oxford: Oxford University Press, 2014), 12.
[19] Ibid., 7.
[20] Ibid.

at will, anywhere on the globe and at any time'. Accordingly, Valéry concludes: 'Works of art will acquire a kind of ubiquity.'[21]

If Valéry and Benjamin were concerned mainly with works of art, then Gopinath and Stanyek have much more catholic interests; their scholarship is addressed not only to a range of global dance idioms but also to novel means of noise control, music–body synchronization and the outsourcing of listening to mobile devices. Still, their theoretical maxim remains the same: 'To state the obvious, mobility and ubiquity are . . . undeniably bound up with one another.'[22] This central claim is summed up by the Gramophone advertising slogan, 'anytime, anywhere', which Gopinath and Stanyek use – accompanied by a question mark – in the title of the introduction to their volume. However, we might wish to challenge what they call the 'rather commonplace notion that the early twenty-first century is *the* era of "mobility"'.[23] I need hardly point out that a number of writers on the nineteenth century have addressed issues of travel, migration and mobility.[24] And the key term of 'portability' has been theorized in relation to cultural activity predating the era of sound recording.[25] In fairness to Gopinath and Stanyek, they do acknowledge that: 'Music has been mobile since time immemorial; sound is mobile by definition.' It just so happens that their own work is concerned with how music and sound relate to particular '*ideologies of mobility* (read: cosmopolitanism, free-market economics, globalization)' as well as what they term '*ideologemes of mobility* (read: "freedom," "fluidity," "flexibility," "ubiquity," "instantaneity," "constant contact," and various imaginaries of traveling – globetrotting, journeying, expeditioning, touring)'. Since Gopinath and Stanyek place the emphasis, historically and technologically, on music since sound recording, it makes sense for them to argue that: 'The ideologic and ideologemic coalesce in master marketing tropes such as "anytime, anywhere" and "on the move"'.[26] However, the first of these tropes had little purchase in the Victorian era. By the same token, what they offer as a 'genealogy of "mobile music"' effectively begins with 'The Walkman Effect' discussed by Shuhei Hosokawa in 1984.[27] For Hosokawa, '*musica mobilis*' is defined as: 'music whose source voluntarily

---

[21] Ibid., 12.
[22] Ibid., 13.
[23] Sumanth Gopinath and Jason Stanyek, eds., preface to *The Oxford Handbook of Mobile Music Studies*, vol. 1 (Oxford: Oxford University Press, 2014), ix.
[24] See, for example, part 1 'Mapping and Movement', in *Victorian Babylon: People, Streets and Images in Nineteenth-Century London*, Lynda Nead (Yale: Yale University Press, 2000), 13–82.
[25] John Plotz, *Portable Property: Victorian Culture on the Move* (Princeton: Princeton University Press, 2008).
[26] Gopinath and Stanyek, preface to *Oxford Handbook of Mobile Music Studies*, vol. 1, ix.
[27] Shuhei Hosokawa, 'The Walkman Effect', *Popular Music* 4 (January 1984): 165–80.

or involuntarily moves from one point to another, coordinated by the corporeal transportation of the source owner(s)'.[28] From this statement, Gopinath and Stanyek tease out key themes in mobile music studies, including 'the relationship between human and nonhuman, transportation and movement, spatial traversal and defined locations, ownership and control'. They also draw attention to Hosokawa's 'capsule sociology of the development of mobile music – portraying an historical process that proceeds from the social and collective to the familial and, ultimately, to the autonomous individual; from aggregate, ambient sound to focused, individuated listening; from musical production to reproduction', a process that is marked as 'fundamentally *urban*'.[29] Once again, this 'capsule sociology' may help us to grasp the significance of music in a world characterized by Walkmans, but it is less clear how it relates to earlier forms of musical ubiquity and mobility. The case of the Old Hundredth, I suggest, provides an opportunity to rethink such ideas in the context of nineteenth-century history.

The first step is to show how far and wide we can track a single piece of music on its travels through the Victorian world. In this sense, the 'movements' of my title can be understood quite literally; I am interested in where this psalm was sung, and how it arrived at its various places of performance. However, I do not aspire to comprehensive coverage; to the extent that my enquiries result in a map or itinerary for the Old Hundredth, it is, at best, a partial and impressionistic picture (though it is also a picture we might distinguish from other maps of globalizing nineteenth-century music, such as Italian opera). What matters more is recognizing the ubiquity of the Old Hundredth as it was remarked upon, or taken for granted, by so many different voices of the period. If the invitation to listen 'anytime, anywhere' has been a hallmark of the era of recorded music then the Victorian discourse on the Old Hundredth holds out an alternative promise. Here music is not marketed as something universally available to an all-powerful consumer but witnessed in action at the frontiers of propriety and civilization. The commonest frame of reference for tunes on the move in Victorian Britain was not global capitalism but a would-be-global Protestantism. The two may be closely related, but the distinction is significant: as well as noting where the Old Hundredth was performed, I am concerned with those groups or institutions that sought to mobilize music in support of a given agenda – this is the other sense of 'movements' in my title. Each of the groups in question had links with the Protestant Church, and each put psalmody to work in distinctive ways. By

[28] Ibid., 166.
[29] Gopinath and Stanyek, 'Anytime, Anywhere?', 5.

following in the tracks of the Old Hundredth we see how music could serve the Victorians as both a vehicle of change and a monument to stability.

Protestantism, globalized

Let us pick up our pursuit of the Old Hundredth at 71° 5′ N and 54° 16′ W, just off the western coast of Greenland. These were the coordinates given in a diary entry of 7 May 1850 by the Scottish man of science Peter Cormack Sutherland. At this point, Sutherland was relatively early in a journey he had helped to organize in search of John Franklin's 'lost expedition' of 1845. As it turned out, Sutherland's party, aboard HMS *Lady Franklin* and *Sophia*, did not find what they were looking for; it would be another 150 years before sonar technology gave us a picture of the final resting place of Franklin's ships, HMS *Erebus* and *Terror*, in the deep water of Victoria Strait. Still, the 1850–51 voyage would make its own kind of history, principally thanks to the detailed log Sutherland kept, and subsequently published, telling of life on and off ship. On 6 May, for instance, we read that: 'The weather was remarkably clear and pleasant. With the exception of a few white clouds on the horizon, the sun performed his daily round upon a cloudless sky.'[30] For Sutherland and the rest of his Victorian shipmates this was not a welcome sight: 'There appeared no signs whatever that our release would be early; for ordinary weather could hardly open the ice, which had been set together so closely. The wind would require to blow with considerable force from east or north-east, before we could look forward to getting clear of the incumbrance [sic] which surrounded us on every side.' This unwanted interruption in the search party's progress allowed for a number of equipment checks – 'ice-anchors, warps, and tow-lines were got ready' – as well as observations on the local fauna: 'The small seal (*Phoca vitulina*) is the only one that comes up through the holes in the ice, which it makes and keeps open for itself.' Fortunately for the seals they were as alert to human behaviour as Sutherland was to theirs: 'The attempts of our sportsmen to shoot them at their holes were always unsuccessful; the sound of footsteps on the ice never failed to reach their acute ears, long before we could approach within rifle-shot of them.' The frustrated explorers took drastic measures: 'Crawling on "all-

---

[30] Peter Cormack Sutherland, *Journal of a Voyage in Baffin's Bay and Barrow Straits in the Years 1850–1851*, vol. 1 (Cambridge: Cambridge University Press, 2014), 50.

fours" . . . behind a white calico screen, which occupied the left hand, while the right held the rifle on full cock, we were enabled to approach much nearer.'[31] But still they had no luck.

The following day, 7 May, brought little change in the weather: 'continued clear and fine; indeed, in all respects pleasant; but it had small gratification for us, who were not permitted to advance a single foot'. The problem, once again, was the ice, which refused to shift sufficiently for the ship to make any headway. On this occasion, however, there was no shooting at seals since the crew were occupied with another matter of local interest: 'In the afternoon a sledge was observed coming towards the ships from the land; and, after a journey of at least twenty miles, in which the poor dog's feet had suffered a great deal, as evident from the blood-stained track, two natives, real "Innuit [sic]," the father and son came on board.'[32] It is worth pausing over Sutherland's reference to the 'poor dog's feet', which serves to preface his introduction of the approaching 'natives'. Whether or not the possessive apostrophe in 'dog's' was misplaced – presumably it took more than one dog to pull two people – the image of blood on the tracks, of red stains gouged into ice, is striking. All the more so when we take into account the time required to travel 'at least twenty miles' from land to ship, during which the stains would have grown ever longer. Given the centrality of purity, innocence and pristine landscapes to what Peter Davidson, following Glenn Gould, calls the 'idea of north', we might wonder how the fluid remains of the sledge-pulling beast appeared to Sutherland and his Victorian readers.[33] Might these bodily traces have been taken, at some level, as a form of wounding, or, in more Freudian terms, as a gash in the virginal Arctic? There is no way of answering such questions conclusively, but they do point towards a set of themes in Sutherland's writing whereby the culture and civilization embodied in the modern ship are placed in unusual proximity to elemental and existential concerns. This is doubly significant when we recall that the stated purpose of the journey was to recover the remains of Britons lost at sea. And it is worth keeping this in mind when considering the place of music in Sutherland's somewhat drastic discourse on exploration and encounter.

'Like the Esquimaux at Leively', Sutherland writes, the father and son who came on board on 7 May 'were very respectful in their manners, and answered questions put to them without being in the least excited'.[34] Especially after their

[31] Ibid.
[32] Ibid., 52.
[33] Peter Davidson, *The Idea of North* (London: Reaktion Books, 2005).
[34] Sutherland, *Journal*, 52.

bloody introduction the reader might have been expecting something less measured and restrained. But Sutherland is at pains to praise the ship's latest guests: 'They had never heard of the Expeditions we were in search of, and they expressed great sympathy for the poor men, who had been so long unheard of by their families and friends.' There is, unsurprisingly, much orientalizing ethnographic depiction. Sutherland notes that the boy's features reveal 'every mark of the Mongolian character. His black, long, and straight hair, black eyes, broad nose, flat and broad cheeks, and sallow skin, at once indicated this variety of the human race'. Yet the crux of the story is Sutherland's citation of the Inuit pair as evidence of the success of European missions. The boy, who remains nameless, 'was not ignorant; for his careful teacher', who we later find out was Danish, 'had bestowed great pains upon him'. One test of the boy's teaching is his response to music:

> When he came into the cabin, his respect, for those whom he considered better than himself, was exhibited by uncovering his head; and when he heard the solemn strains of the Old Hundredth Psalm issuing from our barrel organ, he hung his head, and appeared wrapt in humility, before what he had been taught to believe was the language of another world.[35]

At the very moment Sutherland broaches the psalm tune, he underscores how a shared earth might comprise multiple worlds. To repeat an earlier distinction, the Old Hundredth is not figured as something available *anytime, anywhere* since this formulation would be too generalizing, too neutral. Rather, the audition of music at the fringes of Christendom serves as a reminder of the uncharted territory over which Europeans exercised, at best, partial control. The gap between Sutherland's recognition of 'the solemn strains of the Old Hundredth' and the otherworldly grammar apparently perceived by the visiting 'Esquimaux' is written into his journal as a fundamental lack on the part of the non-Europeans: 'In many respects', Sutherland confides, the boy 'was to be envied, for he was really happy. He knew none of the evils of the world, and, at the same time, possessed all the blessings of the Christian religion'.[36] This portrait of an Inuit adolescent seems to describe a distant cousin of Rousseau's noble savage – a Protestant savage, perhaps – who welcomes the improvements brought to his icy state of nature by a southern form of modernity. This, at any rate, is how he appears to Sutherland, who writes of the boy 'enjoy[ing] all the freedom of

---

[35] Ibid., 53.
[36] Ibid.

his unenlightened ancestors, without exposure to any of the dangers peculiar to their wandering life, or without suffering any of their miseries'.[37]

One theoretical point of reference here is the work of Stephen Greenblatt, whose mobility studies 'manifesto' provides a series of aims for a mode of enquiry that takes seriously the movements not only of bodies and objects but also of ideas and practices.[38] 'First', Greenblatt writes, '*mobility must be taken in a highly literal sense*'. The italics are his, and the list of examples he offers makes clear his interest in the routine details of how people move: 'Boarding a plane, venturing on a ship, climbing onto the back of a wagon, crowding into a coach, mounting on horseback, or simply setting one foot in front of the other and walking: these are indispensable keys to understanding the fate of cultures'.[39] Greenblatt's preference, then, is to move from specifics to abstractions: 'Only when conditions directly related to literal movement are firmly grasped will it be possible fully to understand the metaphorical movements: between center and periphery; faith and skepticism; order and chaos; exteriority and interiority'.[40] Sutherland's journal lends itself to this kind of analysis: not only does it involve close attention to the shifting surfaces of the ice, and the texture of life after 'venturing on a ship', but it also raises questions about borders, limits and edges – where something as mundane as a Sunday psalm tune might illuminate the chasm between worlds.

Greenblatt's second aim – '*mobility studies should shed light on hidden as well as conspicuous movements* of peoples, objects, images, texts, and ideas' – also applies. The history of Arctic exploration has not typically placed music and theatre at the centre of enquiries. Yet, as we shall see, life afloat could be structured by different sorts of musical participation. It is Greenblatt's third point, however, that is most apposite: '*mobility studies should identify and analyze the "contact zones" where cultural goods are exchanged*. . . . A specialized group of "mobilizers" – agents, gobetweens, translators, or intermediaries – often emerges to facilitate contact, and this group, along with the institutions that they serve, should form a key part of the analysis'.[41] The Old Hundredth, I suggest, is best understood in the context of contact zones and mobilizers, but with one crucial caveat. Greenblatt's 'contact zones', like the 'encounters' described by

---

[37] Ibid.
[38] Stephen Greenblatt, 'A Mobility Studies Manifesto', in *Cultural Mobility: A Manifesto*, ed. Stephen Greenblatt (Cambridge: Cambridge University Press, 2009), 250–3.
[39] Ibid., 250.
[40] Ibid.
[41] Ibid., 251.

Annegret Fauser at the 1889 World's Fair, should not be mistaken for spaces of free and equal exchange.[42] The Old Hundredth was part and parcel of an attempt to expand British territory. Despite all stylistic appearances to the contrary, it was a cutting-edge tool, an instrument of a violent Victorian avant-garde.

By the time the Old Hundredth breached the Arctic Circle, aboard Sutherland's mid-century voyage, it had long been associated with the work of charting and converting the outer reaches of the known world. In fact, 1850 was not even the first mention of the tune's presence in the icy north. In the decade following the end of the Napoleonic Wars, William Edward Parry found fame by leading a series of voyages in search of a North-West Passage. Among Parry's surviving possessions is a barrel organ, complete with bells, drums and triangle built by the London firm of John Longman at 131 Cheapside.[43] In a precursor of Sutherland's account, Parry's journal from 1821 includes observations on the use of music for on-board exercise when bad weather prevented the men from leaving ship: 'they were ordered to run round and round the deck, keeping step to a tune on the organ'.[44] In a later journal, of 1824, we also find Parry remarking on an encounter with 'Eskimos' at Winter Island: '[they] derived great amusement from our organ, and from anything in the shape of music, singing, or dancing, of which they are remarkably fond'.[45] Speaking of one woman in particular, the captain continues: 'it was enough . . . just to make the motion of turning the handle of the organ, which conveying to her mind the idea of music and merriment, was always sure to put her immediately into high spirits'. Since five of the barrels that travelled with the instrument remain intact, we have a good idea of tunes available on this expedition. Unlike later, Victorian accounts of mechanical organs dominated by operatic excerpts, the only theatre music available on these polar voyages took the form of songs familiar from British dramas such as *Speed the Plough* or *Ramah Droog*. We also find the obligatory national anthem. And, just as importantly, the first of the two extant barrels of church tunes begins with the Old Hundredth.

This was not an isolated example. In 1830, not long after Parry's barrel organ could be heard sounding out the polar regions, a cousin of the same instrument

---

[42] Annegret Fauser, *Musical Encounters at the 1889 World's Fair* (Rochester: University of Rochester Press, 2005).
[43] Clive Holland and F. R. Hill, 'Sir William Edward Parry's Barrel Organ', *Polar Record* 16, no. 102 (1972): 413–44.
[44] William Edward Parry, *Journal of a Voyage for the Discovery of a North-west Passage from the Atlantic to the Pacific: Performed in the Years 1819–20* (London: John Murray, 1821), 124.
[45] William Edward Parry, *Journal of a Second Voyage for the Discovery of a North-west Passage from the Atlantic to the Pacific: Performed in the Years 1821, 1822, 1823* (London: John Murray, 1824), 163.

was dispatched to Henry Williams, a naval veteran turned leader of the Church Missionary Society in New Zealand. Stephen Banfield, in an essay on the musical 'exports' of the British Empire, notes how Williams's instrument was the first organ of any description in that territory. Based on the single barrel that survives, Banfield lists the music that Williams and his fellow colonists had at their disposal: 'It played four hymn tunes, including the Old Hundredth – plus the national anthem.'[46] One of Williams's missionary colleagues, Samuel Marsden, laid claim to an earlier export of the same psalm tune when he sailed from New South Wales to the Bay of Islands in time for Christmas Day 1814. Marsden's memoirs record, in some detail, his version of events: 'About ten o'clock we prepared to go ashore, to publish for the first time the glad tidings of the gospel. I was under no apprehension for the safety of the vessel; and, therefore, ordered all on board to go on shore to attend divine service, except the master and one man.'[47] If the expedition to the Arctic had placed Sutherland, and Parry before him, in a landscape of fear and uncertainty, Marsden's account of his carefully choreographed arrival in New Zealand is also marked by the potential for violence. The local welcoming party, he tells us, 'marched into the inclosure [sic] to attend divine service. They had their swords by their sides, and switches in their hands'.[48] After Marsden and his men took their seats, they found themselves surrounded: 'The inhabitants of the town, with the women and children, and a number of other chiefs, formed a circle round the whole.' What could have been an unnerving, uncontrollable situation is converted, in Marsden's memoirs, into a moment of collective calm: 'A very solemn silence prevailed – the sight was truly impressive.' After bearing witness to the intensity of the atmosphere generated by this novel assembly, Marsden continues with a passage that would be much quoted down the years: 'I rose up and began the service with singing the Old Hundredth Psalm; and felt my very soul melt within me when I viewed my congregation, and considered the state they were in.'[49] It is unclear how to read this last line: Was 'the state they were in' one of abject barbarity or tender attention? We know from Marsden's own account that 'The natives ... could not understand what [he] meant' when preaching the Gospel

---

[46] Stephen Banfield, 'Towards a History of Music in the British Empire: Three Export Studies', in *Britishness Abroad: Transnational Movements and Imperial Cultures*, eds. Kate Darian-Smith, Patricia Grimshaw, and Stuart Macintyre (Melbourne: Melbourne University Press, 2007), 63–89 (67).

[47] J. B. Marsden, *Memoirs of the Life and Labours of the Rev. Samuel Marsden of Paramatta, Senior Chaplain of New South Wales: And of His Early Connexion with the Missions to New Zealand and Tahiti* (Cambridge: Cambridge University Press, 2011), 102.

[48] Ibid.

[49] Ibid.

of St Luke. Marsden also tells us that, during the service, 'the natives stood up and sat down at the signals given by Koro Koro's switch, which was regulated by the movements of the Europeans'. Such a performance of enforced, disciplined mimicry belies easy explanation. What we do know is that, from Marsden's evangelical perspective, the most suitable liturgical tool for this historic occasion was the Old Hundredth.

Indeed, the Old Hundredth seems to have suited all manner of occasions and congregations: after leaving England for Australia, with a cargo including five Merino sheep and over four hundred convicts, Marsden tells of a sermon he preached one Sunday while standing 'on the long boat'.[50] He recalls it as 'a solemn time, many of the convicts were affected'. He also specifies that: 'We sang the Hundredth Psalm in the midst of a large fleet.' His highly mobile missionary career thus shows the same tune employed as both a gateway hymn for the heathens of New Zealand and a solid standby for the guilty transported. Unsurprisingly, it was the first of these two uses that Victorian commentators chose to emphasize. In an 1854 history of the psalm tune – the one by Havergal helpfully cited in G.A.C.'s aforementioned letter – we read that: 'It cannot be the least interesting fact of any, which may be told respecting the Old Hundredth, that it was the first tune ever sung at divine service, conducted by a clergyman, in New Zealand.'[51] The author goes on to quote the passage from Marsden's memoirs given above, placing the following sentence in italics: '*I rose up and began the service with singing the Old Hundredth Psalm, and felt my very soul melt within me, when I viewed my congregation.*' Marsden's consideration of 'the state they were in' is expunged from this version of his account, as are the details about lack of comprehension and compulsion to congregate. Instead, we move directly to another illustration of the tune's inaugurating powers: this time in Blackburn, where the foundation stone of a new district church was apparently celebrated by 'a chorus of some ten thousand Lancastrians ... all singers of a scientific sort' who rendered the Old Hundredth in 'a magnificent burst of harmony in all the four regular parts'.[52]

Ten years later, in *The Quiver*, we find more responses to Marsden's mission: sandwiched between features titled 'The Pre-Calvary martyrs' and 'We Would See Jesus' is a piece by one Rev. W. Pakenham Walsh: 'Sunday, the 25th December,

---

[50] Ibid., 51.
[51] W. H. Havergal, *A History of the Old Hundredth Psalm Tune, with Specimens* (New York: Mason Brothers, 1854), 47.
[52] Ibid., 48.

1814, was a memorable day in the annals of New Zealand. It was the first time that a Christian service was ever held, or a Christmas Day celebrated, on that hitherto barbarous and savage shore.'[53] The illustrations, centred in each page of text, offer the reader an image of the dark-skinned, tattooed bodies awaiting conversion. The first authority cited for a description of the 'inhabitants' is none other than Captain Cook, 'who visited the islands five times between 1769 and 1777' and understood the locals to be 'a brave but ferocious people. Their wild wardances and their cannibal festival were enough to strike terror into the bravest hearts, and few were adventurous enough to touch upon their inhospitable shores.'[54] In case the sense of exotic danger was not already clear enough, Pakenham Walsh adds that: 'A short time before the Christmas which we are about to describe, a ship called the *Boyd* was attacked, and the entire crew killed and eaten in Wangaroa Bay. . . . It was to a race like this, and under such adverse circumstances, that the Rev. Samuel Marsden paid his visit of love and mercy.' In preparation for quoting Marsden's own description of the Christmas Day service, Pakenham Walsh adds a celestial blessing to the missionary venture: 'As Marsden lay awake that night, there shone above him one of the most glorious constellations of the southern hemisphere – the Cross, formed by a group of four brilliant stars.' We then read of the same solemn silence, and the same singing of the Old Hundredth, before joyous conclusions are drawn for *The Quiver*'s readers:

> Such was the first Christmas Day; such the first Christian service in New Zealand. What changes have been wrought there since! How fully have the hopes and desires of that great, good man, who has laid the foundation of the missions been realised! New Zealand is now not savage, but civilised; not cannibal, but Christian – the most signal triumph of the Gospel that has been witness in modern times.[55]

By now the pattern should be clear: for Victorian writers, the Old Hundredth was repeatedly implicated in stories of confidence and conversion. The preface to Havergal's 1854 history, written by the then bishop of New York, gives further examples, this time from a North American perspective: '[the Old

---

[53] W. Pakenham Walsh, 'Gleanings from the Great Harvest Field', *The Quiver* (17 December 1864), 244–6 (244). In keeping with the global narrative of this chapter, Pakenham Walsh was born in Ireland, married in England and died in the United States. One of his sons, William Sandford Pakenham Walsh, would go on to work in China with the Church Mission Society.
[54] Ibid.
[55] Ibid., 246.

Hundredth] has been known in this country from its first settlement. It was in all probability used by the earliest Church of England missionaries in Virginia, and it was certainly one of the songs of the Puritan fathers of New England'.[56] This last fact is backed up by citing the inclusion of the hymn in Ainsworth's Psalms, a collection that early settlers brought with them from Europe. More evocatively, we read how the Old Hundredth was 'one of the tunes to which the wild forests in this new world were first made vocal with the praise of God'. In the bishop's account, this enchantment of the wilderness was followed soon after by an enrolment of native peoples: 'its lofty strains were taught by [European settlers] to the inhabitants of the forest they found here; it was sung by the new-made converts of the missionary John Elliot [who translated the Bible into the Massachusett language], and in the various missionary settlements amongst the Indians it may yet be heard'.[57] At the time Havergal's book was going to press, the Old Hundredth could also be heard in the Taiping Heavenly Kingdom (centred in modern-day Nanjing) where it was used, with different words, as the state national anthem. The choice was that of the revolutionary leader Hong Xiuquan, a convert to Christianity following the First Sino-British War of 1839 and the arrival of Protestant missionaries from Missouri.[58]

In 1860, readers of *The Sabbath Scholar's Treasury and Juvenile Missionary Record*, a Church of Scotland publication based in Edinburgh, could enjoy an account of a 'School feast in India' written by another literary clergyman, one Rev. C. Green, 'for the school children in his former parish in England'. Green told of a 'very beautiful island about six miles from Bombay, named Elephanta, with some wonderful caves and temples carved out in the rock among the hills'. After recalling his trip to the island by steamer, Green goes on to recount a highlight of the excursion: 'One of our friends had brought an accordion, and the music, as it was floating through the caves, and echoed from side to side, and from roof to floor, was very beautiful.' As you might expect for a missionary discourse, the beauty of the occasion was closely linked to its efficacy in spreading a biblical text: 'We got into a little square chamber, and sang the Old Hundredth Psalm, and delightful it was to hear the dark-faced children singing the praises of God in a heathen temple – for these caves were hewn out for that purpose, to make temples for the heathen gods.' The trip was rounded off with

---

[56] Havergal, *History*, iv.
[57] Ibid.
[58] Wai-Chung Ho, 'China: Socio-political Constructions of School Music', in *The Origins and Foundations of Music Education: Cross-Cultural Historical Studies of Music in Compulsory Schooling*, eds. Gordon Cox and Robin Stevens (London: Bloomsbury Academic, 2011), 190–1.

'plum cake, just like English cake. All the afternoon we played in the shade, very much as we should have played in the field at Lambeth; and then there were bats and balls, and skipping-ropes, and hide-and-seek, till the sun went down'. All was decidedly English. And that, of course, was the point.[59] The Old Hundredth was deployed by the likes of Rev. Green as a means of claiming territory and converting populations. It was exactly the sort of behaviour that we would now wish to subject to postcolonial critique and the hermeneutics of suspicion. But it was also the sort of behaviour that was openly mocked by Victorian audiences when satirized on the musical stage.

Utopia, Limited

I did not mention Arthur Sullivan in my earlier roundup of the Old Hundredth's popular appearances, but I could have done. His Civil War opera *Haddon Hall* (1892), with a libretto by Sydney Grundy, features a scene in which Rupert the Cavalier converses with a group of Puritans about the strictures of the new society. A Roundhead by the name of Kill-Joy boasts that: 'We have robbed the devil of his best tunes'. Rupert responds with comic equivocation: 'to give that ingenious gentleman his due, he has to some extent circumvented us; for, by the simple expedient of playing the Old Hundredth in double time, he has succeeded in evolving from that venerable air something suspiciously resembling the carnal and pernicious polka'.[60] A similar anecdote was included in a book published just a few years later, entitled *Stories of Famous Songs*:

> One summer afternoon when I was playing at the Presbyterian Church, Rochester, I made a discovery. It was that sacred music played quickly makes the best kind of secular music. It was quite by accident that playing the 'Old Hundredth' very fast, I produced the air of Get out o' de Way Old Dan Tucker; this was the first of a good many minstrel songs that I composed, or rather adapted, from hymn tunes played quickly. Among them are 'Lucy Long,' 'Ober de Mountain,' and 'Buffalo Gals'.[61]

---

[59] Rev. C. Green., "School Feast in India," in *The Sabbath Scholar's Treasury and Juvenile Missionary Record*, vol. 1 (1860): 99–100. I take it that, notwithstanding the English accent, those readers of Green's account who were affiliated with the Church of Scotland nevertheless took comfort from reports of Protestant progress in India.
[60] Sydney Grundy and Arthur Sullivan, *Haddon Hall* (London: Chappell & Co., 1892), 18–19.
[61] Quoted in 'G. J. Adair Fitz-Gerald, *Stories of Famous Songs* [review]' in *The Spectator* (22 January 1898), 23.

The claim to authorship of 'Old Dan Tucker' is doubtless apocryphal, but the inadvertent proximity of the Old Hundredth to minstrelsy is the sort of cultural short circuit worth taking seriously. When Sullivan reunited with Gilbert in 1893 to produce *Utopia, Limited; or, The Flowers of Progress* the subject of the opera was the misplaced confidence of both financial and colonial adventures. In one number, scored in the style of a minstrel band, King Paramount of Utopia reflects on the advancement of his people as measured against the state of affairs in England. 'Society has quite forsaken all her wicked courses', he sings, 'Which empties our police courts, and abolishes divorces'. The chorus interjects in ironic fashion: 'Divorce is nearly obsolete in England.'[62] Another chorus line, equally ironic, provides a summary:

> In short, this happy country has been anglicized completely
> > It really is surprising
> > What a thorough Anglicizing
> We have brought about – Utopia's quite another land;
> > In her enterprising movements,
> > She is England – with improvements,
> Which we dutifully offer to our motherland![63]

It seems clear to me that the Old Hundredth – which became a *de facto* imperial hymn, sung from the steps of St Paul's to mark Victoria's Diamond Jubilee – was part of the same mission pilloried in *Utopia, Limited*. For all the British voices expressing belief in sacred music's ability to traverse the globe and convert the natives, there were others less certain of the ethics or efficacy of hymnal persuasion. Indeed, by interrogating the nature of musical ubiquity in the Victorian world we not only learn more of the extent of Protestant ambition but also sound out its limits. Therefore, my final example of the Old Hundredth in action underscores just such a dynamic of testing limits and attempting the seemingly impossible, all in an explicitly biblical and imperial context.

The hymn's carrier, in this case, was the Calvinist Methodist minister John Mills who was born in Llanidloes, Montgomeryshire, in 1812. His early life was dominated by an interest in music, which led to his preparation of one of the first musical grammars in the Welsh language, *Grammadeg Cerddoriaeth*, published from his hometown in 1838. The name of Llanidloes would soon be associated with a Chartist uprising the following April. Mills, however, found his calling a

---

[62] W. S. Gilbert and Arthur Sullivan, *Utopia Limited; or, the Flowers of Progress* (London: Chappell & Co., n.d.), 39.
[63] Ibid., 40.

long way from the working people of Mid Wales: in 1846 he moved to London as a missionary to the 'British Jews', the subject of his next book, published in 1853. This was followed by two visits to Palestine, in 1855 and 1859, about which he wrote a Welsh-language study, *Palestina* (1860), and his final publication, *Three Months' Residence at Nablus and an Account of the Modern Samaritans* (1864). By this point Mill's authorial credentials, spelt out on the title page of *Residence at Nablus*, placed him among the great and the good of Victorian science and learning. As well as a reverend he was a fellow of the Royal Geographical Society and a member of the Royal Astronomical Society. He also belonged to the Syro-Egyptian Society and was honorary secretary of the Anglo-Biblical Institute. We might further note that his last work, like the earlier *British Jews*, includes several musical observations. Some of these observations relate to the use of singing or 'cantillation' in religious practice, others concern the division of the octave in what Mills classifies as Arab, Samaritan and European music. He also notes, and notates, the only melody he encountered 'having a marked European resemblance'. Mills is anxious to impart atmosphere as well as factual detail:

> It was at Jerusalem. It was in the minor mode, and had a very pleasing effect. At midnight, during the month of Ramadan, the garrison struck it up, the stillness of the night heightening its charm. The second night after my arrival I was awakened by the music; and being very much pleased with the melody, I struck a light and wrote it down.[64]

Mills' dictation exercise makes for curious reading. The pleasing melody is made to fit sixteen bars of what the Welshman understood as standard notation, but Mills is aware of the shortcomings of his transcription: 'let [any European] try to write their music according to our notation, and he will find it impossible to express it correctly. Their arrangement of the octave makes it incompatible with our mode of writing musical sounds; and it imparts to their melodies a colouring which our notation cannot convey'. He also observes how a 'native singer' will struggle with European melody, and likewise Europeans cannot 'sing their melodies without infinite practice, the progression being so different from our own'. The dividing line Mills considers is a predictable one: 'Perhaps our cultivation of harmony disqualifies our ears from rightly appreciating their melodious passages as well as our voices from executing them.'[65] We might keep

---

[64] John Mills, *Three Months' Residence at Nablus and an Account of the Modern Samaritans* (London: John Murray, 1864), 231.
[65] Ibid., 232.

in mind the cultural significance of European vocal harmony when turning to another key descriptive passage in Mills' Nablus account.

After an introductory chapter discussing biblical lands, Mills continues with a first-person pilgrimage and invites us to join him:

> We must now pass down from patriarchal times to the time of Joshua and the conquerors. Our reader will probably recollect that to this very place Joshua led the host of Israel after they had crossed the Jordan. Moses had commanded them, when they should have passed over Jordan, to march westward, until they should come to the mountains of Gerizim and Ebal, and there hold a public and religious assembly in honour of the God who had delivered them from the bondage of Egypt. We shall now briefly recount the circumstances.[66]

We are then reminded of the story of the blessings and cursings, of the pitching of tents on the plain between the two mountains, and Joshua's reading of the laws to the people of Israel. Mills invites us to

> pause for a moment to review this wonderful event. . . . The vast congregation filled the valley; and the women and children covered the sides of the mountains like locusts. The Levites on Mount Gerizim then read the blessings, and the Levites on Ebal read the cursings – to which the vast assembly responded, Amen! What a sublime sight! A congregation and a service, compared with which all other assemblies the world has ever witnessed dwindle into insignificance![67]

Not content with asserting the wonders of the assembled masses, Mills proceeds to walk us through the sacred landscape: 'Those who have seen the spot, and have examined it, can readily realize the scene. Just where the two mountains approach each other nearest are the two lower spurs, looking like two noble pulpits prepared by nature, and here the Levites would stand to read.' The picture Mills paints is that of an open-air cathedral: 'The valley running between looks just like the floor of a vast place of worship. The slopes of both mountains recede gradually, and offer room for hundreds of thousands to be conveniently seated to hear the words of the law.' As Mills puts it: 'the whole scenery struck me forcibly, as if Divine Providence had conformed its physical features on purpose to meet the requirements of the occasion'.[68]

But our guide is also alert to the sceptics among his readers: 'To this simple narrative an objection has been brought, alleging that the distance between the

---

[66] Ibid., 55.
[67] Ibid., 57.
[68] Ibid., 57–8.

two mountains is too great for the human voice to traverse.' Mills counters with general observations about 'the great difference in the state of the atmosphere in that country compared with that of our own; and how much farther one can see and hear in Palestine than in Great Britain'. He cites unnamed 'travellers ... surprised at these apparent phenomena in Palestine and Syria' before adding his own testimony: 'One day when passing down the valley, we heard two shepherds holding conversation. One was on the top of Gerizim, out of our sight, and the other was close by us in the valley.'[69] The reader has now been through pages of solid prose dedicated to the proof of an outdoor whispering gallery. Clearly this was a subject dear to Mills' heart, and his endeavours speak to the entanglement of scientific and religious knowledge in the Victorian mind. Mills writes of how, before leaving the country, he and two friends, Rev. David Edwards of Newport and Mr John Williams of Aberystwyth, 'resolved to make the experiment' on the very spot in question: 'We had pitched our tent in the valley near the foot of Gerizim, on the line between the two mountains, where I have supposed the ark to have formerly stood. I clambered up Gerizim, and Mr. Williams up Ebal, Mr. Edwards remaining with the men at the tent.' As the account continues, the men's actions are exactly as you would expect, their conclusions all foregone.

> Having reached the lower spur, I found myself standing as it were upon a lofty pulpit, and my friend found himself similarly situated on Ebal. Having rested awhile, I opened my Bible, and read the command concerning the blessings in Hebrew; and every words was heard most distinctly by Mr. Edwards in the valley, as well as by Mr. Williams on Ebal. Mr Williams then read the cursings in Welsh, and we all heard every word and syllable.[70]

It is what happened next that especially merits our attention.

Mr Edwards, standing in the valley, requested his friends to sing, 'and gave out, "Praise God from whom all blessings flow," &c'. Mills writes that he 'commenced it upon the tune Savoy, or the Old Hundredth; but as I was standing on a very elevated pulpit, I pitched the tune in a key too high for them to join me.'[71] Quite why altitude should determine a singer's pitch in such a manner remains unclear, but the impression we have of Mills' performance is remarkably clear: 'I was determined ... to sing it through; and if ever I sang well and with spirit, I did so then on Gerizim, and was heard most distinctly by all.' To read

---

[69] Ibid., 58.
[70] Ibid., 59.
[71] Ibid.

these lines as self-congratulation would, I think, be to miss the point: 'it was our impression at the time, and still is', Mills continues, 'that, if the whole area before and around us had been filled with the hundreds of thousands of Israel, every soul amongst them would have heard every note and word with perfect clearness'.[72] His auditory re-enactment was, of course, an article of faith: if Mr Edward's had not heard his fellow Welshman up the mountain, he would no doubt have stayed quiet. It is their collective fantasy of projection that comes through most clearly: Mills wanted to reach both back in time to his biblical forebears, and out across the landscape to an imaginary assembly of Israel. For one reason or another – or from sheer force of habit – he chose to channel this ambition through a trusty old psalm tune. Yet this left him in a faintly ridiculous pose: without the vocal support of his friends, and without any hint of the harmony that supposedly distinguished European music from that of Arabs, Jews or Samaritans, the reverend was left belting out the Old Hundredth to the glory of his God, and any passing sheep who cared to listen.

It is tempting to conclude that Mills's confidence was misplaced, that the psalm tune he sent forth into the Palestinian air (at an uncomfortably high pitch) offered no proof of biblical miracles, only the folly of imperial missions. We might even think of Mills unwittingly foreshadowing Gilbert and Sullivan's operatic send up of Victorian adventure and hubris. Nevertheless, the way that Mills found himself singing this psalm in this place is, I find, strangely moving. Among the myriad examples of a tune played for laughs and for power, in the heart of empire and the furthest reaches of its grasp, it is hard to discern any consistent pattern of emotional engagement. While I have showed how the Old Hundredth went up and down the cultural scale, and tracked some of its journeys north, south, east and west, the resulting sketch describes a mode of ubiquity that defies simple definition. What I began by calling one of the most popular tunes in Victorian Britain was certainly well travelled, but it was not uniformly received. To misquote a well-known psalm: it seems that all people on earth did not sing or hear alike. And we can all say Amen to that.

---

[72] Ibid., 59–60.

4

'The Son of God goes forth to war'

The Imperial Martyr's Hymnbook

Brian H. Murray

For Thomas Carlyle, 'Hero Worship' was 'the germ of Christianity itself'.[1] But although the lives of exemplary men and women were a staple of Victorian print culture, Christian hagiography was a contested genre. Saints' lives were enthusiastically adopted by the Oxford Movement as evidence for the Catholic continuity of the Church of England, yet for many Protestants such texts were theologically unsound accretions, fictive distractions from the divinely authored text of scripture. The figure of the martyr, in particular, occupied an ambivalent position in the contest between text and tradition. On one hand, the elaborate rituals connected with martyrs and the veneration of their relics by Catholics had long been the target of reformist revulsion and mockery. On the other hand, martyrdom could be interpreted as a solidly biblical phenomenon. The account of St Stephen's testimony before the Sanhedrin, and his subsequent execution by stoning – narrated in Acts 7 and 8 – gave many of the key martyrological tropes a scriptural provenance and origin: persecution, trial, righteous acts of witnessing and grizzly execution. The centrality of the term 'martyr' (gk. μαρτυς, *mártys*, literally 'witness') is emphasized at the beginning of *Acts*, when the resurrected Christ commands the apostles to 'be witnesses [μαρτυρες] ... unto the uttermost part of the earth' (Acts 1.8). Indeed, tales of persecution and violent martyrdom were foundation myths for almost every Protestant tradition too. For Anglophone Protestants, this legacy was famously preserved in the perennially popular *Acts and Monuments* of John Foxe ('Foxe's Book of Martyrs', 1563). Foxe had made a powerful claim of continuity between the earliest martyrs of Palestine, North

---

[1] Thomas Carlyle, *On Heroes, Hero-Worship, and the Heroic in History* (London: Chapman and Hall, 1840), 15.

Africa and Rome and the Protestant Marian martyrs of Britain.[2] The body of the martyr was a site of conflict precisely because it was central to the theological and historical claims made by almost every branch of Christianity.

If the cult of the martyrs was a Catholic trope, appropriated and reconfigured by radical reformed Protestants, we might say the opposite for another key nineteenth-century religious development: the singing of hymns. In the first decades of the nineteenth century, hymnody was still controversial. The authors of the popular hymnals in English were almost all Nonconformists or evangelical Anglicans. But by the end of the nineteenth century, the journalist W. T. Stead could confidently declare that, regardless of denomination, the 'songs of the English-speaking people are for the most part hymns. For the immense majority of our people to-day the only minstrelsy is that of the hymn-book. And this is as true of our race beyond the sea as it is of our race at home'.[3] Given the size of the corpus, it is understandable that most studies of Victorian hymns have aimed to address broad trends in the culture of hymnody. In many cases, however, this approach has led to a flattening out of the picture, and individual works are too often reduced to mere examples of broader developments or fashions. I want to invert this model by following the journey of a single hymn – the 'The Son of God goes forth to War' or 'St Stephen's Day' by Reginald Heber (1783–1826) – through a variety of devotional and performance contexts and a range of musical settings. Tracing the reception and performance history of this hymn will shed light on two parallel and related developments: first, how High-Church Anglicans came to embrace the hymn book and utilize its devotional and liturgical power; second, that Anglican hymn writers mined a much earlier literary form – martyrology – to craft hymns that looked simultaneously back to the origins of episcopal tradition and forward to the global missionary project. My case study will thus explore how the musical activities of parochial and metropolitan Britons impacted upon and influenced the ambitions and objectives of those 'English-speaking people' who moved 'beyond the sea'.

---

[2] On Foxe's nineteenth-century reception, see Elizabeth Evenden, 'John Foxe, Samuel Potter and the Illustration of the Book of Martyrs', *Bulletin of the John Rylands Library* 90, no. 1 (2013): 203–30 and Dominic Janes, 'John Foxe and British Attitudes to Martyrdom after the French Revolution', in *Martyrdom and Terrorism: Pre-Modern to Contemporary Perspectives*, ed. Dominic Janes and Alex Houen (Oxford: Oxford University Press, 2014), 179–96.

[3] W. T. Stead, *Hymns that have Helped* (New York: Doubleday, 1904), 14.

Reginald Heber and the High-Church hymn

Heber's hymns and secular poetry were produced in a milieu that privileged inventive literary reappropriation of the grand themes of biblical and Classical antiquity. These preoccupations were exemplified by the two major undergraduate English poetry prizes at Oxford and Cambridge: the Newdigate and the Chancellor's Medal. The terms of the Newdigate specified 'a copy of English verse of fifty lines and no more in recommendation of the study of the ancient Greek and Roman remains of Architecture, Sculpture, and Painting'.[4] The successful entry was almost always a long poem in blank verse or heroic couplets exploring an object of Classical art or archaeology, often through the lens of Christian providentialism. Two of the earliest winners of the Oxford prize, Heber in 1803 (for *Palestine*) and Henry Hart Milman in 1812 (*The Belvedere Apollo*), went on to become successful clergy, popular poets, influential hymnodists and close friends.

It was while serving as rector in the rural parish of Hodnet, Shropshire, in 1812 that Heber began his early experiments with devotional verse. His first religious lyrics appeared in the evangelically inclined *Christian Observer* in 1811 and 1812, prefaced with a defence of the role of hymns in Orthodox Anglican worship:

> The following hymns are part of an intended series, appropriate to the Sundays and principal holydays of the year, connected in some degree with their particular Collects and Gospels, and designed to be sung between the Nicene Creed and the sermon.[5]

By placing the singing of hymns in a precise liturgical niche, 'between the Nicene Creed and the sermon', Heber attempted to ward off potential criticism of hymns as a distraction from either the Prayer Book or the sermon. As Susan Drain has suggested, Heber's experimental hymns were part of a broader plan 'to unify thematically three parts of Anglican worship, the liturgy of the Prayer Book, the sermon of the preacher, and the singing of the people'.[6] Although expressing admiration for some evangelical Anglican hymnodists – including Newton and

---

[4] 'An Irish Winner of the Newdigate', *Irish Monthly* 6 (1878): 630–33.
[5] Amelia Heber, *The Life of Reginald Heber, D.D. Lord Bishop of Calcutta, by his Widow. With Selections from his Correspondence, Unpublished Poems, and Private Papers; Together with a Journal of his Tour in Norway, Sweden, Russia, Hungary, and Germany and a History of the Cossaks*, 2 vols (London: John Murray, 1830), 1.131.
[6] Susan Drain, *The Anglican Church in Nineteenth-Century Britain: Hymns Ancient and Modern (1860–1875)* (Lewiston: Edwin Mellen, 1989), 85.

Cowper's *Olney Hymns* (1779) – Heber was careful to distinguish his productions from the 'enthusiastic' and fleshy effusions of Nonconformists like Wesley and Watts. His own hymns, he claimed, contained: 'no fulsome or indecorous language ... no erotic addresses to Him whom no unclean lips can approach; no allegory, ill understood and worse applied'. He did not condemn outright the use of erotic or romantic allegory in Christian poetry, but feared the consequences of allowing a lay congregation to feel as if they were on a level of familiarity or physical intimacy with Christ. The 'brutalities of a common swearer', Heber thundered, 'can hardly bring religion into more sure contempt ... than certain epithets applied to Christ in some of our popular collections of religious poetry'.[7] As J. R. Watson notes, the most striking feature of Heber's chaste rejection of Nonconformist enthusiasm was his marked preference for first person plural (a congregational 'we') over Wesley's first person singular (an enthusiastic 'I').[8]

In October 1820, Heber wrote to the bishop of London (William Howley) with a view to seeking episcopal authorization for an Anglican hymnbook to be compiled with 'the powerful assistance of my friends Scott and Southey'.[9] Heber was writing at a time when the future of hymns in the Church of England was far from certain. In the same year, the bishop of Peterborough had condemned the use of hymns in services as illegal.[10] But in his letter to the Howley, Heber defends the legitimacy of the place of hymns within the liturgy, asserting that 'whole stream of precedent in the Christian Church, from the remotest antiquity, authorises and encourages the use of hymns as well as of the Psalms of David'. He concludes, however, on a pragmatic note. Hymns are here to stay. And if they are not provided by the Established Church, people will seek them elsewhere.

> Every clergyman finds that, if he does not furnish his singers with hymns, they are continually favouring him with some of their own selection; their use has been always the principal engine of popularity with the dissenters, and with those who are called the 'Evangelical' party.... And it may, therefore, be thought unwise to surrender to the service of our enemies a means which is, in their hands, so powerful in attracting the multitude, and of which we ourselves might make so good a use.[11]

---

[7] Amelia Heber, *Life of Heber*, 2.22–27.
[8] J. R. Watson, *The English Hymn: A Critical and Historical Study* (Oxford: Clarendon, 1997), 321.
[9] Amelia Heber, *Life of Heber*, 2.27.
[10] Ian Bradley, *Abide with Me: The World of Victorian Hymns* (London: SCM Press, 1997), 16.
[11] Amelia Heber, *Life of Heber*, 2.24–5.

In his response, Howley praised Heber's hymns and recommended publication but also expressed doubt 'that any publication of this nature, however well executed, will obtain sanction from [Church] authority'.[12] Undiscouraged, Heber next wrote to his friend Milman – who had just decided to run for the Oxford Professor of Poetry – outlining his hope that the hymnal could be licensed for use 'in Churches in the same manner as Tate and Brady's version of the Psalms' and inviting Milman to submit some verses of his own.[13]

In her discussion of John Keble (another Oxford Professor of Poetry), Kirstie Blair suggests that High Anglican poets 'reacted to the Evangelical stress on personal feeling by arguing that while there was a place for strong religious feeling, it was always potentially dangerous and had to be handled carefully'.[14] Blair cites Keble's claim, in a review of a biography of Scott, that poetic form 'shapes out a sort of channel for wild and tumultuous feelings to vent themselves by; feelings whose very excess violence would seem to make the utterance of them almost impossible'.[15] We see a similar attempt to 'channel' religious feeling through acceptable 'forms' in Heber's efforts to find particular hymns to *fit* within a given space in the approved liturgy and church calendar.[16] Heber's hymnal contained no index of authors or first lines – or even suggestions for appropriate tunes – indicating that liturgical occasion was to be the primary organizing principle. The contents page consisted of a simple church calendar with a hymn assigned to each Sunday and feast day. This circular model of annual devotional time had also long been the organizational principle of martyrology, so hymns on the feasts of saints and martyrs offered an ideal opportunity to assimilate these two convergent traditions.[17]

Heber's appointment as bishop of Calcutta in 1823 'left little time . . . for any employment not immediately connected with his diocese', and the hymnal remained unpublished on his death three years later. However, his manuscript

---

[12] Ibid., 2.30.
[13] Ibid., 2.32.
[14] Kirstie Blair, *Form and Faith in Victorian Poetry and Religion* (Oxford: Oxford University Press, 2012), 29.
[15] John Keble, 'Life of Walter Scott', in *Occasional Papers and Reviews*, ed. E. B. Pusey (Oxford: James Parker, 1877), 1–80 (17). Quoted in Blair, *Form and Faith*, 33.
[16] See, for example, Heber to Milman, 28 December 1821: 'There are not . . . many *lacunae* in the portion of the year which this little book contains. In the other half year they are more numerous; and even those Sundays which I have supplied with appropriate hymns, may very well carry double or even treble, if you will supply them with any thing of your own, or selected from other quarters.' *Life of Heber*, 1.49–50.
[17] As Watson has argued: 'Heber and Milman are important in the history of hymnody, because they helped to make hymns respectable . . . through the connection of those hymns with the regularity and Christian order of the Church's year' (*English Hymn*, 320).

was subsequently edited by his widow Amelia (née Shipley) and published by John Murray as *Hymns, Written and Adapted to the Weekly Church Service of the Year* in 1827.[18] Along with Heber's compositions, the hymnal included several hymns by Milman and a smattering of old favourites 'of former times'. These included compositions by Walter Scott and (more surprisingly) Charles Wesley – though the latter's authorship went unacknowledged.[19] Heber's calendar of devotional verses thus appeared before the public in the same year as Keble's hugely successful *The Christian Year* (1827). Although never attaining approval as an authorized Anglican hymnal, Heber's *Hymns* were sufficiently popular to warrant twelve editions within the first twenty years of publication. Significantly, the 'seasonally' arranged hymnal soon became the standard Anglican format, an important legacy of Heber's insistence that hymns could complement existing notions of devotional and liturgical time.[20]

The martyrdom of Bishop Heber

Reginald Heber's short stint as bishop of Calcutta began in June 1823 and ended with his sudden death on 3 April 1826 at Trichinopoly (Tiruchirappalli), while conducting a lengthy tour of Ceylon and southern India. Apparently struck by a fit of apoplexy in the bath, Heber's demise was not as dramatic as some colonial bishops. But immediate accounts of his death and poetic memorials did much to position the self-sacrificing bishop in a tradition leading back to the first generation of apostolic martyrs. Like his predecessor, Thomas Middleton, friends and family complained that Heber's ill health was brought on by the arduous task of ministering to the inhabitants of an impossibly large diocese. His remit included not only the whole of India and Ceylon but also Australia and parts of southern Africa. In the preface to her biography of her husband, Heber's widow and editor, Amelia, complained that the first three bishops of Calcutta had 'already fallen by this kind of voluntary martyrdom'.[21] Heber's hagiographer

---

[18] Reginald Heber, *Hymns, Written and Adapted to the Weekly Church Service of the Year*, ed. Amelia Heber (London: John Murray, 1827), vii.

[19] Heber excerpted a snippet from Scott's *Lay of the Last Minstrel* for the 'Sixth Sunday after Epiphany' (43) and included George Whitefield's revision of Wesley's 'Hark the Herald Angel's Sing' for Christmas Day (15–16).

[20] Drain, *Anglican Church*, 240. In 1864, Milman presented a bound manuscript copy of Heber's collection to the British Museum with the title *Hymns for the Christian Year, copied and chiefly composed by Reginald Heber, Bishop of Calcutta*. British Library, MS 25704 A-B.

[21] Amelia Heber, *Life of Heber*, 1.ix–x.

in chief was Thomas Robinson, archdeacon of Madras and domestic chaplain to the bishop during his short term. Robinson's memoir, *The Last Days of Bishop Heber* (1828), painted a saintly portrait of 'this beloved Apostle of the East'.[22] As Geoffrey Cook has argued, in one of the few scholarly articles on Heber's Indian career, missions to the East in this period were often imagined as pilgrimages to 'the Apostolic age of the New Testament'.[23] References to the 'crown' and 'palm' of martyrdom abound in the immediate memorializing of Heber's mission. Felicia Hemans lamented the loss of him who 'unto death hast bow'd! / In those bright regions of the rising sun, / Where Victory ne'er a crown like thine hath won'.[24] The radical Quaker poet and novelist Amelia Opie counted the bishop's death a loss to poetry but a gain to salvation. She pictures Heber abandoning his 'laurel' wreath won on the 'banks of the Isis' (Oxford) for 'a crown of the amaranth's flowers, / Enwreathed with the *palm*' and the 'Christian's rough labour, the martyr's reward'.[25] In his 'Sonnet on the Bishop of Calcutta Passing Through Allahabad', G. A. Vetch likewise envisions Heber adorned with the 'Christian's palm and poet's wreath combined'.[26] Robert Southey, elegized the Heber's time in Calcutta in even more dramatic terms, imagining the bishop hauling Indians from 'from beneath the wheels / Of that seven-headed Idol's car accurst' and saving helpless women from 'the widow's funeral pile'. More importantly, Southey insists that Heber's self-sacrifice will rouse the youth of England to follow his example.

> Thither our saintly Heber went,
> In promise and in pledge
> That England, from her guilty torpor rous'd,
> Should zealously and wisely undertake
> Her awful task assign'd:
> Thither, devoted to the work, he went,
> There spent his precious life,
> There left his holy dust.[27]

[22] Thomas Robinson, *The Last Days of Bishop Heber* (Madras: W. Taylor, 1829), vi.
[23] Geoffrey Cook, '"From India's Coral Strand": Reginald Heber and the Missionary Project', *International Journal of Hindu Studies* 5, no. 2 (2001): 131–64 (147).
[24] Hemans, included in the prefatory material to Reginald Heber, *Palestine, and Other Poems* (Philadelphia: Carey, Lea and Carey, 1828), lxiv.
[25] Amelia Opie, 'To the Memory of Reginald Heber, Bishop of Calcutta', in Reginald Heber, *Palestine*, lxv–lxvi.
[26] G. A. Vetch, 'Sonnet on the Bishop of Calcutta Passing Through Allahabad on a Visit to the Upper Stations of India', in *Life of Heber*, ed. Amelia Heber (London: John Murray, 1830), 2.252.
[27] Robert Southey, 'On the Portrait of Reginald Heber', in *Life of Heber*, ed. Amelia Heber (London: John Murray, 1830), 2.514–20.

In the spirit of Heber's hymns, Southey's account of the bishop's martyrdom threads a fine line between manly Protestant reticence and Catholic piety. The 'holy dust' left behind by the departed 'saint' echoes the burial service from Anglican Prayer Book, but this phrase also suggests the sacred ashes collected from the Roman catacombs by devotees of the first Christian martyrs. By the second half of the century, Heber was an established hero in the popular genre of missionary biography. His portrait adorned the frontispiece to Charlotte Yonge's *Pioneers and Founders: Or, Recent Workers in the Mission Field* (1874), in which he was praised as both missionary martyr and 'the real originator in England of the great system of appropriate hymnology, which has become almost universal'.[28] The publisher and hymn writer, S. W. Partridge, who specialized in Christian adventure biographies for the Sunday School audience, included a volume on *Reginald Heber: Bishop of Calcutta, Scholar and Evangelist* (1894) in his popular series of colourful, illustrated prize books. The choice of subjects in Partridge's series offers something like a canon of Protestant martyrs: David Livingstone, John Williams, Henry Martyn, Bishop James Hannington of East Africa and Bishop John Coleridge Patteson, the 'martyr of Melanesia'.[29]

By the time Heber's hymnal appeared, a year after his death, his paeans to manly self-sacrifice and missionary heroism were already charged with added poignancy. As Amelia underscored in her later account of Heber's deliberations over whether to accept a colonial bishopric: 'were he alone concerned...he would cheerfully go forth to join in that glorious train of martyrs, whose triumphs he has celebrated in one of his hymns'.[30] The hymn to which Amelia here refers was composed for the first saint's day after Christmas. The feast of St Stephen (26 December) was a fitting point in the liturgical calendar to contemplate transition and renewal. The story of Stephen's martyrdom in *Acts* serves as a hinge between two eras of Christian history: the (scriptural) apostolic age – Stephen as an early disciple of Christ – and the (apocryphal) 'age of martyrs'. Heber's appointed hymn for the day, commonly referred to by its first line ('The Son of God goes forth to war'), attempts to bridge this gap. In eight quatrains of rousing ballad metre, Heber takes us from the crucifixion of Christ – via St Stephen's martyrdom – to the persecution of the early Church Militant by imperial Rome.

---

[28] Charlotte Yonge, *Pioneers and Founders, or, Recent Workers in the Mission Field* (London: Macmillan, 1871).

[29] Arthur Montefiore, *Reginald Heber: Bishop of Calcutta, Scholar and Evangelist* (London: S.W. Partridge & Co., 1894).

[30] Amelia Heber, *Life of Heber*, 2.95.

St. Stephen's Day

The Son of God goes forth to war,
A kingly crown to gain:
His blood-red banner streams afar!
Who follows in his train?

Who best can drink his cup of woe,
Triumphant over pain,
Who patient bears his cross below,
He follows in his train!

The martyr first, whose eagle eye
Could pierce beyond the grave;
Who saw his Master in the sky,
And call'd on Him to save.

Like Him, with pardon on his tongue,
In midst of mortal pain,
He pray'd for them that did the wrong!
Who follows in his train?

A glorious band, the chosen few
On whom the spirit came;
Twelve valiant saints, their hope they knew,
And mock'd the cross and flame.

They met the tyrant's brandish'd steel,
The lion's gory mane:
They bow'd their heads the death to feel!
Who follows in their train?

A noble army – men and boys,
The matron and the maid,
Around the Saviour's throne rejoice,
In robes of light array'd.

They climb'd the steep ascent of Heaven,
Through peril, toil and pain!
O God! to us may grace be given
To follow in their train.[31]

---

[31] Heber, *Hymns*, 17–18. The inconsistent capitalization of synonyms and pronouns referring to God or Christ lends some ambiguity to the precise subject of each stanza. But this had been standardized by Murray's second edition of 1828 (e.g. 'Who follows in His train?').

In series of vignettes we are brought from the example of Christ on the cross, to the sacrifice of Stephen (the 'martyr first') and the apostles ('Twelve valiant saints'), and finally to the plight of all persecuted Christians who have since followed 'in the train' of these early exemplars ('A noble army, men and boys, / the matron and the maid'). The call to arms in the repeated refrain ('Who follows in his train?') would have been powerfully enforced by contemporary accounts of Heber's own apostolic life and martyr's death. The evening before Heber's death at Trichinopoly, Thomas Robinson recalled him repeating 'several lines' from Charles Wesley's 'Head of Thy Church Triumphant', a hymn which climaxes in 'dying [Stephen's]' ecstatic vision of Christ enthroned 'at God's right hand'.[32] Delivering his Bampton Lectures on 'The Character and Conduct of the Apostles' a year after Heber's death, Henry Hart Milman echoed his friend's hymn, praising the 'resolute perseverance' of St Stephen to his 'cause, and ... conviction of the Lord's ascent into heaven ... like his Master submitting to his destiny, like his Master praying for his enemies, the first martyr fell asleep in the Lord'.[33]

The legacy of Heber's hymns

Catalogue figures for the years 1821–1900 – when close to one thousand separate hymnals were published – demonstrate that the Victorian period was the zenith of hymn publishing in Britain.[34] Heber's timely posthumous publication offered a High-Church alternative to popular evangelical and Dissenting collections. The acceptability of hymns within mainstream Anglican culture was confirmed with the publication of *Hymns Ancient and Modern* in 1861. Although never an official text for Anglican worship, it sold 4.5 million in its first seven years.[35] The main portion of *Ancient and Modern* was again laid out to correspond to the liturgical calendar and the hymnal also included a specific section devoted to 'Martyrs etc'. This section was headed up by Heber's 'The Son of God' set to the tune of the 'Old 81st' by the music editor, William Henry Monk (organist of

---

[32] Robinson, *Bishop Heber*, 180.
[33] Henry Hart Milman, *The Character and Conduct of the Apostles Considered as an Evidence of Christianity* (Oxford: Oxford University Press, 1827), 120–2.
[34] John Wolffe, '"Praise to the Holiest in the Height": Hymns and Church Music', *Religion in Victorian Britain*, vol. 5, ed. John Wolffe (Manchester: Manchester University Press, 1997), 59–99 (p. 64).
[35] Jeffrey Richards, *Imperialism and Music: Britain, 1876–1953* (Manchester: Manchester University Press, 2001), 369. On the origins of *Hymns Ancient and Modern*, see Watson, *English Hymn*, 387–421.

King's College London). This psalm tune had been first printed in John Daye's edition of Sternhold and Hopkins' *Whole Booke of Psalms* (1562) and offered a solidly Protestant musical context for Heber's potentially divisive High-Church sentiments. Daye was best known as the original publisher of 'Foxe's Book of Martyrs', and this clever pairing of first-century narrative with sixteenth-century tune may have allowed evangelicals to read Heber's account of Stephen and the early martyrs through the lens of England's Protestant martyrs. Psalm 81 also had the advantage of being itself a celebration of sacred music ('Sing aloud unto God our strength: make a joyful noise unto the God of Jacob') and this text was frequently cited as a scriptural endorsement of congregational hymn-singing.[36] More practically, the 3/4 tune matched the ballad metre favoured by both Heber and English vernacular psalmodists, while the key (E-flat major) was conventionally used to evoke sombre and heroic majesty.[37]

By the second half of the century, Heber's compositions had become emblematic of High-Church tact in the face of dangerous evangelical 'subjectivity' and 'enthusiasm'. It was in this spirit that the liberal bishop of Oxford, John Fielder Mackarness, wrote to the revision committee for the 1874 edition of *Hymns Ancient and Modern*, questioning the 'the fitness of introducing a class of *sentimental* hymns'. An Anglican hymnal, thought Mackarness, 'should consist *mainly* of hymns suitable for worship, dwelling on the majesty and mercy of God, rather than on experience and feelings of men. Bp Heber's Trinity Sunday Hymn is just what I mean'.[38] Yet despite Heber's evident success in pioneering a fashion for Anglican hymnody, the ubiquity of his compositions did not inspire a cult of the author. As the editors of *Heber's Hymns, Illustrated* lamented in 1867, Heber's productions were the 'valued possession of Christendom' yet 'scarcely recognised as the Hymns of one author'.[39] Sampson Low's lavish illustrated edition of *Heber's Hymns* sought to correct this injustice by endowing each of the ninety-one hymns with multiple engraved illustrations.

During the dramatic conflicts between Anglo-Catholic 'ritualists' and the British State in the 1870s, acts of repression and resistance often centred on music and its place in the liturgy. In November 1876, newspapers across the nation reported daily on the activities of the Rev. Thomas Pelham Dale, rector

---

[36] Or in Sternhold and Hopkins's English metrical version: 'Be light and glad in God rejoice, who us our strength and stay; / Be joyful, and lift up your voice to Jacob's God alway.'
[37] Popular uses of E-flat major include Beethoven's *Symphony No. 3* ('The Heroic') and *Emperor Concerto*, Richard Strauss's *A Hero's Life*, Holst's 'Jupiter' and Elgar's 'Nimrod'.
[38] Drain, *Anglican Church*, 133; citing The Bishop of Oxford to W. Pulling, 29 January 1872.
[39] Reginald Heber, *Heber's Hymns, Illustrated* (London: Sampson Low, Son, and Marston, 1867), v.

of St Vedast, Cheapside, who had recently fallen foul of the 'Court of Arches for not complying with the order . . . to refrain from ritualistic practices'. On 8 November 1876, the *Lancaster Gazette* reported that Dale had presided from behind a candle-covered altar in 'a cloth of gold cope, such as is worn by Roman Catholic priests of benediction' before ascending the pulpit to preach a sermon against the 'the folly and wickedness' of the Public Worship Act. During the same service, Dale and his junior clergy had processed into the church behind a surplice-clad choir, wafting incense, 'holding high a cross' and singing 'The Son of God goes forth to war'.[40] In this case, Heber's hymn to St Stephen served as a protest against state control of liturgical practice. As Dominic Janes has shown, ritualist agitators like Dale, who were often fined and imprisoned for their defiance of Church law, frequently identified as persecuted martyrs.[41] But it is also striking that the singing of hymns – so long associated with Low-Church and evangelical practice – had by the 1870s become part of the armoury of Anglo-Catholic 'ritualism'.

Given that Heber's hymns had been carefully composed for convenient integration into Anglican liturgy, his popularity in Anglican hymnbooks is unsurprising. From the beginning, however, evangelicals and Nonconformists also made use of Heber's verses in their own hymnals. The evangelical Edward Bickersteth included several of Heber's occasional hymns in his popular *Christian Psalmody* (1834).[42] In Josiah Conder's *Congregational Hymn Book* (1836) – explicitly framed as a 'Supplement to Dr. Watt's Psalms and Hymns' – the authors of individual hymns were not listed. But the proudly Nonconformist editor magnanimously announced the presence of Protestants of all stripes in his preface.

> The Editor cannot close these Prefatory Remarks, without adverting to the pleasing demonstration which such a collection as this exhibits, of the essential and indestructible unity of the Church of Christ, and of the unison of sentiment . . . when Protestant Christians, who differ about more important matters, can still agree in their hymns of prayer and songs of praise. The productions of Bishops Ken and Heber, of Wesley and Toplady, of Doddridge

---

[40] 'Ritualism in London', *Lancaster Gazette*, 8 November 1876, 3.

[41] Dominic Janes, *Victorian Reformation: The Fight over Idolatry in the Church of England, 1840–1860* (Oxford: Oxford University Press, 2009); Dominic Janes, *Visions of Queer Martyrdom from John Henry Newman to Derek Jarman* (Chicago: University of Chicago Press, 2015).

[42] Edward Bickersteth, *Christian Psalmody* (London: L.B. Seeley and Sons, 1834). On the theology of Bickersteth's influential collection, see Martin V. Clarke, '"Meet and Right it is to Sing": Nineteenth-Century Hymnals and the Reasons for Singing', in *Music and Theology in Nineteenth-Century Britain*, ed. Martin V. Clarke (Farnham: Ashgate, 2012), 21–36.

and Hart, Cowper and Newton, Fawcett and Beddome – Episcopal clergymen, Moravians, Wesleyan Methodists, Independents, and Baptists, all harmoniously combining in this metrical service, prove ... that there actually exists throughout that body, a 'Communion of Saints'.[43]

Heber's 'The Son of God' also appeared in the *Supplement to the Congregational Hymn Book* (1875) at the head of a section on 'The Christian Life: Christian Warfare'.[44] The thematic arrangement of evangelical and Nonconformist hymnals reflects the fact that hymns were more often 'chosen to reflect and reinforce the sermon rather than to supplement the liturgy'.[45] In the official *English Baptist Hymnal* (1876), the 'The Son of God' appears in the section devoted to 'The Christian Life: Perseverance'. Here it stood alongside Catholic convert John Henry Newman's 'Lead Kindly Light', suggesting that Nonconformist hymnodists had little problem with the doctrine of individual authors once their general sentiments were sound or expressed with sufficient vagueness.[46] Some light editing was occasionally necessary. For example, Nonconformist hymnals generally dropped Heber's original title ('St Stephen') – the hymn's only explicit reference to the veneration of saints – and listed the poem under its opening line.[47] Yet even while most hymnals announced their sectarian affiliation on their title page, the most popular hymns demonstrated a remarkable power to transcend theological and ecclesiological differences. As John Wolffe has argued, Victorian hymnbooks provided 'a notable island of calm amidst the storms between and within different Christian traditions'.[48]

As we have seen, for W. T. Stead, the hymn was the key poetic and musical form of the expansive and transnational Anglo-Saxon race: 'No Chinese wall of protective tariffs will ever prevent the two great English-speaking nations practising free trade in hymns'.[49] By the 1860s, Heber's editors could claim likewise that his compositions were 'treasured as Sacred Household Words

---

[43] Josiah Conder, ed., *The Congregational Hymn Book: A Supplement to Dr. Watt's Psalms and Hymns*, revised edn (1836; London: Jackson and Walford, 1844), x.
[44] *Supplement to the Congregational Hymn Book: Published for the Congregational Union of England and Wales* (London: Hodder and Stoughton, 1875), no. 1161.
[45] Wolffe, 'Praise to the Holiest', 82.
[46] *The Baptist Hymnal: A Collection of Hymns and Spiritual Songs* (London: Marlborough, 1879). The *Primitive Methodist Hymnal* (1882) does not include Heber's 'The Son of God', although it does feature fifteen other Heber hymns.
[47] A more extreme case is James Martineau's Unitarian collection, *Hymns for the Christian Church and Home* (London: Longman, Brown, Green, Longmans and Roberts, 1859), which includes twenty-eight of Heber's hymns but subjects each to extensive theological bowdlerization.
[48] Wolffe, 'Praise to the Holiest', 72.
[49] Stead, *Hymns that have Helped*, 5.

wherever the English language is spoken'.⁵⁰ Heber's hymn was published in New York⁵¹ in the same year that the first London edition appeared, and 'The Son of God' was subsequently included in a doctrinally diverse range of North American hymnals too.⁵² The culture of Christian Revivalism, which had originated in North America, also adopted many of Heber's lyrics. Ira Sankey's *Sacred Songs* (1873), which sold an incredible eighty million copies in Britain in its first fifty years of publication, includes both 'The Son of God' and 'From Greenland's Icy Mountains'.⁵³ From the 1870s, American hymnals usually matched Heber's words with 'All Saints New', a rousingly triumphant 4/4 tune by the Bostonian Anglo-Catholic Henry Stephen Cutler, choirmaster at the Gothic-Revival Trinity Episcopalian Church in Manhattan. Cutler's enthusiasm for all-male choirs, antiquarian vestments and chanted psalms aligned with Heber's High-Church sentiments. The Trinity Male Choir's 1922 recording of 'The Son of God' for the Victor label may have further popularized the hymn and Cutler's setting continues to appear in American Lutheran and Episcopalian hymnals today.⁵⁴

Who follows in his train?

Widespread republication in hymnals testifies to the enduring popularity of Heber's 'The Son of God'. But to answer *why* this hymn engaged diverse audiences across the century, we must turn to contemporary accounts of services and performances. Many documented performances in explicitly military contexts suggest that audiences were encouraged to read metaphors of Holy War and the Church Militant as literally as possible. In 1859, the *Belfast News-Letter*, for example, republished Heber's 'The Son of God' under a completely new title:

---

⁵⁰ *Heber's Hymns, Illustrated*, v.
⁵¹ Heber, *Hymns, Written and Adapted to the Weekly Church Service of the Year* (New York: G. & C. Carvill, 1827).
⁵² For example, 'The Son of God' appears in the *Official Hymnal of the Methodist Episcopal Church* in a section on 'The Christian Life: Activity and Zeal'. *The Methodist Hymnal: Official Hymnal of the Methodist Episcopal Church and the Methodist Episcopal Church, South* (New York: Eaton & Mains, 1905).
⁵³ Ira D. Sankey, James McGranahan, and Geo. C. Stebbins, *Sacred Songs: Compiled and Arranged for Use in Gospel Meetings, Sunday Schools, Prayer Meetings, and Other Religious Services* (New York: Biglow and Main, ND). On the success of Sankey's *Songs*, see Michael Ledger-Lomas, 'Mass Markets: Religion', in *The Cambridge History of the Book in Britain, 1830–1914*, ed. David McKitterick (Cambridge: Cambridge University Press, 2009), 324–59 (352).
⁵⁴ Reginald Heber (lyric) and H. S. Cutler (composer), *The Son of God Goes Forth to War*, Trinity Male Choir (Victor, 1922) [on 78 rpm disc].

'The Christian War-Song'.[55] Heber's martial imagery chimed with the Victorian cult of Protestant militarism, 'in which the language of warfare was associated with the individual's commitment to Christ, and the worldwide proclamation of the Gospel'.[56] The Harrow schoolmaster John Farmer included Heber's 'The Son of God' in *Christ and His Soldiers* (1878), a 'children's oratorio' taken up by school and college choirs as far afield as Manitoba.[57] In Juliana Horatia Ewing's novel *Story of a Short Life* (1885), 'The Son of God' is the favourite hymn at a West Country barracks. An officer's son, crippled for life in a coaching accident, begs on his deathbed for the battalion to sing it once more. By the time the soldiers reach '[a] noble army, men and boys' every stiff upper lip in the barracks is suitably aquiver.[58] The hymn was also reportedly a favourite of Florence Nightingale. On her death in 1910, it was sung at memorial services across the nation, underlining her popular status as a Christian military martyr.[59]

As Jeffrey Richards has argued, the 'militarization of Christianity' in the second half of the nineteenth century was paralleled by the 'Christianization of the Army'.[60] An 1891 account of the ceremonial opening of a garrison chapel at Winchester offers a telling snapshot of the kind of liturgical and ecclesiological context in which congregations encountered Heber's hymn. After a 'stirring sermon' delivered at the cathedral by the Chaplain-General John Cox Edghill – a noted Tractarian and author of *The Work of the Church in the Army* (1890) – the 'service ended by the troops singing heartily "The Son of God goes forth to war," to the music of their band'. The assembled troops next marched to the new garrison chapel singing 'Onward Christian Soldiers' only to be rewarded by another 'long and earnest sermon from Dr. Edghill'. The final dedication took place in an apse beneath 'three lancet windows, representing the Crucifixion, the Blessed Virgin Mary and St. John ... gifts of the Rifle Brigade, the Royal Rifles, and the Hampshire Regiment'.[61]

As Britain became more comfortable with its status as an imperial power, the expansion of Christianity in general – and Anglicanism in particular –

---

[55] 'The Christian War-Song', *Belfast News-Letter*, 8 December 1859, 4.
[56] John Wolffe, *God and Greater Britain: Religion and National Life in Britain and Ireland, 1843–1945* (London: Routledge, 1994), 213.
[57] John Farmer, *Christ and His Soldiers: A Sacred Oratorio* (Harrow: J. C. Wilbee, 1878); J. M. Bumsted, *St. John's College: Faith and Education in Western Canada* (Winnipeg: University of Manitoba Press, 2006), 43.
[58] Juliana Horatia Ewing, *The Story of a Short Life* (London: Christian Knowledge Society, 1885).
[59] 'The Lady with the Lamp', *Leamington Spa Courier*, 26 August 1910, 8. 'Salehurst', *Hastings and St Leonards Observer*, 27 August 1910, 3.
[60] Richards, *Imperialism and Music*, 376.
[61] 'Church News', *Worcester Journal*, 31 January 1891, 6.

borrowed from narratives of imperial military heroism. In light of Heber's status as a 'martyred' colonial bishop, 'The Son of God' was a reliable rallying cry for foreign missions and Bible societies. In the aftermath of the Indian Mutiny, the Rev. C. F. Childe, a principal of the Church Missionary College in Islington, addressed the citizens of Ipswich on the mission to the Peshawar region. Chants of 'hear, hear' rose from the crowd as Childe narrated how the CMC's soldier-evangelists, like later day Stephens, 'went into the open streets of Peshawar' proclaiming the gospel in what was 'reported to be the most fanatical city in the whole world'. The soldiers who stood most firmly against the treacherous sepoy, claimed Childe, 'were the very men who had taken an interest in the Missionary cause'.

> And he would in conclusion ask whether a work such as this did not present itself enough to young ardent spirits to make them long to be part of it.... He would ask – young men of Ipswich, do you not long for the privilege of taking part in it?
>
> The Son of God goes forth to war,
>   A kingly crown to gain:
>
> His blood red banner streams afar –
>   Who follows in his train?
>
> Men of Ipswich! answer. (Much applause.)[62]

Childe's strategic, emotive use of Heber's lines may strike us as sinister now. But Heber's most enduringly popular missionary hymn, 'From Greenland's Icy Mountains', had originally been deployed in a very similar context. It was first published under the title 'Intended to be sung on occasion of his preaching a sermon for the Church Missionary Society, in April, 1820'.[63] In fact, Heber had written the hymn a year earlier at the request of his father-in-law (the Dean of Asaph) for a service in aid of the more High-Church Society for the Propagation of the Gospel in Foreign Parts.[64] Heber's later CMS sermon, however, delivered at Whittington, Shropshire, offers a fitting gloss on his rousing missionary anthem. Although he had no experience of India as yet, Heber had travelled widely across Europe and Russia in his youth, and he began his sermon with a stirring image of:

---

[62] 'Church Missionary Society: Meetings at Ipswich', *Ipswich Journal*, 2 October 1858, 4.
[63] Heber, *Palestine*, 157.
[64] Amelia Heber, *Life of Heber*, 1.490.

Millions who have lost the knowledge of the one true God amid a multitude of false or evil deities; who bow down to stocks and stones; who propitiate their senseless idols with cruel and bloody sacrifices; who lose sight of their dying friends with no expectation of again beholding them, and who go down to the grave themselves in doubt and trembling ignorance without light, without hope, without knowledge of a Saviour![65]

In what must be an echo of his earlier St Stephen hymn, he concludes by reminding the congregation that it is 'our duty to desire and contend for the extension of Christianity. Wherever she goes, civilization follows in her train.'[66] In combination with this sermon, Heber's latest hymn would have provided a powerful stimulus to the charitable instincts of the congregation as the CMS collection plate was passed around:

> From Greenland's icy mountains,
> From India's coral strand;
> Where Afric's sunny fountains
> Roll down their golden sand;
> From many an ancient river,
> From many a palmy plain,
> They call us to deliver
> Their land from error's chain!
>
> What though the spicy breezes
> Blow soft o'er Java's isle,
> Though every prospect pleases,
> And only man is vile:
> In vain with lavish kindness
> The gifts of God are strown;
> The Heathen, in his blindness
> Bows down to wood and stone![67]

In the opinion of John Betjeman, 'From Greenland's Icy Mountains' is 'typical of one kind of missionary hymn – the descriptive and comparative approach (look how poor, ignorant and deprived the heathen are; see what blessings we civilised

---

[65] Reginald Heber, 'The Conversion of the Heathen' [16 April 1820], in *Sermons Preached in England*, ed. Amelia Heber (London: John Murray, 1829), 200.
[66] Heber, 'The Conversion of the Heathen', 203–4.
[67] Reginald Heber, 'Before a Collection made for the Society for the Propagation of the Gospel', in *Hymns*, ed. Amelia Heber (London: John Murray, 1827), 139.

Christians enjoy – and be generous)'.⁶⁸ But its popularity was undeniable and, like 'The Son of God', it easily transcended barriers of sect and denomination in the Anglosphere. A manuscript copy was exhibited at the Great Exhibition in 1851 and W. T. Stead called it 'the favourite missionary hymn of the English-speaking world'.⁶⁹ Yet 'From Greenland's' complacent racism clearly assumes an audience of white metropolitan Christians, and by the early twentieth century such hymns were losing ground to the softer universalism of compositions like John Oxenham's 'In Christ there is no East or West', composed in 1908 for London Missionary Society's mammoth *Pageant of Darkness and Light* at the Royal Agricultural Hall, Islington.

The continuing power of Heber's legacy into the twentieth century, however, was also evidenced by the calibre of his critics. In October 1925, Mohandas Gandhi, who had recently served two years in prison for sedition against the Raj, addressed a meeting of missionaries at the Calcutta Y.M.C.A.

> You, the missionaries come to India thinking that you come to a land of heathens, of idolators, of men who do not know God. One of the greatest of Christian divines, Bishop Heber, wrote the two lines which have always left a sting with me: 'Where every prospect pleases, and man alone is vile.' I wish he had not written them. My own experience in my travels throughout India has been to the contrary. I have gone from one end of the country to the other, without any prejudice, in a relentless search after truth, and I am not able to say that here in this fair land . . . man is vile. He is not vile. He is as much a seeker after truth as you and I are, possibly more so.⁷⁰

Heber's lament for the 'vile' humanity of the tropics was written before his appointment as bishop of Calcutta, but he used similar language in contemporary sermons in support of missions, bemoaning 'those sixty millions of our fellow men . . . who in India still bow the head to vanities, and torment themselves, and burn their mothers, and butcher their infants, at the shrine of a mad and devilish superstition'.⁷¹

---

[68] John Betjeman, *Sweet Songs of Zion: Selected Radio Talks*, ed. Stephen Grimes (London: Hodder and Stoughton, 2007), 61.
[69] Richards, *Imperialism and Music*, 387; Stead, *Hymns that have Helped*, 176.
[70] M. K. Gandhi, 'Christianity and Hinduism', in *M.K. Gandhi: Select Speeches*, ed. B. K. Ahluwalia (New Delhi: Sagar, 1969), 179–80.
[71] Heber, 'The Conversion of the Heathen', 203–4. Patrick Brantlinger suggests that the sensationalist preoccupation with 'suicidal zeal and widow burning' in hymns and sermons by Heber and his contemporaries anticipates later colonial discourse. *Rule of Darkness: British Literature and Imperialism, 1830–1914* (Ithaca: Cornell University Press, 1988), 86.

It was during an expedition in search of 'Afric's sunny fountains' (or the sources of the Nile) that Britain gained another notable missionary martyr in 1873. Although David Livingstone was Scottish Congregationalist who began his career in the service of the London Missionary Society, the outpouring of public grief during his public funeral and burial at Westminster Abbey – eulogized by the liberal Anglican Dean A. P. Stanley – ensured his status as an ecumenical national martyr.[72] In the wake of Livingstone's death an extraordinary trade in his 'relics' sprung up among missionary enthusiasts. The patriotic Protestant subscribers who handed over cash for crosses made from the tree under which Livingstone's heart was buried could rest assured that their flirtation with heathen idolatry and the cult of celebrity was all in a good cause: proceeds went to funding the activities of the London Missionary Society and related organizations. A commemorative presentation box issued by Blantyre Missionary Press (in Livingstone's home town) enclosed two withered leaves 'gathered from the tree under which Livingstone's heart was buried'.[73] These fragile relics are framed by two anonymous verse quotations: The first from Robert Browning's valedictory 'Epilogue' to *Asolando* (1889), the second from Heber's 'The Son of God goes forth to war'.

> He climbed the steep ascent of heaven,
> Through peril, toil and pain;
> O God, to us may grace be given,
> To follow in his train.

This is a slight misquotation. Heber's 'They/their' has become 'He/his'. By appropriating lines referring to collective salvation as a tribute to the sacrifice of an individual martyr, this Protestant reliquary further enforces a cult of individualized hero worship. Whereas Heber's original hymn had traced an expanding cast – from Stephen, to a 'chosen few', to the 'noble army' – here Livingstone is just one in a long line of solitary sacrificial victims.

With the onset of world war, the equation of heroism with violent self-sacrifice came under increasing pressure. In 1916, a reforming American economist and pacifist, Simon Nelson Patten, published his collection of *Advent Songs: A*

---

[72] Clare Pettitt, *Dr Livingstone, I Presume? Missionaries, Journalists, Explorers and Empire* (London: Profile, 2007); Joanna Lewis, 'Empires of Sentiment; Intimacies from Death: David Livingstone and African Slavery "at the Heart of the Nation"', *Journal of Imperial and Commonwealth History* 43, no. 2 (2015): 210–37.

[73] The leaves had been collected in Northern Rhodesia by the explorer and colonial administrator Robert Codrington. For images and discussion of these and other Livingstone relics, see Sybren Renema and Timmy van Zoelen, *You Took The Part That Once Was My Heart* (Glasgow, 2012).

Revision of Old Hymns to Meet Modern Needs. A professor at the University of Pennsylvania, Patten thought Americans should reject 'the expressions of war, depravity, and woe, upon which . . . earlier hymns depends' and look towards a progressive future of peace, abundance and social harmony. Irrepressibly optimistic, Patten even managed to reinvent Heber's 'Son of God' as a hymn to peace and love: 'The Son of God goes forth in love, / Who follows in His train? / All ye who put world peace above / What war or greed may gain'.[74]

Conclusion

> Lo, all our pomp of yesterday
> Is one with Nineveh and Tyre!
> Judge of the Nations, spare us yet,
> Lest we forget – lest we forget![75]

Written for Queen Victoria's Diamond Jubilee in 1897, Kipling's 'Recessional' is an obvious epilogue to the history of the nineteenth-century imperial hymn. Its stark Old Testament imagery and sombre refrain offered a timely warning against imperial hubris, and it was quickly absorbed into hymn books on both sides of the Atlantic.[76] But I conclude this chapter with an earlier Kipling text: his short story 'The Man who would be King' (1888). In this satirical imperial fable, two Anglo-Indian ne'er-do-wells, Daniel Dravot and Peachy Carnehan, strike out for the remote province of 'Kafiristan' determined to make themselves rulers of the native pagan tribes. Initially successful, Dravot is eventually undone by his arrogance and hubris and is executed by his subjects. While Kipling's story embodies many of the empire's chauvinistic assumptions, it is also stinging critique of colonial complacency and engages pointedly with the cult of imperial martyrdom. Dravot's death is presented as a sort of burlesque of the military martyr trope. He boldly resolves to 'die like a gentleman' but the cause for which he lays down his life is greed and self-interest. When Carnehan

---

[74] Simon N. Patten, *Advent Songs: A Revision of Old Hymns to meet Modern Needs* (New York: B. W. Huebsch, 1916), ix, 35. For more on Patten, see Daniel M. Fox, *The Discovery of Abundance: Simon N. Patten and the Transformation of Social Theory* (Ithaca, NY: Cornell University Press, 1967).
[75] Rudyard Kipling, 'Recessional'. First published in *The Times*, 17 July 1896: 13.
[76] Richards, *Imperialism and Music*, 393. Gareth Atkins, '"The Ships of Tarshish": The Bible and British Maritime Empire', in *Chosen Peoples: The Bible, Race and Empire in the Long Nineteenth Century*, eds. Gareth Atkins, Shinjini Das and Brian H. Murray (Manchester: Manchester University Press, 2020), 84.

recovers his mangled 'body caught on a rock with the gold crown close beside', we are confronted by a counterfeit of Christian martyrdom, complete with an ill-fitting 'crown'. As if working backwards through the stanzas of Heber's 'St Stephen's Day', we next hear of Carnehan's own botched crucifixion: 'They used wooden pegs for his hands and his feet; and he didn't die. He hung there and screamed, and they took him down next day, and said it was a miracle that he wasn't dead.' This darkly comic Gothic finale appears to flirt profanely with the gospel narrative, but the conclusion assures us that there is no salvation in this passion. In the final sequence, the narrator encounters Carnehan, reduced to drunken beggary and carrying the shrunken head of Dravot in a 'mass of rags round his bent waist'.

> I saw a crooked man crawling along the white dust of the roadside, his hat in his hand, quavering dolorously after the fashion of street-singers at Home. There was not a soul in sight, and he was out of all possible earshot of the houses. And he sang through his nose, turning his head from right to left: –
>
> 'The Son of Man goes forth to war,
> A golden crown to gain;
> His blood-red banner streams afar –
> Who follows in his train?'
>
> I waited to hear no more, but put the poor wretch into my carriage and drove him off to the nearest missionary for eventual transfer to the Asylum. He repeated the hymn twice while he was with me whom he did not in the least recognize, and I left him singing to the missionary.[77]

In Kipling's cynical take on the civilizing mission, the 'missionary' is left to confront the sordid reality of an idealized martyr myth. Carnehan's 'dolorous' quavering is a grotesque parody of precisely the kinds of fervour and missionary zeal that hymnodists like Heber hoped to inspire in their congregations. And yet, again, this is a mangled version of Heber's verse. The original 'Son of God' has become the 'Son of Man', an alternative title for Christ in the Gospels, which foregrounds the human frailty of the incarnate Jesus and emphasizes Christ's physical affinity with fallen humanity.[78] Moreover, the conquerors of Kafiristan

---

[77] Rudyard Kipling, 'The Man Who Would Be King', in *The Phantom Rickshaw and Other Tales* (Allahabad: A.H. Wheeler, 1890), 66–104 (102–4).

[78] Larry Kreitzer notes that this error 'cleverly shifts the focus of the hymn as a declaration of deity to it as a proclamation of humanity . . . [emphasising] the humanity of Carnehan and Dravot, at the expense of any false claims to divinity, claims which, as the story relates, result ultimately in death and crucifixion'. Larry J. Kreitzer, '"The Son of God Goes Forth to War": Biblical Imagery in Rudyard

have sought not Heber's 'kingly crown' – representing an abstracted Christian nobility – but a 'golden crown' – suggestive of mere material gain and temporal power. Carnehan's misreading leaves open the possibility that Kipling's critique is not directed so much at Christian missionaries who advocate a heroic ideal of martyrdom, but those who choose to misread metaphors of Christian warfare as literal vindications of imperial violence and exploitation. On which side of the line Reginald Heber stood is a matter for debate. But by revealing connections between two historical moments, the missionary ambitions of the late Georgian Church of England and the imperial strategies of late Victorian Britain, this chapter has demonstrated the central role of hymns in forging religious, national and ethnic identities in an age of expanding empire.

Kipling's "The Man Who Would be King'", in *Borders, Boundaries and the Bible*, ed. Martin O'Kane (Sheffield: Sheffield University Press, 2002), 99–125 (115).

The Song of Zion in Nineteenth-Century Europe

Sacred Choral Music, Emancipation and Modernity in Jewish Liturgy

Rachel Adelstein

In a tastefully decorated house of worship in London in the late nineteenth century, the morning service is about to begin. Dressed in their best clothes, men and women sit still and quiet in the pews, waiting. The pipe organ begins to play, filling the sanctuary with a stately descending scalar figure in waltz time. The choir of men and women stands ready to burst into song, their voices proclaiming the first prayer of the liturgy in classical four-part harmony. However, this Sabbath service takes place on a Saturday morning, the house of worship is a synagogue and the choir has begun to sing Louis Lewandowski's setting of *Mah Tovu*, the opening prayer of the Sabbath morning liturgy. Like much of the liturgy, the text is derived from small portions of the Hebrew Bible. The opening line of the text comes from the book of Numbers, while the remainder consists of selections from several psalms:

> How lovely are your tents, O Jacob, your dwelling places, O Israel! (Num. 24.5)
> As for me, through Your abundant grace, I enter your house to worship with awe in Your sacred place. (Ps. 5.8)
> O Lord, I love the House where you dwell, and the place where your glory tabernacles. (Ps. 26.8)
> I shall prostrate myself and bow; I shall kneel before the Lord my Maker. (Ps. 95.6)

> To You, Eternal One, goes my prayer: may this be a time of your favor. In Your abundant love, O God, answer me with the Truth of Your salvation. (Ps. 69.14)

Such a scene, of a synagogue congregation listening in silence as the trained voices of their mixed-voice choir give a refined, polished sound to the prayers of the liturgy, might take place in London, or Manchester, or Berlin or Hamburg. The choir might be large or small. It might sing a cappella, or it might be accompanied by an organ, a piano or a harmonium. But regardless of the specifics, the presence of the choir in itself serves as a musical advertisement of the synagogue's carefully negotiated engagement with nineteenth-century Western modernity.

The nineteenth century represented a moment of significant legal and social change for European Jewish communities. Especially in Germany and Britain, legal emancipation allowed Jewish communities to become full participants in public life. As much as Jewish communities welcomed their release from legal disabilities, emancipation created the new challenge of establishing and maintaining a communal identity that was both part of modern European culture and identifiably Jewish at the same time. As Jewish communities became part of European society, they began to incorporate elements of Western thought, Western dress and Western cultural tastes into both their private and public lives. As part of this cultural shift, Jewish music as a distinct entity, and not merely individual Jewish musicians, entered the larger web of European culture. Philip Bohlman has observed that music can often serve as a locus for cultural debates, both because it offers 'a panoply of ways to fix indeterminate meanings' and 'a powerful language to negotiate with the other'.[1] I argue that, as the synagogue became a public space in which German and British Jews negotiated and debated their position in increasingly emancipated modern societies, the music of the liturgy came to serve as a particularly potent tool in these negotiations. The role of the *hazzan*, or cantor, the degree to which congregations should participate in the liturgy, and the question of whether or not to introduce instrumental music all played a role in these debates. But in many ways, it is the rise of the synagogue choir that most fully demonstrates the increasingly complex connections being made in the nineteenth century between European modernity and the twin ideas of biblical and political nationhood.

---

[1] Philip V. Bohlman, *Jewish Music and Modernity* (Oxford: Oxford University Press, 2008), 80.

The sounds of this modernity can be discerned from the significant body of surviving printed music, some of which is still performed today by both concert and synagogue choirs, especially in Britain. The choral repertoire of the nineteenth-century European synagogue is heavily based on biblical texts. In addition to the psalms sung during worship, many of the prayers of the liturgy, such as *Mah Tovu*, cited above, are adapted from selections from the Hebrew Bible. The settings obey the rules of common-practice harmony, sometimes adapted to take advantage of similarities between Jewish prayer modes and European modes, especially the resemblance between the Jewish mode *Magein Avot* and the Western natural minor mode. Melodies may be adaptations of Jewish chant or popular Protestant chorales, or they may be original compositions. This music does not represent the imagined timelessness of Jewish liturgy. Rather, it is the sound of a particular moment in European Jewish community and liturgical life. It is the sound of a specific strand of Jewish thought in Germany and Britain, and it is the sound of a specific moment in time in which many of the current cultural features of Western classical music practice were established.

Enlightenment and emancipation

Reform Judaism, with its radically modernized liturgy and innovative approaches to liturgical music, emerged in Germany in the early nineteenth century, in the wake of two separate Enlightenments in Europe. One was the secular European Enlightenment of the seventeenth and eighteenth centuries, whose proponents placed great value on reason and logic as tools for understanding the world and also engendered the concept of the secular nation. The other was the Jewish Enlightenment, or *Haskalah*. This movement began in the late eighteenth century and was similar to the European Enlightenment in that the *maskilim*, the proponents of the *Haskalah*, prioritized freedom of thought and cultural criticism in their approach to Jewish life and practice. The historian Shmuel Feiner observes that the *maskilim* were 'the first who were conscious of being modern Jews, and the first to advocate a modernist, transformational ideology'.[2] It is partly from this consciousness and this ideology that the Reform movement emerged. I should observe here that, although much of this article

---

[2] Shmuel Feiner, *Haskalah and History: The Emergence of a Modern Jewish Historical Consciousness*, trans. Chaya Naor and Sondra Silverston (Oxford: Littman Library of Jewish Civilization, 2002), preface, n.p.

focuses on the Reform and other progressive movements, the encounter with modernity does not exclude Orthodox Judaism. Orthodoxy did not come into being as a movement in its own right until Reform Judaism emerged and became something separate; in its own way, Orthodox Judaism is as modern as Reform, as different as its expression of that modernity may be.

Jewish emancipation came as part of the growth of the philosophy of secular, constitutional national government. The political changes and innovations wrought by the French Revolution led national governments during the Enlightenment to debate the nature of citizenship and the virtues of full participation in civil society and consider the question of extending citizenship and full civil rights to minorities. Many Western and Central European countries granted citizenship to the Jewish communities living within their borders, a process known as emancipation. Full emancipation came to Britain in 1858, and when Germany became a nation in 1871, it was with an emancipated Jewish minority.

Among other things, legal emancipation allowed Jews and Gentiles to engage with each other on an equal footing in civil society. This engagement caused a variety of reactions among Jewish communities. Although the legal pressure to convert to Christianity eased, social pressures and popular religious prejudices remained firmly in place for decades. Some Jews took the opportunity to assimilate entirely into their host cultures, in some cases giving up their Jewish identity and converting to Christianity. Some Jews retained and strengthened their traditional religious practice, imposing new strictures over the decades, leading to what we now recognize as Jewish Orthodoxy.

However, some Jewish thinkers sought the middle ground in their response to their host societies. They observed the way that their gentile neighbours interacted with the world, compared it to their own body of religious laws that governed both ritual practice and everyday life, and looked for ways to reconcile the two ideas. Upon encountering Western European modernity, they declared that many of their traditional religious practices were not modern: these included gender-segregated seating, and a liturgy, drawn heavily from the Bible, that was chanted in Hebrew in modes constructed using small motivic cells, much like Middle Eastern *maqamat*. Composers such as Salomon Sulzer and Louis Lewandowski, who will be discussed in greater detail below, were especially horrified at both the florid recitative style of liturgical chant as sung by the hazzan, and the sound of congregants chanting the liturgical responses in their own individual rhythms and at their own speeds, accompanied by physical movement including swaying, bowing and taking small, shuffling steps. Sulzer lamented in 1865, in his preface to the second volume of his collection of choral works for the synagogue, that

> for too long, the weight of the medieval era, the curse of dark centuries has burdened the Jews, until the rhythm of the soul, without which the free, joyful art of harmony cannot hope to develop naturally, was crippled.[3]

Lewandowski wrote in 1871, in the preface to one of his own collections, *Kol Rinnah u-T'Fillah*:

> Prior to the introduction of choral singing, the congregations were entirely dependent on the often strange performances of *hazzanim*. They [congregations] participated or expressed their displeasure only through noisy praying.[4]

These thinkers who sought the middle ground wished to become modern while still remaining distinctly Jewish. The musicologist Abraham Zvi Idelsohn remarks:

> The idea was so to remodel Judaism that it should not be a stumbling block by reason of its Orientalism and Medievalism, that it should be as easy to observe as Christianity, that, furthermore, the modern Jew should not be offended by its strangeness and should be attracted by its European exterior.[5]

The solution to the problem was the Reform movement, which arose in Germany at the beginning of the nineteenth century.

The first successful Reformer was Israel Jacobson (1768–1828), who founded a new temple in 1810 in Seesen, Westphalia. The order of worship at this temple included many changes to the musical aspects of the service as well as ritual and theological innovations. Jacobson eliminated the hazzan, as well as the practice of chanting the weekly readings from the Torah and the *Haftorah*. In their place, he instituted newly composed congregational hymns, sung in German, to Christian chorale tunes with organ accompaniment. Other Reformers in Germany tried out similar changes to the worship service, according to their wishes, the wishes of their congregants and the availability of suitable music. The

---

[3] Salomon Sulzer, *Schir Zion: Gesänge für den israelitischen Gottesdienst; revidiert und neu herausgegeben von Joseph Sulzer* (Leipzig: M. W. Kaufmann, 1905), 5. Quote translated by author.
[4] Cited in Geoffrey Goldberg, 'Neglected Sources for the Historical Study of Synagogue Music: The Prefaces to Louis Lewandowski's *Kol Rinnah U'T'Fillah* and *Todah W'Simrah* – Annotated Translations', *Musica Judaica* 11 (1989): 41.
[5] Abraham Zvi Idelsohn, *Jewish Music in Its Historical Development* (1929; New York: Schocken Books, 1972), 233.

first of the Reformers' negotiations with modernity took place with their own rabbis and congregants.

Over the course of the three decades following Jacobson's establishment of his temple in Seesen, Reform congregations in Germany, and later in Britain, accepted the mixed choir singing chorale-like tunes, sometimes accompanied by an organ or a harmonium, but retained both the hazzan and some of the older chanted prayer melodies.[6] Their experiments culminated in 1845, when the leaders of the Berlin Reform Congregation codified the alterations to their worship prior to the High Holy Days. The final product, which had enormous influence on other Reform congregations, included an abbreviated liturgy, a sermon and some prayers in the vernacular, and called for a mixed-voice choir, which might be accompanied by an organ. Both the Jewish Reformers themselves and the rulers of some of the German states also directed congregations to behave with dignity and decorum, in order to eliminate the uncontrolled sound of individuals chanting prayers in their own voices, to their own rhythms and speeds.[7]

Some German states imposed further changes on synagogue music in their efforts to integrate Jews into the local bureaucracy. They equated the Jewish hazzan with the Lutheran *Kantor*, placing the hazzan into the category of religious functionaries who were required to obtain a state education certification.[8] The certification programmes were standardized and regulated, and included a required course of instruction in Western music theory, history and performance, which cut deeply into the time available for students to learn traditional synagogue chant. As a result, students in these German institutions began to rely on notated scores to learn the music of the synagogue and lost the mastery of the hazzan's art that would have allowed them to improvise in the free-metered, flexible style of earlier generations of *hazzanim*.[9] As the repertoire of German cantors became more closely aligned with contemporary standards of art music, the sonic space of the synagogue became more compatible with the sound of a choir.

The intent behind these reforms, on the part of both local governments and Jewish Reformers themselves, was to make Jewish worship more modern,

---

[6] Ibid., 243–4.
[7] George L. Mosse, *Confronting the Nation: Jewish and Western Nationalism* (Hanover, NH: Brandeis University Press, 1993), 137.
[8] Geoffrey Goldberg, 'The Training of *Hazzanim* in Nineteenth-Century Germany', *Yuval* 7 (2002): 'Studies in Honour of Israel Adler', special issue ed. Eliyahu Schleifer and Edwin Seroussi, 308.
[9] Ibid., 356.

according to the standards of the day. In doing so, the Reformers required a model for the idea of modern worship, and they found that model in local Christian practices. In selecting a choir, whether mixed voice or single sex, as a means of musical expression, the Reformers also aligned themselves with a wider cultural marker of nineteenth-century European modernity.

The choir in the age of Industrial Revolution

The choir as it is understood today is largely a product of the nineteenth century. Prior to the nineteenth century, choirs were small groups of ten to thirty singers, primarily professional singers rather than amateurs.[10] This situation changed over the next thirty years. The first part of the change was the rise, first in Britain in the late eighteenth century and later in the rest of Europe, of populist performances of Handel's oratorios that might involve a thousand massed singers. However, the greatest aid to the development of the popular choir in Europe was the Industrial Revolution.

The Industrial Revolution provided both the circumstances under which popular choirs could exist and the materials that they needed to function. The swelling population of cities brought enough people together that they could form various societies for entertainment and education, and the growth of the middle class produced people with enough leisure time to take advantage of activities such as amateur music-making. Advances in printing technology allowed publishers to produce print runs of sheet music large enough and cheap enough to supply the growing demand for scores for amateur music societies. These music societies formed at a great rate in Europe. They had names like Academy of Music, *Singakademie*, *Singverein* and Philharmonic. There were societies devoted to particular composers, notably Bach, Handel and Haydn, and many themed music festivals. While many of the choral societies started out singing oratorios, they required new music as well, inspiring composers to produce a wide variety of both sacred and secular works for chorus and orchestra.

Choral music also became part of children's education, especially in Britain, where a new compilation of Jewish liturgical music would take advantage of new methods of music pedagogy aimed at middle- and working-class children.

---

[10] Chester Alwes, 'Choral Music in the Culture of the Nineteenth Century', in *The Cambridge Companion to Choral Music*, ed. André de Quadros (Cambridge: Cambridge University Press, 2012), 29.

Training middle-class children in sight-singing ensured a steady supply of voices for the music societies. Middle-class educators also believed that training working-class children to sing would provide them with an opportunity for moral and spiritual improvement. In 1841, the British Congregational Church decided to improve church singing by finding a cheap and efficient way for Sunday schools to teach poor children to sing. To this end, the minister and educator John Curwen (1816–1880) adapted an idea from Sarah Glover (1785–1867), a teacher from Norwich, to produce tonic sol-fa notation.[11] In this system, each scale degree is represented by the first letter of its solfege syllable (do, re, mi, fa sol, la, ti), and note values are represented by periods, colons, dashes and underlines. Curwen published several instructional manuals for teachers and for students, including *Singing for Schools and Congregations* in 1843 and *The Teacher's Manual of the Tonic Sol-fa Method* in 1875.

Because tonic sol-fa could be printed using only letters and punctuation marks, it was cheaper to mass-produce than staff notation. Instruction books and complete scores of choral oratorios sold briskly, especially after Curwen's son raised the profile of the method and brought it to the attention of the middle class beginning around 1880.[12] David Wright observes that 'Tonic Sol-fa notation (cheap to produce and quick to learn) gave many their way into music, and some subsequently learned staff notation in order to broaden out their musical interests'.[13] As Erin Johnson-Williams explores in Chapter 9 of this volume, evangelical missionaries, temperance societies and schools all used tonic sol-fa notation to bring choral singing, both of hymns and of secular works, to the general public.

Tonic sol-fa notation also appears in an influential Anglo-Jewish publication. In 1899, Rabbi Francis Lyon Cohen (1862–1934) of Borough Synagogue in London and David M. Davis (*c.* 1853–1932), choirmaster of the New West End Synagogue in London, published a volume called *Kol Rinnah V'Todah* (The Voice of Prayer and Praise), commonly known as the Blue Book, under the auspices of the British Chief Rabbi, Hermann Adler. The Blue Book contains harmonized settings of the prayers, hymns and congregational responses used in Anglo-Jewish worship at the time. Although the Blue Book was compiled for

---

[11] Charles Edward McGuire, *Music and Victorian Philanthropy: The Tonic Sol-fa Movement* (Cambridge: Cambridge University Press, 2009), 17.
[12] Ibid., 24.
[13] David Wright, 'The Music Exams of the Society for the Encouragement of Arts, Manufacturers and Commerce, 1859–1919', in *Music and Institutions in Nineteenth-Century Britain*, ed. Paul Rodmell (Farnham: Ashgate, 2012), 173.

Figure 5.1 First line of a setting of *Mah Tovu* by Abraham Saqui (1824–1893) of Liverpool in the Blue Book, *Kol Rinnah V'Todah*, with tonic sol-fa notion of the soprano and alto lines. Francis L. Cohen and David M. Davis, *The Voice of Prayer and Praise: A Handbook of Synagogue Music for Congregational Singing* (1899; London: Office of the United Synagogue, 1933), 28.

use by member synagogues of the Orthodox United Synagogue, it contained melodies composed by influential Reform composers, both British and German, and was used in Reform as well as Orthodox synagogues. The Blue Book remains well known in Britain today, although it is no longer the only source of liturgical music.

Tonic sol-fa notation appears in the Blue Book precisely because it was so popular in schools (see Figure 5.1). The preface to the original 1899 edition declares:

> Remembering the extent to which our choir-boys and the pupils of Religion Classes are drawn from Elementary Schools, the Editors have presented the Soprano and Alto parts in the Tonic Sol-fa as well as in the Staff Notation. In the latter, the four vocal parts are printed in 'compressed score', to facilitate accompaniment on the organ or pianoforte in the choir-room or domestic circle.[14]

Cohen and Davis create an explicit picture of their ideal Anglo-Jewish household at the turn of the twentieth century. The imagined audience for the Blue Book is middle class and financially stable enough to afford a piano, printed sheet music for the piano and piano lessons for at least one member of the household. Families have the leisure time to spend both gathered around the piano singing and at rehearsals for their synagogue choir. Their children attend local state schools, where they learn to sing in parts from tonic sol-fa notation, very likely using

---

[14] Rabbi Francis L. Cohen and David M. Davis, *The Voice of Prayer and Praise: A Handbook of Synagogue Music for Congregational Singing* (1899; London: Office of the United Synagogue, 1933), vi.

books containing both English folk songs and popular Christian hymns, either from the Anglican tradition or that of one of the Nonconformist denominations.

This was the bourgeois musical environment into which the Jewish communities of Europe were emancipated. This was the culture that they sought to enter as educated, contributing members of society. Well-to-do Jewish ladies and gentlemen could sing in the choir of the *Singakademie* in Berlin, which included members of the wealthy Itzig and Mendelssohn families, and which formed an important part of the Bach revival, thanks to the collection of Sara Itzig Levy.[15] Jewish schoolchildren in England could learn to sing in choirs from tonic sol-fa instructional manuals. Choral music was the music both of modern Christian worship and the secular religion of civil society. To the emancipated Reformers, it was a clear choice to bring the modernity of choral music into the synagogue.

The first and most famous of the nineteenth-century composers of choral synagogue music was Salomon Sulzer (1804–1890), who became Chief Cantor of Vienna in 1826. Although he was not an adherent of the Reform movement, he did wish to modernize the music of Jewish worship. To that end, he assembled his monumental work, *Schir Zion* (The Song of Zion), in two volumes, between 1839 and 1865. *Schir Zion* contained compositions by Sulzer and by other composers whom he commissioned.[16] Both volumes consisted of hymns and selections from the liturgy, in Hebrew, for solo cantor and four-part choir. In Sulzer's synagogue, this choir was all male, with young boys singing the soprano and alto parts. Although instrumental accompaniment was becoming an option for modernized Jewish worship, Sulzer did not include accompaniment in his first volume, possibly following the contemporary fashion for a cappella singing in secular men's choruses.[17]

Sulzer had an enormous influence on the music of Jewish worship, both cantorial and choral. Synagogues that did not find his music too church-like for their tastes installed choirs of their own. They called themselves *Chor-shuln*, or 'choral synagogues', advertising at least their commitment to modern worship, if not outright Reform.

---

[15] Christoph Wolff, 'A Bach Cult in Late-Eighteenth-Century Berlin: Sara Levy's Musical Salon', *Bulletin of the American Academy of Arts and Science* 58, no. 3 (2005): 27.

[16] Abraham Lubin, 'Salomon Sulzer's *Schir Zion*. Volume One: A Survey of its Contributors and its Contents', *Musica Judaica* 8 (1985): 24–5.

[17] Thomas Albrich, 'Oberkantor Salomon Sulzer: Sein Leben und seine Zeit', in *Von Salomon Sulzer bis "Bauer & Schwartz:" Jüdische Vorreiter der Moderne in Tirol und Vorarlberg*, ed. Thomas Albrich (Vienna: Haymon, 2009), 26.

The sound of Jewish modernity

The presence of a choir in a nineteenth-century synagogue can be read as a sign of that synagogue's sympathy to, experimentation with or wholesale adoption of the ideals of modern European life. But what does this modernity sound like? What nuances and ambiguities might one hear in the song of a synagogue choir? Most composers of music for synagogue choirs have had to strike a delicate balance in their composition: incorporating features that render the piece suitable to be sung by a four-part choir in recognizable Western classical harmony, as well as features that would allow the congregation to identify the music as Jewish, such as the use of synagogue modes, cantorial melodies and Hebrew-language texts based on the biblical verses of the liturgy. They worked with and adapted the expected compositional tools of melody, harmony, rhythm, mode and metre. In addition, they experimented with combinations of choral voices and solo lines, judicious use of language and considered the charged question of instrumental accompaniment.

One of the composers who was most successful in this negotiation was the Polish-born Louis Lewandowski (1821–1894). His compositions are still sung in synagogues of all denominations, accompanied or a cappella, in mixed or single-sex choirs, and as unison melodies by congregations that do not have a choir. Lewandowski began his compositional training as a teenager. One of his teachers was Salomon Sulzer, and he also received support from Alexander Mendelssohn, a cousin of Felix Mendelssohn. With Felix Mendelssohn's recommendation, Lewandowski studied at the Royal Prussian Academy of Arts, being the first student of Jewish descent.[18] He was appointed choirmaster of the Berlin Synagogue in 1840 and became choirmaster of the Neue Synagogue on Oranienburgerstraße around 1866. The choir was initially composed of men and boys; however, at an unknown date during Lewandowski's tenure, it changed to a mixed-sex group. It was for this synagogue that he composed his most famous works.

Lewandowski's compositional style encapsulates many of the ways in which Reformers and their congregations negotiated their encounter with the sound of modern worship. His music is not purely Western art music, but neither is it recognizable as the chanting of a hazzan. It is a blend of the two styles. In

---

[18] Jascha Nemtsov and Hermann Simon, *Louis Lewandowski: 'Love Makes The Melody Immortal!'* (Berlin: Hentrich and Hentrich Verlag, 2011), 14.

his first collection, *Kol Rinnah u-T'fillah* (1871), Lewandowski used simple melodies in two-part harmony, making his settings accessible to choirs and to congregations as well.[19] In *Mah Tovu*, which appears in the first volume of his second collection, *Todah W'Simrah* (1876), he employs both a hazzan and a four-part (SATB) choir. Initially, both hazzan and choir sing in Western harmony, in waltz time. Later, the hazzan has a solo section in the free rhythm of traditional Hebrew chant, with the choir returning in strict rhythm at the end. This division is typical of Lewandowski's approach to amalgamating Jewish and Western elements in his composition. His writing for the solo hazzan's voice remains firmly within the modal and recitative-like chant style of traditional Central and Eastern European synagogue chant, while the choir sings in a Romantic style reminiscent of Mendelssohn.[20]

Much of his work is composed for choir and organ; however, relatively few of his organ accompaniments are mandatory, as can be seen in *Mah Tovu* (see Figure 5.2).

In his preface to the first volume of *Todah W'Simrah*, Lewandowski writes:

> The publication of this present work had also to take into consideration those Jewish communities that do not employ musical accompaniment. The entire contents had to be re-arranged to accommodate their needs. The focus of the work had to be placed here. Obbligato treatment of the organ had to be abandoned, the choral writing had to be addressed independently, and the accompaniment had to be used only as support for the vocal parts.[21]

That Lewandowski specifically wrote his organ accompaniments to be optional indicates both the delicacy of his musical negotiations with modernity and the reason that it is the choir and not the organ that served as the most enduring vehicle of this negotiation. Much has been written about the introduction of the organ into German, and later British, Jewish worship. Some congregations, including the West London Synagogue, adopted the instrument as part of their adaptation to perceived modern methods of worship. Tina Frühauf and Walter Hillsman have observed that adopting the organ was a cause for great debate among, respectively, German and British Jewish congregations. Rabbis and congregations worried about a sound that they associated with Christianity,

---

[19] Tina Frühauf, 'The Reform of Synagogue Music in the Nineteenth Century', in *The Cambridge Companion to Jewish Music*, ed. Joshua S. Walden (Cambridge: Cambridge University Press, 2015), 197.

[20] Nemtsov and Simon, *Louis Lewandowski*, 40–2.

[21] Goldberg, 'Neglected Sources', 46.

Figure 5.2 First page of Lewandowski's setting of *Mah Tovu* from *Todah W'Simrah*. Louis Lewandowski, *Todah W'Simrah: Vierstimmige Chöre und Soli für den israelitischen Gottesdienst* (Berlin: Ed. Bote and G. Bock, 1876), 3.

whether or not playing and pumping an organ on the Sabbath counted as work and might therefore be forbidden, where to place the instrument within the synagogue building and whether or not organ music might displace the voice of the hazzan. In Germany, Frühauf explains, the organ

[Became] an integral component of liberal Jewish identity; it was not adopted, however, by way of creating a 'synagogue organ' as a counterpart to the 'church organ' but by binding the instrument into the sacred space even if it had to be combined with elements of Jewish life that were considered traditional.[22]

In London, Professor David Woolf Marks, senior minister at the West London Synagogue, drew on biblical precedent and images of the secure situation of Anglo-Jewry in his sermon of 20 September 1859 for the dedication of the newly installed organ. Marks instructed his congregation that:

> The grand scale on which instrumental and vocal music was employed in the Temple of Solomon . . . fell in with the sentiments of a people enjoying peace, security, and a high state of national prosperity.[23]

After describing both the instrumental and the choral forces of biblical Israel at its zenith, he drew an explicit comparison between the practices of biblical Judaism and his vision of a form of Anglo-Jewish worship that reflected the ideals of nineteenth-century modernity.

> With these historical evidences before us, we may fearlessly advance the proposition, that in as much as time has wrought its influence on the forms of worship, the exigencies of time may again be consulted for the purpose of bringing our ritual practices into harmony with our mental, social, and political progress.[24]

The Manchester Reform Synagogue proved even more receptive to the idea of an organ, as that congregation was of heavily German descent, and installed its first organ in 1858, one year after its founding.[25]

However, as bold and attractive a symbol as the organ is, both to those who support its use in Jewish worship and to those who oppose it, it is of limited use in exploring the relationships between Jewish communities and modernity, precisely because it is such a bold symbol. An organ is not just an instrument that, even today, carries an enormous cultural association with formal

---

[22] Tina Frühauf, *The Organ and Its Music in German-Jewish Culture* (Oxford: Oxford University Press, 2009), 74.

[23] David W. Marks, 'The Synagogue and the Organ', in *Sermons Preached on Various Occasions at the West London Synagogue of British Jews by the Rev. Professor Marks, Minister of the Congregation*, vol. 2 (London: Trübner and Co., 1885), 168.

[24] Ibid., 178.

[25] Walter Hillsman, 'Organs and Organ Music in Victorian Synagogues: Christian Intrusions or Symbols of Cultural Assimilation?', in *Christianity and Judaism: Papers Read at the 1991 Summer Meeting and the 1992 Winter Meeting of the Ecclesiastical History Society*, ed. Diana Wood (Oxford: Blackwell, 1992), 428.

Christian worship. It is also a large and expensive object, available primarily to relatively wealthy communities that could either find a space for it in an existing synagogue building or build a new synagogue to accommodate it. The presence of an organ further required a trained organist to play it, most likely hired from a local church, and organ music suitable for Jewish worship for that organist to play.[26] Importing an organ into Jewish worship meant importing not just an instrument, but an entire infrastructure that had to be adapted for a different worship service. As much of a controversy as the organ caused, it was a controversy that remained truly relevant only to those synagogues that could afford the organ infrastructure in the first place.

A choir was a much more affordable way for congregations to experiment with the sound of modern worship. The first and most obvious advantage of a choir was simply that it was cheaper than an organ, whether the singers were paid or not. Because of the popularity of choral singing as a secular leisure activity, it was much easier to find Jewish choir singers and choir directors than Jewish organists. A synagogue could experiment with modernity and new music without having to invest a large sum of money in an organ and its infrastructure up front. The choir was a versatile instrument that could be employed to sound as Western or as Jewish as the congregation wished. Since composers could rely on the liturgical text as something that congregants would be familiar with and recognize as Jewish, they could experiment musically, employing modes, melodies and choral harmonies reminiscent of modern, secular European culture. The choir could sing the familiar biblical texts and psalms of the liturgy either in the original Hebrew or in vernacular adaptations or paraphrases, using language to emphasize how closely any given synagogue wished to affiliate itself with the more radical agendas of the Reform movement. This flexibility allowed the congregation's encounter with modernity to be a true negotiation rather than a hard and binding decision.

Some proponents of the organ argued that the instrument would also serve to control congregations, either by guiding congregational singing during a hymn or liturgical response or by drowning out conversation during a prelude, enforcing the idea of quiet dignity and decorum in worship. A properly trained choir could perform that task as well, by singing arrangements that were complex enough or in which the melody line was set high enough that the average congregant could not join in the singing. The choir could further control a congregation by singing

---

[26] Frühauf, *The Organ and Its Music in German-Jewish Culture*, 89–90.

the congregational responses to the liturgy, removing the need for congregants to participate in worship at all.

Women in Reform choirs

Most contemporary progressive synagogue choirs are mixed, with adult men and women singing together. This was not always the case; many of the most famous nineteenth-century choral synagogues started out with choirs composed of men and boys. The male-voice choir in the West London Synagogue lasted until 1863. In that year, the synagogue officers decided that replacing boys as their voices changed was causing too much turnover in the choir. The Musical Committee addressed this situation, working with the Oxford-educated Anglican musician Charles Garland Verrinder (1834–1904). Hired by the West London Synagogue in 1859 as their first organist, Verrinder served as both organist and choirmaster for forty-five years. He selected a dozen girls from the West Metropolitan Jewish School to integrate the choir.[27] He proved adept and flexible in both recruitment and management of the singers, and the mixed choir has remained at the West London Synagogue into the present day. Other British synagogues soon adopted the practice. The mixed synagogue choir was the musical expression of one of the Reform movement's key changes, bringing women into the public sphere of worship.

The Reformers' reasons for including women were the same as their reasons for the other changes that they made. The first reason was internal; the Reformers believed that worship should be an edifying and spiritually uplifting experience for all participants, including women. One of the reasons that the service was increasingly translated into the vernacular was so that women, who often were not educated in Hebrew, could follow it.[28] The other reason was external; the Reformers were concerned that their worship should adhere to local models of respectability and decorum. Women were increasingly present in public religious life in many Christian churches in the nineteenth century, as women took on the

---

[27] Susan Wollenberg, 'Charles Garland Verrinder and Music at the West London Synagogue, 1859–1904', in *Music and Performance Culture in Nineteenth-Century Britain*, ed. Bennett Zon (London: Ashgate, 2012), 67–9.

[28] Michael A. Meyer, 'Women in the Thought and Practice of the European Jewish Reform Movement', in *Gender and Jewish History*, ed. Marion A. Kaplan and Deborah Dash Moore (Bloomington, IN: Indiana University Press, 2011), 140.

role of guardians of the family's moral and spiritual life. Jewish women in Europe embraced this public status as well.

Although the first synagogues to institute mixed choirs and mixed seating were Reform, this innovation was not limited to Reform worship, just as the idea of modernity was not limited to Reform. Orthodoxy, which did not exist until the emergence of Reform to define it, is as much a product of the modern era as the progressive movements. The fundamentalist ultra-Orthodox communities frame their ever-growing list of religious restrictions as keeping to Jewish traditions; however, these actions are also the product of their own engagements with and reactions to Western ideas of modernity.

Until the middle of the twentieth century, some Orthodox synagogues in Britain employed mixed-voice choirs. Anglo-Jewish communities had enjoyed a much greater level of freedom within the wider community than on the Continent. The various models and methods of engaging with modern cultural life perhaps came easier to British Jews than to Continental Jews, and these engagements penetrated more deeply into more traditional forms of worship. Because this form of congregational music in Orthodox congregations persisted for so long, it remains in living memory, and one can even find accounts of choral activity on websites maintained by existing congregations. Hazzan Jaclyn Chernett, a founding member of Kol Nefesh Masorti synagogue in London, recalled to me the pre-war custom of the Orthodox synagogue where she grew up. 'I was part of the choir in my teens at a very large synagogue in Bayswater, London, which was the New West End, a very beautiful shul, it's still there. And they had a mixed choir.'[29] Similarly, Sheila Levy of Cambridge recalls singing in a mixed-voice choir at the Liverpool Old Hebrew Congregation on Princes Road in the 1960s. 'I joined when I was a teenager. I got my older sister involved, and she's still there.' Levy further recalls that the choir sang every week on the Sabbath, and at weddings, which revealed the synagogue's compromise regarding the propriety of an organ; it was not used during Sabbath services, but was permitted at para-liturgical occasions such as weddings. Levy says that 'Weddings we loved, because A, we sang with an organ, which we wouldn't have done otherwise, and B, we got paid extra.'[30]

---

[29] Cantor Jaclyn Chernett. Interview by author, 30 July 2010. London, England. Digital recording. Private collection.
[30] Sheila Levy. Interview by author, 17 April 2015. Cambridge, England. Digital recording. Private collection.

British Orthodox engagement with this aspect of modernity in worship reached its height in the first half of the twentieth century. Although women did not have much of a formal role in Orthodox worship, some synagogues, including the New West End and Hampstead in London, and the Liverpool Old Hebrew Congregation, maintained mixed-voice choirs with the permission of Chief Rabbi Hermann Adler. It was Chief Rabbi Israel Brodie (1895–1979), who rescinded that permission for all United Synagogue member synagogues. Since then, some of those member synagogues have maintained choirs, but those choirs have been all male. The Liverpool Old Hebrew Congregation is not a member of the United Synagogue and maintains its mixed choir to the present day. Saul Marks, a member of the congregation, writes on the synagogue's website that 'we believe we are now the only Orthodox congregation in the UK to retain a mixed choir. Whilst smaller in number, the musical tradition is still maintained by today's choristers during every service and at many weddings'.[31]

The presence of these mixed-voice choirs, especially in Reform synagogues in Britain, led to other, more profound changes in worship. In Britain, the Reform movement officially did away with the position of hazzan, although some congregations retained the position informally, employing the services of a part-time or lay cantor. In place of the hazzan, the Reform movement elevated the choir and the musical director to the task of leading the musical aspect of prayer and delegated the remaining spiritual leadership to the rabbi.

The continuing legacy of choral modernity

Synagogue choirs were never the only way in which synagogues worked out their relationship to the modern world, nor did every synagogue in the Western world have a choir. Their popularity has risen and fallen over time and in different places, as the needs, resources and ethnic and religious affiliations of Jewish communities have changed. Nevertheless, the rise of the synagogue choir in the nineteenth century and the four-part vocal music that it sang have left an enduring mark on Jewish music.

Prior to the rise of the choir, the hazzan had functioned within the synagogue as the *sheliach tzibbur*, the representative of the congregation before the Divine.

---

[31] Saul Marks, 'Choir', 2012, available at http://www.princesroad.org/#!choir/ctte, accessed 23 November 2016.

Now, the choir joined the hazzan in that representation. The voice of the hazzan was monophonic, the voice of an individual man (in the nineteenth century), representing the voices of a congregation full of individual men, praying individually in each other's company, rather than as a unified group. The voice of the choir is polyphonic, the voices of many men and women working together, singing chords rather than single notes, trading lines back and forth, overlapping each other with words and with music, singing and praying as one entity rather than as a collection of individuals. This distinction has profound consequences, as Philip Bohlman has noted: 'The polyphony of the music in the synagogue, its new form of mystical speech, symbolizes the structural transformation of the Jewish community itself. For the first time, the sanctuary was truly a public space.'[32] The Enlightenment and emancipation allowed Jews access to the larger sphere of European public life. The Haskalah gave Jewish communities the conceptual tools with which they could grapple with their understanding of and choices about what role they might wish to assume in that public life. By blending the biblical texts of ancient Hebrew prayers and psalms and the melodies and motives of synagogue chant with the harmonies, rhythms, and in some cases, the instrumental sounds of contemporary art music and the form of a popular cultural entertainment, Jewish choral composers brought the question of modernity not just into the Jewish community, but into the synagogue itself.

As the appetite for Reform began in Germany, much early Jewish choral composition came from that country. Louis Lewandowski's compositions have become so beloved that many people have forgotten their origins and believe that they are old folk melodies. Indeed, one of Lewandowski's settings of the prayer 'V'sham'ru', the command to keep the Sabbath day as stated in Exod. 31.16-17, has fully entered the oral tradition, learned by ear with multiple small variations to the melody, and having leaped beyond the Friday night service for which it was intended to be used throughout the Sabbath. Lewandowski's setting of Ps. 92 is a mainstay of Sabbath services in Britain, especially the final part, 'Tzaddik Katamar'. Congregants from many synagogues might sympathize with Cantor Zöe Jacobs of Finchley Reform Synagogue when she told me that 'if we didn't do the Lewandowski Tzaddik Katamar pretty frequently, people would feel like, what happened to my community?'.[33]

---

[32] Bohlman, *Jewish Music and Modernity*, 99.
[33] Cantor Zöe Jacobs. Interview by author. 1 May 2015. London, England. Digital recording. Private collection.

The choral tradition of British synagogues came into its own with the music of Julius, or Israel, Mombach (1813–1880), who emigrated to England from Pfungstadt, Germany, in 1828 at the age of fourteen. He arrived in the company of his tutor Enoch Eliasson, formerly the hazzan of Darmstadt, when Eliasson was elected First Reader of the Great Synagogue in London. In 1841, Mombach became director of the newly established choir at the Great Synagogue, where he composed the bulk of his music.[34] His compositions were so popular that they were used in nearly all German synagogues in Britain and the Colonies. Mombach's most enduring work is his setting of 'L'cha Adonai', 'Yours, our Living God', a hymn of praise sung as the Torah is carried through the congregation on the Sabbath, with a text combining 1 Chron. 29.11, Ps. 99.5 and Ps. 99.9.

It was in Britain that the Jewish community engaged with non-Jews most fully through the medium of choral music. Some of the beloved old melodies in the Blue Book were products of neither Reform nor Orthodox composers. Several came from Charles Garland Verrinder. Despite being initially unfamiliar with the language, Verrinder learned enough Hebrew to be able to compose new choral settings of both selections from the liturgy and the psalms. His music has embedded itself in the Anglo-Jewish tradition, especially his setting of Ps. 121, 'Esso Enai', which continues to be sung in synagogues across Britain.

Conclusions

The transition to modernity was not easy for European Jews. That the transition took place amidst an array of rapidly changing legal codes and restrictions very likely made it even more difficult. Between the European Enlightenment and the First World War, ideas about what constituted a legitimate state, the proper role of the citizen in that state, how such a state should be governed and the notion of individuals carrying the burdens of multiple large-group identities affected not only the political, but also social, cultural and religious lives of European Jewish communities. Learned people debated earnestly what it meant to be Jewish and British, or Jewish and German, and they came up with a dizzying array of answers. The debates reached as far as the rituals and practices of worship, entering the synagogue itself, and causing Judaism to divide into multiple movements, each

---

[34] David Conway, *Jewry in Music: Entry to the Profession from the Enlightenment to Richard Wagner* (Cambridge: Cambridge University Press, 2011), 103.

in its own way a response to the challenges of modernity. The choir singing the biblical texts of Jewish worship provided a flexible and multifaceted arena in which synagogues could explore their changing relationship to religious traditions and to the modern world. Through their choirs, communities could use the words of the Bible to debate questions of language, gender, ritual practice and public vocality, locating ways for those communities to retain and to shape their Jewish identities in the face of a rapidly changing engagement with the world around them. It is a process that continues even into the present day, as Jewish choirs continue to sing old favourites and newly composed works, helping their communities to find their place in a world that continues to change and grow.

6

A Temperament of 'ideal cast, lofty tone, sacrificial flame and haughty purity'

Jenny Lind's Faith and Her Career

Matildie Wium

A short-lived and poorly received musical production opened in Her Majesty's Theatre on Thursday, 12 April 1849: *Il flauto magico* (Mozart's *Die Zauberflöte*) with Jenny Lind singing Pamina, but performed in a non-staged concert format, without costumes or action. One annoyed reviewer remarked on the opera's 'state of unwarrantable nakedness', with Lind 'supplying her share as coolly and deliberately as if she were singing the solos in the *Messiah* or the *Creation*'.[1] Because the concert did not draw the revenue that Benjamin Lumley (the manager of Her Majesty's) had hoped for given Lind's stardom, and had left the audience and critics underwhelmed, he cancelled the rest of the planned series of similar 'grand classical performances' of operas.[2] The experiment had proved ill-advised. But why had Lumley tried it in the first place? The concept of this concert-version production (not common in this period) was a compromise between Lumley and Lind, who as the *prima donna* of Her Majesty's in 1847 and 1848 had ensured highly successful seasons. However, her singing in the 1849 season was the source of conflict with Lumley. In Lumley's version of the story, Lind could not decide if, nor when, she wished to retire from the stage and consequently 'kept [Lumley] in a state of harassing suspense as to the reappearance on the stage of her who had proved in latter years my chief attraction'.[3] In the version told in the biography of Lind sanctioned by her husband, she had decided to retire after the 1848 season and had not signed a contract for 1849, but Lumley, worried

---

[1] *The Musical World*, 21 April 1849 (review reprinted from *The Morning Herald*).
[2] Benjamin Lumley, *Reminiscences of the Opera* (London: Hurst & Blackett, 1864), 244.
[3] Lumley, *Reminiscences*, 230.

about the finances of his theatre, nevertheless hoped that he would be able to convince her to sing after all.[4] The latter is the more likely: numerous letters from 1848 express her decision to retire that year, and her daughter's biography points out that the entry in her journal of her performance of Donizetti's *La Figlia del Reggimento* in Brighton on 3 November 1848 is thickly underlined and followed by eight exclamation marks, so that 'we may safely assume that she intended this to be her last appearance on the stage'.[5] Lind's determination to end her operatic career, though, was not the whole reason behind the unstaged format of the *Magic Flute* performance: although she had intended to retire for a number of years, she had recently developed strong religious objections to acting, a result of her involvement with Methodism. The concert version of Mozart's opera therefore allowed her to sing her part without playing the role. The religious motivation for this choice is further contextualized by the venue originally proposed for the series of concert-opera performances, namely Exeter Hall, regularly used for evangelical religious meetings.[6] (Lumley ultimately convinced Lind and her fiancé, Claudius Harris, to consent to the concerts being held in Her Majesty's Theatre instead of the Exeter Hall.[7]) The denouement of the failed production is complicated: in order to save the theatre's finances, she agreed despite her scruples to give four final opera performances, but they precipitated such disagreement with her pietistic fiancé, whose objections to the theatre were much more radical than her own, that their engagement was broken off. The following year, she embarked on a spectacularly lucrative concert tour to the United States promoted by P. T. Barnum, and at the end of the tour, in February 1852, she married her accompanist Otto Goldschmidt, who had converted to Christianity for her sake. Although the Methodism that had precipitated her retirement from the stage was not a lasting commitment, she never considered

---

[4] Henry Scott Holland and W. S. Rockstro, *Jenny Lind the Artist, 1820–1851: A Memoir of Madame Jenny Lind Goldschmidt, Her Art-life and her Dramatic Career: From Original Documents, Letters, Ms. Diaries, &c., Collected by Mr. Otto Goldschmidt* (London: John Murray, and New York: Charles Scribner's Sons, 1891), II, 275.

[5] Jenny Maria Catherine Goldschmidt Maude, *Life of Jenny Lind* (London, Toronto, Melbourne and Sydney: Cassell & Co, 1926), 107–10. For example, Maude includes a translation of a letter Lind wrote in July 1848 to Josefine von Kaulbach, the wife of painter Wilhelm von Kaulbach (1804–1874), saying 'It was very hard for me to take upon myself again the frightful responsibility of supporting the Opera here. But it was my duty to do so, as it rested with me whether Lumley should be ruined . . . or not. . . . I go this year also to the English provinces; but then I shall have done, and shall leave my "grand carrière" behind me, and shall only work in Sweden for my pleasure, that is, for my school.' This school was a charitable project Lind intended to establish, on which more below.

[6] On Exeter Hall, see Chapter 7 of the present volume.

[7] Lumley, *Reminiscences*, 243.

revoking her decision: she went on to maintain a fairly active concert and oratorio career, settling in England from 1858 until her death in 1887.[8]

Even a cursory glance at the considerations that Jenny Lind brought to bear on the crucial personal and career decisions she made between 1848 and 1852 reveals that her religious convictions exerted a profound influence on her choices: through Lind's person, then, religion determined musical performance in concrete ways. This discussion aims to contextualize the role of Lind's religious convictions with respect to other factors that may have motivated her decisions, and to consider the consequences of those decisions with respect to music practice. Through this case study of Jenny Lind's retirement from the operatic stage and her subsequent career, I hope to contribute to an understanding of the influence of evangelicalism on music life in mid-nineteenth-century Europe and the United States, an understanding which should in turn elucidate the place of musical performance in nineteenth-century thought on personhood, morality and spirituality.

* * *

Long before Lind's desire to leave the stage became controversial public knowledge in 1848-9, her Protestant piety was an important constituent of her image. At the beginning of her public career, this piety was associated with Lutheranism, then the state religion of Sweden, in which she had been raised.[9] In December 1845 the *Berlinische Zeitung* explicitly praised the earnestness with which she seemed to portray religious feeling as Agathe in Weber's *Der Freischütz*:

> In the grand Aria . . . the most heart-felt love and the tenderest breath of maidenhood were blended together and hallowed, both of them, with sincerest piety. The singer was not contented with continuing her prayer so long only as it was indicated in the music: she retained it in her soul, that it might ring forth as a thank-offering even in the ecstasy of love that occupied her to the last moment.

---

[8] Lumley notes wryly that '[p]erhaps in this matter Mademoiselle Jenny Lind may be cited as a rare and almost solitary instance of artistic stability in the announcement of a "last farewell"'. Lumley, *Reminiscences*, 246.

[9] Many biographers attribute her strong religious sentiments from an early age to the influence of her maternal grandmother Tengmark. Maude, *Life of Jenny Lind*, 2; Gladys Denny Shultz, *Jenny Lind: The Swedish Nightingale* (Philadelphia and New York: J. B. Lippincott Company, 1962), 25; Joan Bulman, *Jenny Lind: A Biography* (London: James Barrie, 1956), 8-9.

> No singer has ever before adhered so closely, or with such warmth and clearness, to the religious tone with which Weber has coloured this entire scene.[10]

The perception among her English audience of moral excellence inspired by her faith was probably established by the *Morning Post* critic Rumsey Forster (as George Biddlecombe has explained), who had 'defined the image of Lind in terms of the essential desiderata of bourgeois Victorian womanhood: saint-like purity allied to attributes such as serenity and sensibility'.[11] Because of the 'deception' it involved, acting was considered especially inappropriate for women whose 'simplicity and sincerity' were valued above all.[12] This sentiment is quite clear from a review of a play in which Lind acted as a ten-year-old in the Royal Theatre in Stockholm, where she was being educated:

> Little Jenny Lind acts excellently, we would almost say too well. Such spirit and theatrical assurance, such utter lack of shyness in a little girl appearing before an audience of twelve hundred people, is an exception to the normal course of nature. We hope, however, that it will have no adverse influence on the moral training of the grown woman.[13]

It is therefore informative to observe how Lind's operatic interpretations could be construed as consonant with the ideals of femininity: a familiar trope for resolving this tension was explaining the success of acting by effectively negating it, by stressing the authenticity of the emotions enacted.[14] The guileless drabness of the ideal Victorian woman is an obvious subtext for the observations recorded by Priscilla Pole-Wellesley (Lady Westmoreland) that Lind 'could not render anything in which there was a suggestion repugnant to her own higher nature' but 'expressed every varying emotion of the character perfectly because she really felt it', and that at the beginning of her international career she 'was very careless of outward appearances' and 'disliked the artificial adjuncts of rouge, &c., which are a necessity of the stage, and as a natural result was often unbecomingly dressed', so that she needed to be helped to dress appropriately for her roles.[15] Thus, even before Lind became convinced of the force of those specific religious objections

---

[10] Translation from Holland and Rockstro, *Jenny Lind*, I, 311.
[11] George Biddlecombe, 'The Construction of a Cultural Icon: The Case of Jenny Lind', in *Nineteenth-Century British Music Studies*, ed. Peter Horton and Bennet Zon ([n.p]: Ashgate, 2003), III, 47–8, 51.
[12] Alison Byerly, *Realism, Representation, and the Arts in Nineteenth-Century Literature* (Cambridge: Cambridge University Press, 1997), 55.
[13] Translation from review in the *Dagligt Allehanda* of 30 November 1830 in Bulman, 16.
[14] In this vein, the well-known actress Fanny Kemble distinguished between insincere 'theatrical' acting and sincere 'dramatic' acting. Byerly, *Realism*, 54.
[15] Cited in Holland and Rockstro, *Jenny Lind*, I, 199.

to acting that prompted the concert performance of Mozart's *Zauberflöte*, her profession as a respectable and pious actress certainly required finely nuanced definition in terms of her public image – and also, perhaps, of her self-image. When Nassau Senior asked Lind about her acting, she is said to have replied that she regarded it 'a sort of fraud' to think of herself or the audience when she was performing a part: 'I scarcely ever think of the effect I am producing, and, if the thought does sometimes come across me, it spoils my acting. It seems to me, when I act, that I feel fully all the emotions of the character I represent.'[16] The incompatibility of piety and acting in the public imagination at the time is evident from the way in which Lind's intimacy with the family of Edward Stanley, the bishop of Norwich, is discussed by Holland and Rockstro. They report that in inviting Lind to stay with his family during her week-long visit to Norwich as part of her post-opera-season tour in 1847, the bishop had 'bravely broken through the conventional scruples of religious people in receiving at his palace, as a friend, one fresh from the boards', and that the singer's conversations with the Stanleys at this time 'had all turned on her power to purify the drama by her influence'.[17] The authors contextualize religious prejudices against the theatre as having relaxed at their time of writing (1891) with reference to the same episode, stating that '[i]n those days, such an invitation to one who was engaged at the Opera, was remarkable enough. English society, and especially English religious society, was strangely and stupidly conventional'.[18] When Lind decided to retire from the stage, some critics assumed that Bishop Stanley had played a role despite his well-known tolerant views.[19]

In fact, although the Stanleys probably approved of her decision, Lind's religious conviction that she should end her opera career was not instigated by them but through her involvement with evangelical pietism. In 1848, Josephine Åhmansson became Lind's companion and chaperone, replacing Lind's childhood friend Louise Johansson, who had held this position from 1842 to 1847. Åhmansson was a cousin of the wife of Lind's former singing teacher Isak Berg, and she would remain in Lind's service until after her marriage.[20] She was Methodist and seems to have exerted a strong influence on Lind. While Holland and Rockstro merely remark that Lind was 'much impressed' by Åhmansson's

---

[16] Holland and Rockstro, *Jenny Lind*, II, 70.
[17] Holland and Rockstro, *Jenny Lind*, II, 342.
[18] Ibid., 311.
[19] Lumley, *Reminiscences*, 228. See also *The Musical World*, 21 April 1849, review of *Il Flauto Magico* reprinted from *The Morning Herald* and a letter to the editor of *The Musical World*, 28 April 1849.
[20] Shultz, *Jenny Lind*, 132, 316.

'strong piety' and that Åhmansson influenced her against opera, Lind's later biographer Gladys Shultz writes that whereas Lind had formerly preferred to attend Lutheran services but had also 'felt at home with the ceremonies of the Church of England', under Åhmansson's influence she began 'going frequently to little, out-of-the-way chapels where the "true gospel" might be found'.[21] Most probably, this 'true gospel' refers to an emphasis on personal salvation, devotion, holiness and charity as the distinguishing characteristics of Christianity as opposed to participation in the ceremonies of established religion. This pietistic Methodist influence may be what Holland and Rockstro had in mind when they wrote that 'the religious convictions, which [Lind's] English surroundings fostered and developed, were steadily increasing their hold upon her; and, as their pressure grew, her repugnance to the theatrical mode of life . . . grew also'.[22] Interestingly, Shultz's account suggests that Lind may have been seeking solace in religious exercises for the trauma that Mendelssohn's death in November 1847 had caused for her.[23] While Bulman also interprets Lind's greater devotion to religion as having 'taken increasing refuge' in meditations, exercises and Bible readings with Åhmansson, the background she implies for Lind's need of consolation is the troubled nature of her engagement to Julius Günther, a tenor with whom she had sung at Stockholm and with whom she had been romantically involved since 1844.[24] They had become engaged in the first months of 1848 (before Lind sailed to England in mid-April), but broke it off in October for reasons that are not clear, although more than one biographer has suggested that Lind realized that it would be difficult for her to retire from the stage if she married an opera singer.[25]

Evangelical condemnation of the theatre formed part of a general disdain of secular activities, since, as Doreen Rosman has explained, evangelicals' 'otherworldly view of life as a time of probation in which man prepared himself and was prepared for heaven created an intensive concern for the way in

---

[21] Holland and Rockstro, *Jenny Lind*, II, 339; Shultz, *Jenny Lind*, 132.
[22] Holland and Rockstro, *Jenny Lind*, II, 339.
[23] Shultz, *Jenny Lind*, 131-2. Lind had formed a close friendship with Mendelssohn since meeting him in Berlin in 1844 and sang under his direction in Gewandhaus concerts (1845 and 1846) as well as at the Lower Rhine Festival of 1846. She often met him socially, too, and they kept up a warm correspondence. George Biddlecombe has suggested that there was a relationship between Mendelssohn and Lind; see his 'Secret Letters and a Missing Memorandum: New Light on the Personal Relationship between Felix Mendelssohn and Jenny Lind', *Journal of the Royal Musical Association* 138(1), 47–83.
[24] Bulman, *Jenny Lind*, 203.
[25] Shultz, *Jenny Lind*, 136; Holland and Rockstro, *Jenny Lind*, II, 339; Bulman, *Jenny Lind*, 201.

which this life was spent'.²⁶ Beliefs on what constituted time well spent varied considerably, with the strictest groups sanctioning religious pursuits only, but most saw music as a meaningful endeavour nevertheless.²⁷ Specific objections to the theatre (which non-evangelicals shared to some extent) included profane material in plays, actresses' reputation for loose morals and the specious appeal to the senses.²⁸ Plays were held to indoctrinate theatregoers in anti-religious values and to encourage them to set aside their moral judgement, while acting was thought to foster vanity and female brazenness.²⁹ A further objection to acting which resonates particularly well with Lind's correspondence, and explains her passionless delivery of the part of Pamina in Mozart's opera, was the threat that it seemed to hold to one's autonomy of self.³⁰ During her operatic career, as we have seen, she asserted that all the emotions she portrayed when acting were authentic and emerged from a self-forgetful immersion in her character, so that the transition to oratorio and concert singing, requiring no acting, represented a significant relief for her. In July 1849, for example, she wrote to Charlotte Birch-Pfeiffer (her former German teacher whom she often addressed as 'mother') that she had begun to sing oratorio, since in this genre 'the words make me feel a better being', and Holland and Rockstro similarly argue that, contrary to the emotional strain of the opera, she 'could pass straight on to the concert platform from her inner musings, and could there deliver herself of her full message, just as it burned within her to give it'.³¹

Lind's Methodist-inspired objection to acting was part of a holistic dissatisfaction with her life as an opera singer that had been growing for years, and it is noteworthy that Harriet Grote, remembering a conversation with Lind to this effect that took place in 1845, listed a number of reasons that are not religiously motivated (with the single exception of the unwanted association with people who were not respectable):³²

---

²⁶ Doreen Rosman, *Evangelicals and Culture* (London: Croom Helm, 1984), 58.
²⁷ Rosman, *Evangelicals*, 55, 135–6.
²⁸ D. W. Bebbington, *Evangelicalism in Modern Britain: A History from the 1730s to the 1980s* (London: Unwin Hyman Ltd, 1989), 130.
²⁹ Rosman, *Evangelicals*, 77.
³⁰ Boyd Hilton, *The Age of Atonement: The Influence of Evangelicalism on Social and Economic Thought, 1785–1865* (Oxford: Clarendon Press, 1988), 18.
³¹ Holland and Rockstro, *Jenny Lind*, II, 352, 436. The oratorios Lind performed at this stage of her career were the same ones that would become iconic constituents of her repertoire: Mendelssohn's *Elijah* (he had composed the aria 'Hear Ye, Israel' to show off the pleasing quality of Lind's high F-sharps), Haydn's *The Creation* and Handel's *Messiah*.
³² This is consonant with what we know of her behaviour during her employment at the Royal Theatre in Stockholm. Her disdain of Emilie Högqvist, for example (who was the prima donna of the theatre in the 1830s and was famous for her affairs – including with King Oscar I and with Julius Günther

Among the things Jenny said to me during these two days, one was that her earnest desire was, to have done with the stage, and to retire to private life as speedily as was consistent with pecuniary independence. I manifested some surprise at hearing her speak of her profession with such dislike. She went on to say 'that it was the theatre, and the sort of "entourage" it involved, which was distasteful to her. That, at the opera, she was liable to be continually intruded upon, by curious idlers, & exposed to many indescribable "ennuis" – that the combined fatigue of acting & singing was exhausting, that the exposure to cold "coulisses", after exertion on the stage in a heated atmosphere, was trying to the chest, the labour of "rehearsals" tiresome to a degree. & altogether she longed for the time to arrive when she should be rich enough to do without the theatre' – adding, 'my wants are few – my tastes simple – a small income would content me.'[33]

In addition to these professional frustrations, she also wanted to have a family, as more than one contemporary observer remarked.[34] Writing to Charlotte Birch-Pfeiffer after her split from Harris, Lind herself, too, explains that 'I have, indeed, greatly wished [to be married], for few people have a truer feminine feeling than I, the feeling of a loving woman, and it would have been a blessing for me to be able to call a child *my very own*'.[35] Lind may also have felt that changing to concert singing was a smart career move: The music critic Henry Chorley, commenting in 1862 on her retirement, thought that her limited opera repertoire 'must have exposed her on every side to comparisons, should she have remained on the stage till enthusiasm cooled, as it must inevitably have done', and that by contrast the 'wild, queer, northern tunes' and oratorios she sang in concerts were her strong suit.[36]

During 1848, then, while she was engaged to Günther, Lind began to make more concrete plans for her retirement. She hoped to work as a concert singer in Sweden after their marriage, raising money in this way to establish a charitable school. The dissolution of the engagement meant that these plans had to change,

---

before he was engaged to Lind), extended to her reacting with indignation at Högqvist's inclusion in a memorial service for three Swedish artists the year after she passed away. Oscar Wieselgren, 'Emilie Högqvist: Ett livsöde ur vårt 1800-tals teaterhistoria', in *Nordisk Familjeboks Månadskrönika, Andra Årgången, Häfte 8*, ed. Yngve Lorents (Stockholm: Nordisk Familjeboks Förlags Aktiebolag, 1939), 525.

[33] Harriet Grote, 'Memoir of the Life of Jenny Lind (written 1855–6)', manuscript, Jenny Lind Archive, Royal Academy of Music, 29.

[34] Holland and Rockstro, *Jenny Lind*, II, 329; Simpson, *Many Memories*, 91.

[35] Translation from W. Porter Ware and Thaddeus C. Lockard, Jr, *PT Barnum Presents Jenny Lind: The American Tour of the Swedish Nightingale* (Boston, Rouge and London: Louisiana State University Press, 1980), 171.

[36] Henry Chorley, *Thirty Years' Musical Recollections* (London: Hurst and Blackett, 1862), I, 312.

of course. At the time of the breakup with Günther, though, Lind was already being courted by Claudius Harris, to whom she was engaged between January and May 1849. The contemporary descriptions of this engagement allow the nuances of Lind's Methodist convictions at this time to emerge more clearly. Harris was a relation by marriage of Harriet Grote's, who acted as Lind's patron during her tenure at Her Majesty's Theatre, and he met Lind through Grote during Lind's 1848 provincial tour. Evangelical religion was a specific point of mutual interest between them. Reporting Lind's engagement in April 1849 to her sister Frances von Koch, who had supported Lind in similar ways during her early career in Stockholm, Grote wrote that Harris had 'won Jenny by his intense passion for her, and also by his virtuous character tending toward the pious, which falls in with her present leanings', and Lind's friend Mary Simpson remembers that Harris's attraction for Lind lay in his 'goodness' and 'pure mind'.[37] However, it soon transpired that Lind's and Harris's religious convictions, however much they may have seemed to converge, differed significantly enough to create tension between them that eventually caused the breakdown of the relationship. The principal points of conflict appear to have been the morality of the theatre, of public musical performances and the proper conduct and rights of married women. It is not clear with which religious group Harris identified. Holland and Rockstro merely state that 'he had been brought up in a strict Evangelical system, which thrust the stage outside the pale of religion'.[38] Lind would later write to her friend Emma Flygare that 'he belonged to a *sect*, did nothing but read psalms and go to church, could talk of nothing but the Last Judgment which was at hand'.[39] His convictions on the immorality of the theatre seem to have been so uncompromising that he regarded Lind's having starred in operas as sins to be confessed and shunned: Lind's adviser in the contractual negotiations, Nassau Senior, would later remember Lind characterizing Harris's family as people who considered 'the theatre a temple of Satan, and all the actors priests of the Devil' and expected her 'to go down to Bath, among people who care for nothing but clergymen and sermons, as a sort of convert or penitent'.[40] Furthermore, he wished her to commit in their marriage contract never to appear in any public performance, operatic or otherwise, and would not consent to her

---

[37] *The Lewin Letters; a Selection from the Correspondence & Diaries of an English Family, 1756–1884. Printed for Private Circulation*, ed. Thomas Herbert Lewin (London: Archibald Constable & Co. Ltd, 1909), II, 65.
[38] Holland and Rockstro, *Jenny Lind*, II, 341.
[39] Translation from Bulman, *Jenny Lind*, 219.
[40] Holland and Rockstro, *Jenny Lind*, II, 344.

having control over the earnings she had already amassed up to that point, since such independence of a wife seemed to him 'unscriptural'.⁴¹ That these terms were unacceptable to Lind indicates that while Methodism partly motivated her decision to end her operatic career, she did not share the most fundamentalist evangelical convictions of her day. Had she come to hold convictions similar to Harris's, her marriage would clearly have constituted the end of her public career. (David Kennerley's recent exploration of conduct literature from the mid-eighteenth to the mid-nineteenth century confirms that evangelical authors shared an implicit 'condemnation of the moral character of the women who [worked] professionally as musicians' (i.e. not only as opera singers), and held that 'it was impossible to cultivate diffident modesty and professional excellence at the same time'.⁴²) Interestingly, Lind seems to have been encouraged to break off the engagement by the Stanleys, whose advice throughout their relationship with Lind was offered in the explicit context of religion.⁴³ This observation allows for a counterpointed narrative of the effect of Lind's religion on her career: while it played a role in her conviction that she should end her opera career, it may have played an equally significant role in her decision to embark on a second career. In a letter she wrote to her friend Augusta von Jaeger in 1850, she explains that she interpreted P. T. Barnum's proposition to act as her agent for a tour to the United States as divine providence (as a 'direct answer' to prayer, in fact) to enable her to donate generously to charitable endeavours, particularly her Swedish school project:⁴⁴

> I have for long had the most eager wish to earn, somewhere, a great deal of money, so as to endow a school for poor lost children in my own country. And the invitation to America came as a direct answer; so that I go there in this confidence; and I pray God in Heaven, out of a full heart, that He will guide me thither, as ever before, with His gentle hand; and will graciously forgive me my sins, and my infirmities. I shall have much to encounter; it is a very big undertaking. But since I have no less an aim before me than to help in widening God's kingdom, the littlenesses of life vanish in face of this! My dearest Gusti, my Bible was never more necessary to me than now – never more truly my stay! I drink therein rest, self-knowledge, hope, faith, love, carefulness, and the fear

---

⁴¹ Lumley, *Reminiscences*, 232–3; Holland and Rockstro, *Jenny Lind*, II, 346.
⁴² David Kennerley, *Sounding Feminine: Women's Voices in British Musical Culture, 1780–1850* (Oxford: Oxford University Press, 2020), 48–9.
⁴³ Lumley, *Reminiscences*, 233. For the religious tenor of Lind's friendship with the Stanley family, see Holland and Rockstro, *Jenny Lind*, II, 312–16.
⁴⁴ Eventually, Lind set up a fund for travelling scholarships for Swedish singers, which still makes awards annually.

of God; so that I look at life and the world in quite another fashion to what I did before.[45]

The commitment to charity Lind expresses here, the description of an emphatic change in her outlook and the central place the Bible seems to have held in her experience of faith at this time resonate with David Bebbington's analysis of the unique characteristics of evangelicalism. In his view, 'activism, the expression of the gospel in effort', 'Biblicism, a particular regard for the Bible' and 'conversionism, the belief that lives need to be changed' constitute three of four defining traits of evangelicalism (the last one is 'crucicentrism, a stress on the sacrifice of Christ on the cross').[46]

The period of 1850–1 seems to represent the apex of Lind's involvement with the Pietist revival. Before leaving on her American tour in September 1850, she spent May and June in Stockholm giving recitals, and her refusal to perform in operas as well as her public identification with the revival was controversial. Preserved correspondence among Lind's contemporaries pertaining to her stay in Stockholm in 1850 also shows the most pronounced identification of her faith as Methodist and provides some clues as to its origins. In a revealing letter, Carl Olof Rosenius wrote to his mentor George Scott, a Methodist pastor whose Swedish ministry of 1826–41 Rosenius was continuing,[47] that their group was much maligned because they were perceived as having 'ensnared the Swedish Nightingale'.[48] This document mentions Lind 'seeking private interviews' with Rosenius, and attending the services of Peter Wieselgren and Peter Fjellstedt, itinerant preachers associated with the Swedish Temperance Society (*Svenska nykterhetssällskapet*) founded by Scott. This scenario seems to suggest that Åhmansson may have been converted to Methodism through the evangelism of Scott and Rosenius in Stockholm in the first place. The revival, however, was not specifically Methodist despite Scott's central role: Rosenius preferred that members of the movement should remain members of the Church of Sweden and focused rather on the experience of a relationship with God through faith.[49]

---

[45] Holland and Rockstro, *Jenny Lind*, II, 396.
[46] Bebbington, *Evangelicalism*, 3.
[47] Hans J. Hillerbrand, *Encyclopedia of Protestantism* (Oxon and New York: Routledge, 2004).
[48] *The London Quarterly Review*, XXXII (1869), 316. This source dates Rosenius's letter to 1849, but this is probably erroneous in the light of other contemporary documents. See 'The American and Foreign Christian Union', II, 1851, 293–4.
[49] Mark Safstrom, 'Introduction', in *The Swedish Pietists: A Reader: Excerpts from the writings of Carl Olof Rosenius and Paul Peter Waldenström*, ed. Mark Safstrom (n.p.: Wipf and Stock Publishers, 2015), 4, 7.

A letter of 29 May 1850 from Frances von Koch to Harriet Grote shows the tenor of public opinion of Lind's religion:

> Jenny Lind arrived per steamer from Lübeck a week ago. She has announced six concerts at the theatre.... We have not met.... I have plans for the country after such a prolonged winter ... so I shall not subscribe to these concerts probably, and at all events my relish for her singing is damped by the annoyance of the baggage's resolving never to act any more, because the devil is in such work. They say she is a red-hot methodist; perhaps she thinks we are not holy enough for her company.[50]

A less indignant, more tongue-in-cheek observation of the controversy appears in the memoirs of politician Emil Key, who writes that, although the Stockholm public was outraged at Lind's having left the stage because of her connection with the 'läsare' ('readers', a pejorative name for Pietists),[51] the public yet retained hope that she would change her mind since she dressed as elegantly as ever.[52]

Through her involvement with the revival, Lind became impressed with the hymns of Oscar Ahnfelt, who toured Sweden as a singing evangelist after his conversion through a sermon delivered by Rosenius in 1841. He had set texts by Rosenius and Lina Sandell (the daughter of a central revivalist and, through her songs, an important figure herself), and Lind helped to fund a series of Ahnfelt's songs that appeared between 1850 and 1877.[53] Although some sources claim that she had also popularized them by including them in some of her recitals in the United States, surviving concert programmes and reviews do not mention them.[54]

Lind's public persona during her tour of the United States seems to have continued the identification with evangelicalism generally and Methodism specifically as observed above in London and Stockholm in 1849–50. This is apparent from some of the causes to which she donated money: a salient example is the Jenny Lind Chapel in Andover, constructed through funds she had donated to the founder of the Augustana Evangelical Lutheran Church in

---

[50] Lewin, *The Lewin Letters*, II, 68.
[51] Safstrom, 'Introduction', 1. The 'läsare' movement had its origins in the eighteenth century and exhibited the classic traits of pietism: 'a return to the biblical portrayal of humans as sinners, Christ as redeemer, justification by faith, experiential rather than doctrinal theology, and holiness of life'. Carol M. Norén, 'Origins of Wesleyan Holiness Theology in Nineteenth Century Sweden', *Methodist History* 33, no. 2 (1995): 1. These characteristics have significant theological resonance with Bebbington's four pillars of evangelicalism cited above.
[52] Emil Key, *Minnen av och om [Memories on and on]* (Stockholm: Albert Bonniers Förlag, 1915), 173.
[53] Anders Jarlert, *Piety and Modernity* (Leuven: Leuven University Press, 2012), 292.
[54] Carl Daw, 'Hymnic Anniversaries for 2013', *The Hymn* 63, no. 3 (2012).

America, Lars Paul Esbjörn, who like Scott, Rosenius, Wieselgren and Fjellstedt was associated with the temperance movement in Sweden. Equally revealing of the public opinion of her faith was the fact that when she gave a concert in a Methodist church in Harrisburg, Pennsylvania, the church stewards required the pulpit to be covered with planks, because they felt that 'since some members of Jenny's troupe – notably Otto Goldschmidt – were not Christians, it would be "wicked and ungodly" for anyone except Jenny Lind herself to step on that sacred platform'.[55] Evidence of more direct involvement with Swedish Methodism in America during 1851 comes from her relationship with Olof Gustaf Hedstrom, the minister of a Swedish Methodist community in New York. He was not directly linked with the Stockholm group as he had been converted to Methodism in the United States, although he is often portrayed as Scott's successor in histories of Swedish Methodism. He held services on a 'Bethel Ship' (an unused docked ship in the New York port used as a 'floating chapel') called the John Wesley, which Jenny Lind seems to have attended regularly, having been approached by Hedstrom shortly after her arrival in New York. The historian of religion Henry Whyman reports that 'a pastoral relationship developed [between Lind and Hedstrom] that made it natural for such meetings, at the singer's request, to conclude with a prayer';[56] this 'pastoral relationship' is evidenced by two letters from Lind to Hedstrom, dated October 1851 and March 1852, that indicate some intimacy and trust.[57] Strikingly, there is also a narrative of a conversion-like experience during one of these visits, which centred on Lind's retirement from the stage once more:

> [O]ne day in 1851 she attended the service on the Bethel Ship and heard Hedstrom preach. Lind then followed Hedstrom into his office, and during the ensuing conversation, discussed the matter of her relationship to God. Several indications would seem to reflect that at this period of her life Lind was involved with an inner spiritual struggle. At one point a tearful Jenny Lind fell to her knees and begged Hedstrom to pray for her. The matter of theatrical and operatic performance must have been a part of their conversation. A day or two later, Hedstrom received a letter from Lind expressing gratitude for his kindness

---

[55] Ware and Lockard, *PT Barnum Presents Jenny Lind*, 114.
[56] Henry C. Whyman, *The Hedstroms and the Bethel Ship Saga: Methodist Influence on Swedish Religious Life* ([n.p]: Southern Illinois University, 1992), 105.
[57] They are held by the United Methodist Archives Center at Drew University. Subsequent quotations from them are taken from the translations by Whyman in *The Hedstroms*.

to her. In it she revealed her decision never again to appear in theatre or opera, but only on the concert stage.⁵⁸

That religious objections to the stage as motivation for Lind's career change surface again during her American tour in the context of a conversion narrative is intriguing. It may reveal that the idea of a conversion narrative was likely to have had greater traction with American publics than with European ones, or perhaps the account of her conversion was a spontaneous addition to the Lind legend in the public imagination, being congruent with the earlier European reports of the reasons for her retirement from the stage and her public participation in evangelical religion (not to mention her donations to Christian charitable institutions).⁵⁹ A pietistic identification with Lind endures among some Christians to the present day, with Lind honoured as having sacrificed her 'worldly' career out of religious conviction.⁶⁰ Holland and Rockstro, however, were careful to steer away from such an interpretation of her decision, perhaps because her involvement with evangelicalism seems not to have extended beyond her US tour:

> Even if, at the moment of the actual withdrawal, she was possessed by influences which disturbed her normal conscience, yet even then she repudiated, with hot indignation, any aspersion which implied contempt for her profession. And her determination to withdraw ran back far behind the time when that special form of religious puritanism affected her: and it lasted on, with undiminished strength, long after she had recovered, again, her more habitual judgment. No! It was religion, if you will, that moved her; but it was the simple and wholesome religion of a pious soul, who felt that she *must* retain the plain and primitive peace, which is the secret of all high and noble living.⁶¹

In their gloss on Lind's religious motives, they emphasize rather that her acting was emotionally draining and that her health suffered because of this, whereas

---

⁵⁸ Whyman, *The Hedstroms*, 105. These details are taken from Victor Witting's memoirs, where it becomes clear that the conversion story was handed down to Witting by an old member of Hedstrom's congregation, who seems somewhat defensive, telling Witting that Hedstrom had told the congregation of these events 'privately and publicly' and had shown him the place where Lind had wept on her knees and prayed. Victor Witting, *Minnen Fran Mitt Liv* (Worcester, MA: Burbank & Co. Tryckeri, 1904), 168. The letter in which Lind supposedly resolves never to sing in an opera again has not survived.
⁵⁹ Another account of her attendance of services on the Bethel Ship appears in Gilbert Haven and Thomas Russell, *Father Taylor, the Sailor Preacher* (Boston: B.B. Russell, 1872), 130.
⁶⁰ See, for example, the weblog entry of 18 May 2015 of a member of the Wellspring Mennonite Church, https://comeintothefields.wordpress.com/2015/05/18/time-out/, accessed 21 October 2020.
⁶¹ Holland and Rockstro, *Jenny Lind*, II, 439.

'authentic', non-acting musical interpretation allowed her to retain spiritual composure. It is possible that her husband Otto Goldschmidt was instrumental in her 'recovery of her more habitual judgment': in her 1852 letter to Hedstrom, Lind writes that she regards marriage as a 'spiritual school' and that her husband's 'mild disposition and temperament' had 'already accomplished much good' for her.[62] Goldschmidt, a Jew, had been baptized before their wedding, and both ceremonies were conducted in the episcopal denomination, which may indicate that Lind was turning away from Methodism at the end of her US tour. Again, like she did at many important junctures in her life, Lind experienced her marriage to Goldschmidt as the result of divine intervention. Nevertheless, his Jewish faith was a significant obstacle to her, and it is safe to assume that she would not have married him had he not converted. In March 1852, she wrote to Amalia Wichmann:

> God has sent him to me as my consoler and helper. I am sure of that fact, for the wonderful way in which we two were brought together could not have happened unless a higher Providence had ordained it thus. . . . His parents are Jews, dear Amalia, and I assure you, there are many worthy people in his family. And my husband has been baptised of course, and is a sincere Christian in his heart and soul. I hope that he will become more and more so. I have always regarded two things as special trials and right now I have had to go through both of them: first, marrying a man younger than I, and, second, marrying a Jew. But this is the way God treats us whenever we are self-willed.[63]

Goldschmidt continued his career alongside Lind's, and contributed significantly to Christian church music after their marriage, editing a volume of hymns and composing an oratorio, *Ruth*, which like Mendelssohn's *Elijah* drew on a theme common to the Jewish and Christian traditions. If Lind chose against a union with Harris who had shared her faith but condemned her career, she must have valued Goldschmidt's active professional participation in it, and their different religious backgrounds did not prove an insurmountable obstacle, even though he seems to have compromised far more than she in that respect.

Even if, after her marriage, she ceased to identify with evangelicalism in the exercise of her faith, it is noteworthy that she seemed to profess stricter convictions regarding the immorality of the theatre than ever. When August Bournonville met her in Vienna in 1854 and berated her for 'turn[ing] her back

---

[62] Whyman, *The Hedstroms*, 110.
[63] Translation from Ware and Lockard, *PT Barnum Presents Jenny Lind*, 126.

on the stage forever, and thus bury[ing] the rich talent that had once been the delight and edification of so many', she said that she had 'now learnt that the theatre was nothing but lies and delusions',[64] and in 1865, Lind asserted that her mother had been reluctant to allow her to be trained as an actress and singer because 'she, like myself, had the greatest horror of all that was connected with the stage'.[65] Perhaps these statements indicate that Lind's prejudice against the stage had evolved from professional and personal discontent with theatrical life in the late 1840s, via specifically pietistic objections in 1848–52, to the assumption of a matronly Victorian Puritanism thereafter.

The historical record allows a correlation to be posited between the trajectories of Lind's spirituality and her musical performance, so that Lind's involvement with pietism inspired her career change. Such an easy interpretation should however be challenged by an awareness that the cultural, moral, professional and personal contexts in which she performed likewise influenced her choices and their musical outcomes. As a pioneer of the first generation for whom a singing career composed solely of concert and oratorio engagements became possible,[66] Lind mediated, through her choices, a host of considerations that are revealing of, even as they impacted upon, the intertwined, multidirectional histories of music and spirituality in mid-nineteenth-century Europe and the United States.

---

[64] August Bournonville, *My Theatre Life*, trans. Patricia McAndrew (Middleton, CT: Wesleyan University Press; London: Adam & Charles Black, 1979), 214.
[65] Letter to the editor of the Swedish Biographical Lexicon, quoted in Holland and Rockstro, II, 445–6.
[66] Deborah Rohr, *The Careers of British Musicians, 1750–1850: A Profession of Artisans* (Cambridge: Cambridge University Press, 2001), 103, observes that 'concert singing evolved as a primary career focus in the nineteenth century, particularly for women musicians' and names Elizabeth Rainforth and Charlotte Sainton-Dolby as British examples. Both of these women were exact contemporaries of Lind.

7

Urban Hymns

The Sacred Harmonic Society and Exeter Hall

James Grande

The massed choirs of the Crystal Palace Handel Festivals might seem to represent a kind of apotheosis of Victorian musical life. In pure numerical terms, they stand unrivalled. At the inaugural festival of June 1859, held to mark the centenary of the composer George Frideric Handel's death, we are told that a chorus of 2,765 singers, accompanied by a 457-strong orchestra, performed *Messiah*, *Israel in Egypt* and a selection from other Handelian oratorios in the central transept of the Crystal Palace before a combined audience (over the four days of the festival) of 81,319 (see Figure 7.1).[1] The event brought together a choral festival tradition that in the previous century had been largely based around provincial cathedrals with the new, predominantly urban, phenomenon of the sight-singing movement, with its transformative effect on music education and amateur singing.[2] It was made possible by new technology, both in the glass and steel dome of the Crystal Palace itself and the railways that carried spectators and performers to Sydenham. The festival would be repeated every three years, with ever-increasing numbers, until 1926. Howard Smither's history of the oratorio describes the event as 'a climax of the amateur choral movement': 'At last the metropolis had a continuing festival that outdid those of the provinces and

---

[1] Michael Musgrave, *The Musical Life of the Crystal Palace* (Cambridge: Cambridge University Press, 1995), 39.

[2] As Alain Frogley writes, Britain's 'commercial wealth, relative social openness and cosmopolitanism' made it an 'international clearing-house' for musical culture. In London, this role extended to musical practices from around Britain, as well as (more famously) Continental imports such as Italian opera and Austro-German instrumental music. See Alain Frogley, 'The Symphony in Britain: Guardianship and Renewal', in *The Cambridge Companion to the Symphony*, ed. Julian Horton (Cambridge: Cambridge University Press, 2013), 376–95 (p. 377). On the Congregational minister John Curwen and the development of the Tonic Sol-fa system of music education, see Charles Edward McGuire, *Music and Victorian Philanthropy: The Tonic Sol-fa Movement* (Cambridge: Cambridge University Press, 2009).

Figure 7.1 John Brandard, the Handel Festival at the Crystal Palace ('Israel in Egypt'). Printed by M. & N. Hanhart, published by Chappell & Co. 1859 chromolithograph. © National Portrait Gallery, London.

one that could be seen as a symbol of British musicality and imperial power'.[3] Contemporary accounts emphasized the scale of the venue, the sheer number of performers and the sense of national ritual conveyed by their performances: for the *Musical Times and Singing Class Circular*, writing about the 1857 trial festival, it was 'as though the Palace itself were a great musical instrument'. The 'Hallelujah Chorus' from Handel's *Messiah* 'could be distinctly heard nearly

---

[3] Howard E. Smither, *A History of the Oratorio, Volume 4: The Oratorio in the Nineteenth and Twentieth Centuries* (Chapel Hill: University of North Carolina Press, 2000), 283. Smither notes that for the 1857 trial festival, 1,200 singers came from London and 800 from the English provinces, mainly the midlands and north. The railway companies offered reduced tickets to festival participants.

half a mile from Norwood, and its effect, as the sound floated on the wind, was impressive beyond description, and sounded as if a nation were at prayers'.[4]

The core of the Crystal Palace chorus was drawn from the Sacred Harmonic Society, founded in 1832 and already well established as London's leading choral society, while the organizational impetus was provided by the society's conductor (since 1848) Sir Michael Costa, a Neapolitan composer and conductor who had directed the opera at the King's Theatre, Haymarket and founded the Royal Italian Opera at Covent Garden.[5] Earlier accounts of the Sacred Harmonic Society tend towards the teleological, dwelling on the monumental performances at the Crystal Palace at Sydenham and emphasizing the distance the organization had travelled from its more obscure origins. Cyril Ehrlich and Simon McVeigh characterize its history as a progression towards eventual orthodoxy: 'born of religious dissent and social upheaval during the 1830s', the society was 'later redirected at the Crystal Palace Handel Festival'.[6] In this narrative, the organization appears as an exemplary institution in the musical and moral life of nineteenth-century London, achieving a degree of mid-century middle-class respectability that effectively obscured its more uncertain, even disreputable beginnings.[7] Such narratives follow the influential account by William Weber, which treats the Sacred Harmonic Society as an instance of a new 'mass musical culture', located in the urban lower middle class and closely linked to demographic change and industrial development.[8] This chapter focuses on the early years of the society's existence to re-examine some of these interpretations; in particular, Weber's straightforward equation of musical and political reform. The following account places greater emphasis on the Nonconformist or Dissenting character of the society, its appropriation of the Handelian tradition and its association with a specific place: not the Crystal Palace, but Exeter Hall on London's Strand. This highlights the particular achievement of the Sacred Harmonic Society, which was to take an eighteenth-century Anglican, cathedral and provincial choral

---

[4] Quoted in Musgrave, *Musical Life*, 36.
[5] On Costa's role, see John Goulden, *Michael Costa: England's First Conductor* (Farnham: Ashgate, 2015).
[6] Cyril Ehrlich and Simon McVeigh, 'Music', in *An Oxford Companion to the Romantic Age: British Culture, 1776–1832*, ed. Iain McCalman et al. (Oxford: Oxford University Press, 1999), 249.
[7] The definition of an institution as 'an assemblage that organises, transmits, and validates, and that self-consciously represents itself as doing so', included in a recent study of literary institutions, is also helpful in this context. See Jon Mee and Matthew Sangster, 'Introduction: Literature and Institutions', in *Institutions of Literature, 1700–1900: The Development of Literary Culture and Production*, eds. Jon Mee and Matthew Sangster (Cambridge: Cambridge University Press, 2022), 8.
[8] William Weber, *Music and the Middle Class: The Social Structure of Concert Life in London, Paris and Vienna between 1830 and 1848* (Aldershot: Ashgate, 2004; first pub. 1975), 122.

tradition and give it a distinctive urban and Dissenting incarnation. The chapter goes on to explore the reception of the society's large-scale oratorio performances and the meanings they held for nineteenth-century Londoners. The spectacle of massed choirs singing scriptural narratives has often been treated with a faint air of condescension by music historians. If we shift our gaze away from the vaunted sublimity of the society's performances at the Crystal Palace, however, we can uncover the more complex role that the institution played in the lived cultural and religious experience of nineteenth-century London.

'Heard over all the earth'

Given the Sacred Harmonic Society was established in 1832 it is perhaps inevitable that both contemporary observers and later historians have been quick to identify it with the project of political reform and the modest expansion of the franchise brought about by the Reform Act of the same year. The language of progress, democracy and reform would routinely be invoked to describe the activities of this new choral society: periodical writers described 'the stronghold it now has on the suffrages of the musical public' and heralded 'an important reform in musical affairs'.[9] In the view of the Whig-Radical *Morning Chronicle*, the popularity of this demanding repertoire represented something new in the musical life of the metropolis: 'the crowds who flock to the performances of this great society, where the music is always of the most severe and lofty character, afford the most striking proof of the progress of musical taste among the middle classes of London'.[10] Weber has argued more broadly that the rhetoric of the music press from the 1820s was 'deeply influenced by the movements for parliamentary reform' and that in the 1830s 'the aristocratic cliques that had governed musical life were seriously shaken politically and socially'.[11] However, while the Sacred Harmonic Society has often been seen as a representative body in an age of reform, and its success as an allegory of the reform crisis of 1832, its history might be more closely related to a slightly earlier challenge to the Anglican Establishment: the 1828 Repeal of the Test and Corporation

---

[9] *The Mirror of Literature, Amusement, and Instruction*, 1 February 1840, 66; *The Musical World*, 28 March 1839, 201.
[10] *Morning Chronicle*, 26 June 1838, 5.
[11] Weber, *Music and the Middle Class*, xxi, xxxi.

Acts.[12] These pieces of legislation, which had lain on the statute book since the seventeenth century, severely limited the rights of Protestant Dissenters who refused to conform to the Church of England.[13] The repeal of these laws was a totemic event for Dissenters, extending civil liberties but also undermining the self-image of Dissent as a separate community defined by its opposition to the Established Church.[14]

Dissenters may no longer have been consigned by law to the status of second-class citizens but more insidious forms of prejudice remained. In contemporary novels, for instance, Dissenters were routinely caricatured and ridiculed. To take one prominent example, Charles Dickens's fiction features a long line of greedy, hypocritical, frequently drunk Dissenting clergymen, beginning with the Reverend Stiggins in *Pickwick Papers*, who preaches temperance but is first seen at the Marquis of Granby pub, in front of the fire, red-nosed, drinking 'reeking hot pine-apple rum and water' and devouring hot toast 'with fierce voracity'.[15] The caricature of the gloomy Dissenter is a recurrent type in Dickens's writing, including the 'mournful congregation' of 'Little Bethel' in *The Old Curiosity Shop*, led by a preacher who is 'by trade a Shoemaker, and by calling a Divine', delivering 'a by no means small sermon', and the Reverend Melchisedech Howler in *Dombey and Son*, who 'had announced the destruction of the world for that day two years, at ten in the morning, and opened a front parlour for the

---

[12] Authoritative accounts of the evolution of Protestant Dissent in this period include Michael R. Watts, *The Dissenters, Volume II: The Expansion of Evangelical Nonconformity* (Oxford: Clarendon Press, 1995) and Timothy Larsen and Michael Ledger-Lomas, eds., *The Oxford History of Protestant Dissenting Traditions, Volume III: The Nineteenth Century* (Oxford: Oxford University Press, 2017).

[13] The Corporation Act of 1661 required all holders of municipal office to take communion in an Anglican church, while the Test Act of 1673 made the same requirement of all those who held civil or military office under the crown. Repeal of these acts had been the focus of a long campaign by Dissenters. Parliament voted against motions for repeal in 1787, 1789 and 1790, after which the British reaction to the French Revolution, and the perceived association between political and religious Dissent, delayed repeal for almost four decades. Even in 1828, ultra Tories such as Lord Eldon warned that such a move threatened the relationship between the Established Church and state.

[14] The Dissenting writer William Hazlitt offered a characteristically contrarian response to the Repeal of the Test and Corporation Acts, reflecting in the final year of his life on this long-awaited advance in civil and religious liberty: 'When a thing ceases to be a subject of controversy, it ceases to be a subject of interest. Why need we regret the various hardships and persecutions for conscience-sake, when men only clung closer to their opinions in consequence? They loved their religion in proportion as they paid dear for it. Nothing could keep the Dissenters from going to a conventicle while it was declared an unlawful assembly, and was the high road to a prison or the plantations – take away tests and fines, and make the road open and easy, and the sect dwindles gradually into insignificance.' 'The Spirit of Controversy' (1830), in William Hazlitt, *The Spirit of Controversy and Other Essays*, ed. Jon Mee and James Grande (Oxford: Oxford University Press, 2021), 312–17 (314–15).

[15] Charles Dickens, *The Posthumous Papers of the Pickwick Club* (London: Chapman and Hall, 1837), 276–7.

reception of ladies and gentlemen of the Ranting persuasion'.[16] In *Hard Times*, we are told there are 'eighteen religious persuasions', each occupying 'a pious warehouse of red brick', but which have no hold over the workers of Coketown, who are left 'gazing at all the church and chapel going, as at a thing with which they had no manner of concern'.[17] As the novelist Margaret Oliphant wrote in *Blackwood's Magazine*, Dickens's stereotype of the Dissenting minister reached its culmination in *Bleak House* with the 'detestable Mr. Chadband, an oft-repeated libel upon the preachers of the poor'.[18] Chadband is 'attached to no particular denomination' and is once again greedy, verbose and oleaginous: 'a large yellow man, with a fat smile, and a general appearance of having a good deal of train oil in his system'.[19] As Valentine Cunningham has argued, 'Dickens's unthinking contempt for Christian theology and Christianity's Dissenting practitioners' represents a common response to Dissenting culture in the Victorian novel.[20]

Such prejudices ran deep, making the success of an avowedly Dissenting organization such as the Sacred Harmonic Society more remarkable. Indeed, the society rapidly assumed a central role in London's musical life, extolled by virtually every section of the press. The chorus became widely known as the Exeter Hall Society, or the Exeter Hall Amateurs, and the difficulties that dogged its early years suggest that its ultimate success was inseparable from this particular building on the Strand. The imposing neoclassical structure of Exeter Hall had only been completed a few years earlier, in 1831, on the site of Exeter House, the London residence of the Earls of Exeter, and afterwards Exeter 'Change, home for half a century to a celebrated menagerie. Pidcock's, later Cross's, menagerie occupied the first floor of the building, above a row of small shops, and aimed to satisfy both the scientific curiosity and patriotic spirit of its visitors. One newspaper puff from the 1810s proclaimed:

> The rising generation, on a single visit to the Royal Menagerie, Exeter Change, will obtain a more abundant store of knowledge of Natural History, than can be procured from all the volumes ever yet printed. In this vast assemblage nature is seen in endless variety, in perfect security, and in a state of cleanliness truly surprising; the young British Lions afford unbounded gratification, and are

---

[16] Charles Dickens, *The Old Curiosity Shop* (London: Chapman and Hall, 1841), 214, 20; Charles Dickens, *Dombey and Son* (London: Bradbury and Evans, 1848), 147.
[17] Charles Dickens, *Hard Times* (London: Bradbury and Evans, 1854), 27–8.
[18] Margaret Oliphant, 'Charles Dickens', *Blackwood's Edinburgh Magazine* (April 1855), 451–66 (463).
[19] Charles Dickens, *Bleak House* (London: Bradbury and Evans, 1853), 185–6.
[20] Valentine Cunningham, *Everywhere Spoken Against: Dissent in the Victorian Novel* (Oxford: Clarendon Press, 1975), 190.

taken in the arms of every visitor; the large Lions and other animals are regularly fed at nine in the evening; at that time nature is displayed at the highest point of animation.[21]

The Exeter 'Change menagerie was a fixture on the London tourist itinerary by the turn of the century but these long-standing connections would soon be overwritten by a very different set of associations. In 1828, Exeter 'Change was demolished to allow for the widening of the Strand and construction of Wellington Street and the famous lions and other animals were transferred to the King's Mews at Charing Cross (now the National Gallery) and then to Surrey Zoological Gardens. Exeter Hall was built between 1829 and 1831, creating a meeting place for religious, charitable and scientific associations on a scale that London had never previously seen (see Figure 7.2). Crucially, it was non-sectarian, not being linked to any single denomination, and provided a respectable alternative to meeting rooms in public taverns. It quickly became home to a vast array of improving and evangelical organizations, including the Anti-Slavery Society, the British and Foreign Bible Society, the Ragged School Union, the National Temperance League, the London Missionary Society, the Sunday School Union and the Religious Tract Society. Exeter Hall was somehow both sacred and secular, and by 1869 had even generated a novel, *Exeter Hall: A Theological Romance*, in which the author explained:

> no other place in the world has attracted such crowds of social renovators, moral philosophers, philanthropists, and Christians. Of late years, almost every great measure for the amelioration of the condition of the human family has here had its inception, its progress, and its triumph . . . the voice of Exeter Hall is heard over all the earth.[22]

The African American abolitionist Frederick Douglass appeared at Exeter Hall on his 1845–7 lecture tour of Britain and Ireland and would frequently invoke the venue in his later speeches, telling one audience at Rochester, New York, 'What is bloody revolution in France, is peaceful reformation in England. The friends and enemies of freedom, meet not at the barricades thrown up in the streets of London; but on the broad platform of Exeter Hall.'[23] As James Q.

---

[21] *Morning Chronicle*, 18 April 1818, 3.
[22] William McDonnell, *Exeter Hall: A Theological Romance* (Boston: American News Company, 1869), 3.
[23] Frederick Douglass, 1848 speech, quoted in Tom F. Wright, *Lecturing the Atlantic: Speech, Print, and an Anglo-American Commons, 1830–1870* (New York: Oxford University Press, 2017), 61. Wright also quotes an account from the end of the century, looking back at this period and remembering

Figure 7.2 View of Exeter Hall on the Strand. 1831 etching. © The Trustees of the British Museum.

Davies has recently written, by the mid-nineteenth century, 'Exeter Hall lay at the epicenter of global evangelical reform.'[24]

The Sacred Harmonic Society was founded in October 1832 and initially rehearsed and performed at Gate Street Chapel, a Calvinistic Methodist chapel in Lincoln's Inn Fields. As Wiebke Thormählen has argued, 'the Society's ideals were not initially public-facing: at the heart of its formation was not the

---

how 'statesmen, weighing one policy against another, have had to ask "What will Exeter Hall say?"' (62).

[24] James Q. Davies, '*Elijah*'s Nature', *19th-Century Music* 45, no. 1 (2021): 49–64 (56).

performance of great sacred music, but the *making* of it'.[25] This commitment to amateur music-making ran counter to the increasing professionalization of elite music culture through institutions such as the Philharmonic Society, a process which 'also represented the silencing of the amateur, relegated to the role of educated and critical listener'.[26] After only a year, the society was expelled from Gate Street Chapel after members of the congregation complained about the impropriety of holding public concerts in a place of worship. The society's members were drawn from congregations across the city and various alternative venues were considered, covering a range of denominations: the German Lutheran Church on Savoy Street, the Congregationalist Adelphi Chapel and Orange Street Chapel, the Baptist chapel in Clements Lane and the Moravian Chapel, Fetter Lane. Meetings were held in the Baptist Henrietta Street Chapel in Brunswick Square and the Scottish Chapel in Fleur-de-lis Court, Fleet Street, while the society awaited the result of its application to Exeter Hall. After initially being informed by the directors that a standing resolution of Exeter Hall prohibited public concerts, an agreement was reached when the committee explained that the society 'is in a great degree composed of the Organists, Clerks and members of Choirs of different Churches and Chapels in the Metropolis', the music performed would be '*exclusively* Sacred' and that 'the strictest order and decorum are enforced at all the Meetings, and no signs of approbation or disapprobation, by clapping of hands or otherwise, are at any time allowed to be made use of'.[27] The Sacred Harmonic Society gave its first public concert at Exeter Hall on 7 August 1834.[28]

At this point, the society had fewer than sixty members and subscribers; by the following year, this number had more than doubled; it climbed to over four hundred in 1837 and was approaching seven hundred by 1840. Since women were not admitted as formal members, the membership numbers only include men, and the society's annual reports routinely thank 'the Ladies who have assisted at the Rehearsals and Public Performances'. Most performances seem to

---

[25] Wiebke Thormählen, 'From Dissent to Community: The Sacred Harmonic Society and Amateur Choral Singing in London', in *London Voices, 1820–1840: Vocal Performers, Practices, Histories*, eds. Roger Parker and Susan Rutherford (Chicago: Chicago University Press, 2019), 159–78 (p. 159).
[26] Thormählen, 'From Dissent to Community', 166.
[27] 'Letter addressed to the Secretary of Exeter Hall . . . 6th January 1834', part of 'Sacred Harmonic Society. Special Report. 20th May 1834', 137–8. The account of the early years of the society in this paragraph is based on the handwritten reports covering 1832–6, held at the Royal College of Music, shelf mark 41832.a.4 (1).
[28] This concert included a programme of solemn sacred music in tribute to the musician Charles Wesley (1757–1834), son and nephew of the Methodist founders Charles and John Wesley. See RCM 41832.a.4 (1), 174–5.

have involved around four hundred singers and Exeter Hall was large enough to accommodate the rapid growth in the society's membership, holding an audience of 2,500 in the larger of its two auditoriums.[29] In the cultural imagination, Exeter Hall became associated above all with the phenomenon of the 'May Meetings', when the myriad religious and philanthropic societies held their annual public meetings. These events featured lengthy and passionate speeches from the great and good: we are told that the veteran abolitionist William Wilberforce, in his final year, 'attended ten of these meetings in as many days, and spoke twelve times'.[30] Alongside the 'May Meetings', however, much of the significance Exeter Hall accrued, the special status it assumed in nineteenth-century London, was through music and, specifically, the oratorio concerts by the Sacred Harmonic Society. Oratorio singing would become the sound that accompanied all those high-minded projects of philanthropic improvement and evangelical mission, which radiated out from the Strand across the British Empire. For many Victorians, oratorio (and Handel's oratorios above all) was the definitive form for mediating scripture through song, and the performances of the society provided a sonic supplement to the countless meetings and speeches at Exeter Hall. Oratorio would become one of the foremost ways in which nineteenth-century Britons experienced biblical narratives, through collective performance and a primarily eighteenth-century musical language.[31]

'A flood of harmony'

By the 1840s, the Sacred Harmonic Society was performing on average once every three weeks, to effusive reviews in both the specialist music press (a relatively new development in itself) and the daily newspapers (see Figure 7.3). Indeed, the degree to which its activities were acclaimed by publications from across the political spectrum is striking, and the language of the reviews suggests that it was not just the musical quality of the performances that was being evaluated but the attitudes and behaviour of the Exeter Hall audience and the broader

---

[29] From 1836, the society held its concerts in this larger hall, despite its poor acoustics, which eventually led to alterations for the 1850–1 season. John Edmund Cox, *Musical Recollections of the Last Half-Century*, 2 vols (London: Tinsley Brothers, 1872), II, 49, 62–4; *Times*, 30 November 1850, 8.
[30] F. Morell Holmes, *Exeter Hall and Its Associations* (London: Hodder and Stoughton, 1881), 162.
[31] On other engagements with eighteenth-century culture, suggesting 'how rooted in its immediate predecessor culture the nineteenth century was', see B. W. Young, *The Victorian Eighteenth Century: An Intellectual History* (Oxford: Oxford University Press, 2007), 1.

Figure 7.3 The orchestra at Exeter Hall, during the meeting of the Sacred Harmonic Society. Engraving from the *Pictorial Times*, 10 February 1844. © Look and Learn/Peter Jackson Collection/Bridgeman Images.

significance that the society had come to occupy in the cultural life of the city. The *Times* approvingly observed that 'hundreds of persons who never before ventured into any place of public entertainment have since thronged to Exeter-hall', while the Tory *True Sun* declared that, 'the Sacred Harmonic Society has conferred an incalculable good on the people of this metropolis. To this body of amateurs we owe it, that the grandest musical effects are no longer to be sought exclusively in the Provincial Festivals'; choral singing was 'a mission for elevating the taste, and by that, for aiding the moral improvement of the middle classes of society'.[32] The *Musical World*, the weekly journal of the Novello publishing house, favourably compared the Exeter Hall performances to the long-running Ancient Concerts, claiming a restoration of the true Handelian spirit: 'we are not sorry to see the fame of Handel, who is a popular musician, a man potent over multitudes, taken out of the guardianship of an exclusive aristocratical body, and committed to the affectionate keeping of the public at large'.[33] The *Morning*

---

[32] *Times*, 13 September 1837, 3; *True Sun*, June 1837, quoted in *Fifth Annual Report of the Sacred Harmonic Society* (London, 1838), RCM, 41832.a.4 (1).

[33] *The Musical World*, 25 October 1838, 109. Given the role of the Novello & Co. sheet music publishing business, commercial considerations were no doubt a factor here. By the time of the Crystal Palace Festivals, Novello was guaranteed huge sales of its cheap (1s.) octavo editions of vocal scores for Handel's oratorios. Clara Novello was also a regular, if often criticized, soloist at Sacred Harmonic

Herald went even further, imagining the great composer risen from the grave to hear his works performed by the Sacred Harmonic Society: 'He would feel that his pen had not been employed in vain; and that he had circulated a flood of harmony throughout the land, fertilizing and fructifying, like a mighty river, the regions over which it flowed'; the society's activities 'cannot fail to have a humanizing influence on the mass. We hail them as regenerators'.[34]

We might wonder what these concerts actually sounded like, given the poor acoustics of Exeter Hall, the sheer scale of musical forces deployed and their confident belief that 'Handel's Music . . . permits of the employment of almost unlimited force with increased effect and grandeur'.[35] To do so involves a considerable feat of historical imagination: modern aesthetic preferences have made such a clear break with the nineteenth-century tradition that a great gulf now separates us from the soundworld of Exeter Hall; we are now accustomed to a very different, restrained, period instrument, 'historically informed' approach to this repertoire.[36] And indeed, amidst all the approbation, there is some evidence that the experience of these concerts was not universally appreciated. In March 1839, Thomas Carlyle wrote to his brother about a forthcoming performance of Joseph Haydn's oratorio *The Creation* at Exeter Hall:

> a grand musical performance, which I am to be at on Friday night; the Wilsons had got tickets for Jane and me both, but Jane declines, on account of the hot crowd and the cold weather. I was there once already: above 3,000 people, and some 500 musical performers! You never heard anywhere such a tempest of music. I do not count on going a third time.[37]

Society concerts: according to one retrospect of the 1851 programme, 'The liberties which this lady took with the text of Handel and Haydn were severely commented upon by the press, but her chaste and correct performances in *Elijah* and *St. Paul* were universally extolled. Madame Novello, it is to be hoped, will take counsel, and reflect that what is admissible in Italian opera may be nothing less than impertinent in music which attempts to illustrate the divine admonitions of scripture' (*Times*, 29 September 1851, 6).

[34] *Morning Herald*, 22 October 1840, quoted in *Eighth Annual Report of the Sacred Harmonic Society* (London, 1841), 39.

[35] *Grand Handel Musical Festival at the Crystal Palace in 1857. A Letter Addressed to the Members, Subscribers, and Assistants of the Sacred Harmonic Society* (London, 1856), 15.

[36] As Richard Taruskin has argued, 'The split that is usually drawn between "modern performance" on the one hand and "historical performance" on the other is quite topsy-turvy. It is the latter that is truly modern performance – or rather, if you like, the avant-garde wing or cutting edge of modern performance – while the former represents the progressively weakening survival of an earlier style, inherited from the nineteenth century, one that is fast becoming historical.' See Richard Taruskin, 'The Pastness of the Present and the Presence of the Past', in *Text and Act: Essays on Music and Performance* (New York: Oxford University Press, 1995), 90–154 (140).

[37] Thomas Carlyle to Alexander Carlyle, Chelsea, 13 March 1839, in *The Collected Letters of Thomas and Jane Welsh Carlyle, Volume 11: 1839*, gen. ed. Charles Richard Sanders (Durham, NC: Duke

As Carlyle's arch description suggests, the 'tempest of music' produced by such an army of singers and instrumentalists was not to all tastes. The success of the Exeter Hall concerts cannot be understood on purely aesthetic grounds, however, and must be viewed instead as part of a much wider cultural phenomenon.

The concerts belonged to an emerging discourse of 'rational recreation' during the 1830s and 1840s. Newspapers gave effusive descriptions of the lower-middle-class membership of the society: 'the artizans, who, in all weathers, wend their way from every part of the metropolis and its suburbs to attend the rehearsals and performances', who 'fill their hours of leisure with an industry at once heroic and intellectual'.[38] Such accounts perform a regulatory function, portraying an idealized and sentimentalized image of London's lower middle class. Most members of the society seem to have been artisans or shopkeepers, the same class that a few years before had been routinely mocked in the Tory press as 'Cockney' upstarts with pretensions to high culture.[39] The praise extended to the character of the audiences: for example, an 1843 review in the *Times* placed particular emphasis on the authenticity and sincerity of those attending the concerts:

> the musical audiences at Exeter-hall . . . are not drawn there because it is fashionable, or because they wish to see one another, or because they wish to be seen themselves, but simply because they wish to hear the music. . . . None of the ordinary temptations of the concert-room are held out to them; there is no chance of seeing 'great folks' – there is no opportunity of showing off fine clothes; but the music, and the music alone, attracts them; and, attired in bonnets, and stout great-coats, they paddle through the mud and fog of November and through the snow of December to hear Handel. There is not in London an audience so truly musical. The society owed its origin to a really musical taste in classes of people among whom it was scarcely supposed to exist. . . . If a foreigner desired to know where in London the real unsophisticated taste for music lay, apart from its being considered a fashionable accomplishment, he would necessarily be directed to the audiences of the Sacred Harmonic Society. The applause of such audiences is worth having; we feel it is honest applause.[40]

University Press, 1985), 53. The editors of Carlyle's letters note that he had probably heard Mendelssohn's *St. Paul* performed at Exeter Hall on 1 March 1839.

[38] *Britannia*, 2 November 1844, quoted in *Twelfth Annual Report of the Sacred Harmonic Society* (London, 1845), 62; *Morning Herald*, 7 November 1844, quoted in ibid., 63.

[39] Weber, *Music and the Middle Class*, 118–20, 167. On the 'Cockney' controversy, see Gregory Dart, *Metropolitan Art and Literature, 1810–1840: Cockney Adventures* (Cambridge: Cambridge University, 2012).

[40] *Times*, 16 November 1843, 5.

We cannot, of course, take such descriptions at face value; instead, they demonstrate how the amateur choral movement became part of a wider discourse of music, faith and national identity. *The Musical World* proclaimed that the society 'has bred and diffused a relish for the most sterling music, in the vast population of this mighty metropolis, and, in fact, throughout the empire', while the *Standard* reflected with some satisfaction on what the popularity of the Exeter Hall oratorios said about the national character:

> In no other country of Europe, perhaps, could an audience, consisting of between 2000 and 3000 persons, mostly of rank and education, be collected together, who would sit, not only quietly, but enthusiastically delighted, during the space of three hours listening to sacred music. . . . It may be observed that the popularity which now attends the performance of sacred music in this country is a mark of the sobriety that distinguishes the national character, and that impels a vast number of people, who, from principle, shun the precincts of the playhouse, to seek that relaxation and relief from the cares of life in an oratorio or sacred concert.[41]

The reference to the 'sobriety' of the national character suggests how well the oratorio concerts at Exeter Hall fitted with the venue's association with the temperance movement, while the sense of national superiority no doubt contributed to the evangelical confidence of the missionary societies setting out from the Strand to spread the gospel across the British Empire.

Through such descriptions, a series of oppositions emerges: the success of the Sacred Harmonic Society represented a victory for the amateur chorus over virtuosic soloists, the artisan over the aristocrat, harmony over melody, instruction over amusement and an established canon over the ephemerality of new works. The straw man in all of these oppositions is Italian opera, which forms the explicit point of comparison in one 1838 article on 'The Musician About Town':

> nothing has contributed so effectually to soften, without effeminizing, the national manners, as the increased and increasing cultivation of the science of Music. The springing up of choral societies all over the country – more especially in the dense manufacturing districts – is the result of this improvement in taste. The same effect may be observed in London, where the amateur choral societies are multiplying and increasing to a remarkable and satisfactory extent.

---

[41] *The Musical World*, 2 March 1843, quoted in *Eleventh Annual Report of the Sacred Harmonic Society* (London, 1844), 58; *The Standard*, 8 April 1841, 1.

The performances of the 'Sacred Harmonic Society', at Exeter Hall, now hold an important station in the rank of metropolitan recreations; and the prospect of its three or four hundred members, almost all of them mechanics, or persons engaged during the day behind their counters, performing at night the most lofty compositions of the great musical epic writers, is an object worthy of admiration, and doubtless is producing a beneficial effect upon the thousands who come to improve their moral and intellectual perceptions by listening to those divine homilies. It has frequently been remarked . . . that the lower-middle class of English society are not merely leaving – that they have already *left* – the aristocracy leagues in the rear upon all questions of intellectual refinement. The Italian Opera of London is one example in confirmation of this remark, as regards the cultivation of Music. The compositions listened to night after night by our aristocracy, with so much complacency, at Her Majesty's Theatre, are confessedly, as works of invention and imagination, of the most ephemeral character.[42]

The contrast between the ephemeral operas performed for an aristocratic audience at Her Majesty's Theatre, Haymarket and the performances of sacred choral music at Exeter Hall suggests the society's contribution to what has been described in other contexts as the 'work-concept'.[43] The advocates of the Sacred Harmonic Society claimed that the Handelian tradition had deteriorated into selection concerts in which oratorio excerpts were mixed with other works of sacred and non-sacred music. By the turn of the nineteenth century, Handel's oratorios were rarely performed in full, with the single exception of *Messiah*. By contrast, the society became increasingly invested in the performance of whole works, offering complete biblical narratives instead of theatrical miscellanies. To charges of monotony – all those endless *Messiahs* – the society emphasized its role in reviving a number of Handel's oratorios that had not been performed entire for many years (*Deborah*, *Jephtha*, *Athaliah*) and inclusion of works by Haydn, Mozart, Beethoven, Mendelssohn and Spohr, as well as British composers such as Gibbon, Purcell, Croft and Boyce. The programmes of the Sacred Harmonic Society therefore played a significant role in the emergence of a canon of choral music, a canon which was clearly anchored in the eighteenth

---

[42] 'The Musician About Town', *The Analyst*, 8 (1838), 310–11.
[43] See Lydia Goehr, *The Imaginary Museum of Musical Works: An Essay in the Philosophy of Music* (Oxford: Clarendon Press, 1992). For a rare consideration of this term in relation to choral music, see Nicholas Mathew, '"Achieved is the Glorious Work": *The Creation* and the Choral Work Concept', in *Engaging Haydn*, eds. Mary Hunter and Richard Will (Cambridge: Cambridge University Press, 2012).

century and the compositions of Handel (the 'Milton of music') but remained open to new works.

'The most elevated compositions'

In 1843, a performance at the exclusive Hanover Square Rooms of Louis Spohr's *The Fall of Babylon* (written for the Norwich Festival of the previous year), conducted by the composer, 'resulted in the most lamentable failure and disappointment'.[44] The next day, Spohr received a letter from the Committee of the Sacred Harmonic Society,

> stating, that they felt the scanty attendance to have been a disgrace to the Metropolis, and requesting to be allowed to repeat the Oratorio in Exeter Hall, under the full conviction that there it would attract the attention it deserved.... The truth seems to be, that the appeal was made in the first instance in the wrong quarter and to the wrong class.[45]

Spohr agreed to conduct a performance at Exeter Hall and the *Times* compared the success of the second performance to 'the coldness and apathy with which its first production was met, when the higher prices of admission excluded that class of auditors which usually attends the performances of the society'. At the second performance,

> the immense crowd which filled the hall to the remotest recesses ... and hailed with eagerness the opportunity of hearing this fine composition executed under the immediate direction of the great composer himself, proved that the exertions of the society had succeeded in instilling into a large portion of the public a taste for the higher order of musical beauties, and forming an audience desirous and capable of appreciating the most elevated compositions.[46]

These accounts attest to the price sensitivity of London audiences (10s. 6d. for tickets at Hanover Square Rooms, 3s. at Exeter Hall) and make the striking argument that new choral works on biblical themes were most keenly appreciated not by the cultural gatekeepers of Hanover Square but by the lower-middle-class audience at Exeter Hall.

---

[44] *Eleventh Annual Report of the Sacred Harmonic Society* (London, 1844), 15.
[45] *Spectator*, 22 July 1843, 13.
[46] *Times*, 22 July 1843, 5.

Spohr's success, however, was eclipsed by Felix Mendelssohn, then emerging as the undisputed modern master of oratorio. The Sacred Harmonic Society gave the first London performance of *St Paul* in 1837 and two performances were conducted by the composer at Exeter Hall in 1844. *Elijah* was commissioned by the Birmingham Festival and premiered in 1846 at Birmingham Town Hall though Mendelssohn conducted the first performances of the revised version of the work at Exeter Hall the following year. The work was solemnly performed there again after Mendelssohn's death in November 1847 and then in 1848 with Jenny Lind, finally performing the soprano part that Mendelssohn had written for her. Celia Applegate has asked,

> what would have become of the English oratorio tradition without Mendelssohn's contributions to it of *Paulus* and especially *Elijah*. The least one could say is that he gave a new lease on life to the tradition by rescuing it from endless repetition, invigorating it, giving it the incalculable effect of the new – the thrill of a premier, the fission of his foreignness, as well as the familiarity of his earnestness, all of that.[47]

This interpretation puts what may be an anachronistic premium on novelty: while they welcomed new compositions by Mendelssohn and Spohr, nineteenth-century choral societies were less aware than the modern historian that they stood in need of rescuing from 'endless repetition'. Applegate goes on to argue for Mendelssohn's role in British musical culture as a mediating, conciliatory figure, whose visits 'played a major role in calming the troubled waters and creating a remarkable consensus'.[48] Above all, he represented the ability to move between instrumental and choral music, the latter always 'relegated to a slightly lesser status as a source of pious uplift for the middle-class amateurs and their audiences'.[49]

In similar, faintly condescending fashion, the entry on 'London' in the *New Grove Dictionary of Music and Musicians* claims that although the 'quintessentially Victorian event' of the Crystal Palace Handel Festival was 'much imitated, notably in the USA' it 'was never fully respected by serious musicians'.[50]

---

[47] Celia Applegate, 'Mendelssohn on the Road: Music, Travel, and the Anglo-German Symbiosis', in *The Oxford Handbook of the New Cultural History of Music*, ed. Jane F. Fulcher (Oxford: Oxford University Press, 2011), 234.
[48] Applegate, 'Mendelssohn on the Road', 236.
[49] Applegate, 'Mendelssohn on the Road', 235.
[50] Cyril Ehrlich, Simon McVeigh, and Michael Musgrave, 'London (i) – VI. Musical life, 1800–1945 – 2. Concert Life', *Grove Music Online*. Oxford University Press, https://www.oxfordmusiconline.com/grovemusic/view/10.1093/gmo/9781561592630.001.0001/omo-9781561592630-e-0000016904, accessed 23 March 2023.

The embarrassment surrounding the nineteenth-century obsession with oratorio only intensifies in accounts of 'popular' music. For example, Ronald Pearsall's history of Victorian popular music reluctantly concedes the popular status of oratorio: 'unquestionably the oratorio was a millstone round the neck of Victorian music, and although it was popular it was popular for the wrong reasons'. The popularity of a form bent on self-improvement and high moral purpose, which served a regulatory, even disciplinary, role, is an uncomfortable fact for the modern historian of popular music. Its status is reduced to the merely functional: 'oratorio filled a need; it was the rice-pudding of music – starchy, filling, but rather uninteresting'.[51]

Once more, we can mark the distance created by changing tastes and aesthetic priorities. 'Endless repetition' may appear to us as an alien musical tradition but was a cultural ideal in the 1830s and 1840s, both in terms of the repertoire and in the works themselves. The straw man was, once again, Italian opera, with its constant recourse to novelty and melody. In 1844, an article in the *Morning Chronicle* reflected on the remarkable popularity of *Israel in Egypt*:

> It is hardly possible to imagine a work less adapted, from its construction, to become popular. It is a series of choruses, intermixed with a few solo passages, so trifling both in quantity and character, as to be scarcely worthy of notice . . . the oratorio consists of chorus after chorus, in rapid succession, absolutely astounding the hearer by their colossal grandeur and magnificence. A work of this kind, depending so little on popular melody and the display of vocal power, can be generally pleasing only to audiences who have learned to appreciate and feel the effects of the grand masses and profound combinations of choral harmony. Accordingly, it is only in our own day that *Israel in Egypt* has become popular. Before our time, its performances were 'few and far between'; and it was considered necessary, on those occasions, to *sweeten* it, as it were, and render it more palatable, by an infusion of melody; for which purpose a number of airs were interpolated, taken from Handel's other works, particularly his Italian operas; in which manner, we remember, it was performed at the great Commemoration Festival, in Westminster Abbey, in 1834. This expedient, which produced an incongruous piece of patchwork, is no longer necessary; the oratorio is performed in its original form, preserving the classical simplicity and unity of its design; and an almost unbroken series of gigantic choruses, exhausting all the resources of counterpoint, is listened to by crowded audiences

---

[51] Ronald Pearsall, *Victorian Popular Music* (Newton Abbot: David & Charles, 1973), 147.

with admiration and delight. There cannot be a more striking proof of the progress which music, in its noblest form, has made among us.[52]

The 1834 Handel Commemoration Festival at Westminster Abbey had excluded Dissenters, leading to an influx of new members to the Sacred Harmonic Society and a rival event at Exeter Hall, the Amateur Musical Festival. A decade later, the Sacred Harmonic Society's concerts had eclipsed the establishment version of Handel through their commitment to the integrity of the scriptural narrative in its apparently definitive Handelian form. Few of the works performed by the society have survived in the modern repertoire. But in the mid-nineteenth century the popularity of works so apparently unsuited to popular status was celebrated as an achievement for Dissenting culture, reflecting its cherished values of seriousness, education and collective endeavour. The cultivation of this repertoire spoke to a widely held belief in the potential of music as a vehicle for moral improvement, forcefully articulated in George Hogarth's *Musical History* (1835):

> Music may sometimes be the handmaid of debauchery; but this music never can . . . that man must be profligate beyond conception, whose mind can entertain gross propensities while the words of inspiration, clothed with the sounds of Handel, are in his ears. . . . Wherever the working classes are taught to prefer the pleasures of the intellect, and even of taste, to the gratification of sense, a great and favourable change takes place in their character and manners. They are no longer driven, by mere vacuity of mind, to the beer-shop; and a pastime, which opens their minds to the impressions produced by the strains of Handel and Haydn, combined with the inspired poetry of the Scriptures, becomes something infinitely better than the amusements of an idle hour.[53]

The Exeter Hall concerts became the virtual embodiment of this view of music, one mirrored in the countless choral societies of a newly industrialized nation.

The achievement of the Sacred Harmonic Society also illustrates a broader shift in the status of Dissent. It may not have been in any direct sense a result of the Repeal of the Test and Corporation Acts but it did reflect a changing climate of opinion, in which Dissenters were entering the cultural mainstream. In 1839, *The Musical World* alluded to the stereotype that some Dissenters were rich and philistine, observing that the society 'has extracted patronage from monied

---

[52] *Morning Chronicle*, 7 November 1844, 2.
[53] George Hogarth, *Musical History, Biography, and Criticism: Being a General Survey of Music, from the Earliest Period to the Present Time* (London: John W. Parker, 1835), 430–1.

sources among its religious connexion that have hitherto but little contributed to fertilize the arts'.[54] Descriptions from elite musical culture of the society 'as a medium for the popularizing of high art among the middle classes of this vast metropolis' retain a sense of the separateness of Nonconformist religion and culture: the *Times* described the society as having 'a public of its own'.[55] However, despite such judgements, the society received a level of coverage and approbation from across the London press that would have been inconceivable for a Dissenting institution a generation earlier. By the 1840s, even Queen Victoria and Prince Albert occasionally patronized their concerts.[56] The success of the Sacred Harmonic Society represents a Dissenting appropriation of the Handelian tradition. No longer defined by their outsider status and association with small-d political Dissent, Nonconformists would instead be integral to the nineteenth-century imperial project in its most far-reaching, earnest and evangelical phase.

Conversely, the Sacred Harmonic Society signalled the increasing acceptability of music within Dissent. While music had long been an important part of Dissenting culture, above all through the practice of congregational hymn-singing, the non-verbal aspects of music were often unsettling for Dissenters committed to written revelation and the complete sufficiency of scripture as a guide to faith and practice.[57] For many Nonconformists, oratorio became the definitive way of uniting scripture and song, through what seemed to be a divinely sanctioned form of music. After witnessing several of the society's Exeter Hall concerts during his 1855 visit to England, Richard Wagner described this cultural phenomenon:

> I got to know the true spirit of English musical life there. It is closely intertwined with the spirit of English Protestantism, and thus such an oratorio performance attracts the public far more than the opera; there is a further advantage in that attendance at such an oratorio is considered the equivalent of going to church. Everybody in the audience holds their Handel piano scores in the same way church-goers hold their prayer-books.[58]

---

[54] *The Musical World*, 18 April 1839, 238.
[55] *The Musical World*, 7 November 1846, quoted in *Fourteenth Annual Report of the Sacred Harmonic Society* (London, 1847), 51; *Times*, 30 November 1850, 8.
[56] Cox, *Musical Recollections*, II, 56–9, 62.
[57] See Michael Ledger-Lomas and Scott Mandelbrote, 'Introduction', in *Dissent and the Bible in Britain, c. 1650–1950*, eds. Ledger-Lomas and Mandelbrote (Oxford: Oxford University Press, 2013), 1–2. On the Dissenting hymn, see Isabel Rivers and David L. Wykes, eds., *Dissenting Praise: Religious Dissent and the Hymn in England and Wales* (Oxford: Oxford University Press, 2011).
[58] Richard Wagner, *My Life*, trans. Andrew Gray, ed. Mary Whittall (Cambridge: Cambridge University Press, 1983), 225–6.

By this point, the Sacred Harmonic Society had reached a new pinnacle in 1851, when it put on weekly performances of *Messiah*, *Elijah* and *The Creation* in turn throughout the six months of the Great Exhibition, while the exhibition itself included a scale model of the society's orchestra.[59] The society had become an institution of Victorian London, but its inextricability from a particular building on the Strand is demonstrated by its rapid demise after Exeter Hall was purchased in 1880 by the Young Men's Christian Association. While the society struggled on for a few more years at St James's Hall, the relocation enforced a drastic reduction to a mere three hundred performers and, combined with the ill health and retirement of Michael Costa, effectively precipitated the dissolution of the society. The Handel celebrations at Sydenham were carried on by the Crystal Palace Company, and Exeter Hall would be demolished in 1907. The Strand Palace Hotel opened two years later on the same site and the significance of this meeting place for nineteenth-century Londoners was all but erased.

---

[59] On the vexed status of music within the Great Exhibition, see Flora Willson, 'Hearing Things: Musical Objects at the 1851 Great Exhibition', in *Sound Knowledge: Music and Science in London, 1789-1851*, eds. James Q. Davies and Ellen Lockhart (Chicago: University of Chicago Press, 2016), 227-45.

8

Singing, Playing, Seeing

Scripture and the Multi-Sensorial Gothic Revival in Late Victorian Church Interiors

Ayla Lepine

In 1866, the priest and artist Frederick H. Sutton published the first edition of *Church Organs: Their Position and Construction*. Sutton worked closely with the Gothic Revival architect George Frederick Bodley, and their mutual interest organ case design revolutionized the relationship between music, architecture and interiors in late Victorian churches in Britain and beyond.[1] These micro-architectural organ cases often featured painted inscriptions drawn from biblical sources. By the 1890s, the painting of organ cases and church interiors with biblical inscriptions had taken an important and compelling turn towards the inclusion of square notation and plainsong. The instrument itself became an aesthetic voice in a new way in relation to the production of sacred interiors in which biblical passages set to music were incorporated into stained glass, wall painting designs and even canvas scrolls encircling spaces for worship.

In 1895, the architect and ecclesiastical designer John Ninian Comper completed a memorial chapel dedicated to St Sepulchre in the crypt of St Mary Magdalene in Paddington, London. The chapel, which served as a memorial to the parish's first vicar as well as a place of reservation of the Blessed Sacrament, combined imagery of Christ's tomb and resurrection with imagery celebrating both Mary Magdalene and the Virgin Mary. It represented the culmination of a new and experimental form of Gothic Revival design, in which intensive layers of iconographically rich sculptures, painting and gilding expressed the immersive multi-sensory world of the fin-de-siècle church.[2] This space is simultaneously

---

[1] Michael Hall, *George Frederick Bodley and the Later Gothic Revival in Britain and America* (New Haven: Yale University Press, 2014), 231.
[2] For discussion of this transitional time in Church history, see Frances Knight, *Victorian Christianity at the Fin de Siècle: The Culture of English Religion in a Decadent Age* (London: I.B. Tauris, 2015).

guided by the pivot point between death and new life in the Incarnation and by the women closest to Christ in his ministry. In this subterranean chapel, the relationship between the Bible, music, Gothic Revival interiors and organ cases was refined and innovatively interlaced. Figural representations of saints, angels, the resurrection and the Last Judgement are tightly nested together with scripture and hymns accompanied by musical notation. This case study, which is little known and under-researched, forms the core of a chapter that explores the phenomenon of biblical inscription and musical culture as a crucial aspect of Gothic Revival interiors, in which organ cases and decorative programmes fit together to form a unified whole. Both music and visual representations of music in late Victorian medieval revivalist churches and chapels signalled an important double temporal move. These holy resonating chambers simultaneously looked forward to the new uses of music in Anglican worship on the brink of the twentieth century and turned back to pre-Reformation, Early Church and scriptural sources with stimulating multi-sensorial results.

At St Mary Magdalene, in the undercroft beneath the High Victorian Gothic Revival church designed by George Edmund Street in the 1860s with its mosaics, sculpture and gleaming stained glass windows, Comper's St Sepulchre Chapel designed a generation later contains some of the finest devotional art in London despite its relative hiddenness deep within the cavernous realm of one of north London's tallest churches. The organ (Figure 8.1) at the west end of Comper's St Sepulchre Chapel provides a coherent explication of the relationship between late Victorian revivals of medieval liturgical music and theological claims regarding the significance of the resurrection. Comper's relatively small yet symbolically highly compact instrument is revealed to be a key conduit for the exploration of Gothic Revival and late Victorian church interiors as a whole. I also want to make the case that while the type of instrument and its availability in late Victorian church music circles were somewhat unexceptional, this particular instrument is indeed highly significant, and it is unique in relation to sacred space and to ritual. It is also the first organ case that Comper painted. The organ combines aspects of altarpieces, church architecture and a hymnal, all in one. It is a close descendant of one of the very earliest medieval organs to survive into the modern period. It unifies these elements of revived medievalist sensibility in a single set of surfaces and musical interiors. The object's function is of course primarily musical; through the trifold decorative scheme of pattern, representational image and notation, it is far more than this, particularly

Figure 8.1 Ninian Comper, organ case, St Sepulchre Chapel, St Mary Magdalene, Paddington, London, 1895. Photo: author.

in relation to a richly decorated chapel that recalls the interlacing of music and scripture at several points and in unusual ways. This organ, whether it is being played or not, sings across multiple phases of time and place to draw together centuries of Christian history in the visual arts, in building and in music, and it situates these through the content of the images themselves – whether it's a painted saint or a painted musical note – in the epicentre of God's revealedness in Christ's death, resurrection and sacramental sacrificial beauty.

Organs and the Victorians

Organs can be grouped into three types: portative (which is small enough to carry), positive (which can be moved) and the typical immobile and architecturally integrated church organ.³ Comper's organ for the chapel is positive, in proportion with the chapel. The altarpiece-like wings of Gothic organ cases are uncertain in origin; their practical function was to assist in sound production, and the pipes could be enclosed when not in use.⁴ The highly decorated open panels and more minimalist closed position of Comper's organ at St Mary Magdalene bear strong comparison with altarpieces, whose wings could be closed for penitential periods such as Lent. The first known English organ builder dates from the mid-fifteenth century in York.⁵ One of the most famous and influential chapel organs, the organ at King's College Cambridge, constituted a musical revolution in Britain when it was completed in the first years of the seventeenth century, and Peter Williams has argued that if a 'church had an organ at all by 1600, it would certainly have been no more than a single-manual large-scaled positive of half a dozen stops'.⁶

In both scale and treatment of the painted wings, the organ Comper designed for St Mary Magdalene took its cue from major developments in organ construction and chapel organ provision through canonical musical history; Comper's organ is notably similar to the organ at the west end of Notre Dame cathedral in Valere sur Sion, Switzerland. Unlike Comper's painted case, the Sion organ's wings were painted on canvas and fixed to the wooden panels.⁷ The organ's original position is unknown, and the object and its painted surfaces likely date from the early fifteenth century⁸ – a period that Comper also drew upon heavily for inspiration in designing stained glass, altarpieces, tracery and painted interiors. The Sion organ's right-most wing is the same subject as the right-hand wing of Comper's St Mary Magdalene organ: the *noli me tangere* post-resurrection narrative from St John's gospel. Comper's own interest in organs and his careful study of the Sutton-Bodley partnership and their own rootedness in history mean that Comper would have most likely known the Sion organ and its Magdalene wing.

Kimberley Marshall's study of musical iconography and images of organ-playing in medieval French, Flemish and English manuscripts assists in mapping out organ-playing and the aesthetics of the organ as liturgical object in the Middle Ages. Images of organs accompany various manuscripts in the marginalia, and

---

[3] Michael I. Wilson, *Organ Cases of Western Europe* (London: C. Hurst, 1979), 9.
[4] Wilson, *Organ Cases*, 10.
[5] Peter Williams, *A New History of the Organ* (Bloomington: Indiana University Press, 1980), 131.
[6] Williams, *New History of the Organ*, 133.
[7] Wilson, *Organ Cases*, 39.
[8] Williams, *New History of the Organ*, plate 1 (np).

these texts are, naturally, primarily biblical and usually psalmody. The organs Marshall explores are usually positive or, more commonly, portative. Treatment and decoration of organs changed dramatically from region to region, even when forms were kept somewhat consistent. Painted shutters in the Middle Ages, like those that may have inspired Comper's work at St Mary Magdalene in the 1890s, were no longer popular by the early modern period; they returned in the mid-nineteenth century (though they remained somewhat uncommon); and by the organ revival of the mid-twentieth century shutters were a consistent feature of organ design but they were rarely if ever painted.[9] Between manuscripts, architecture, interior decoration and organs themselves and their surfaces, there is a complex matrix of the relationship between organs, their depiction and biblical inscriptions which the Victorians inherited and manipulated in order to create a new medievalist aesthetic.

Through the mid- to late nineteenth century in Britain, various quests for a credible and adaptable medievalist aesthetic – in architecture, ecclesiastical vestments and in organs and music too – dominated discourse around church-building. The choral revival of the 1860s was a direct descendant of the art and architectural medievalizing of the Ecclesiological Society which itself was a crucial product of the Oxford Movement's intensification through the 1830s and 1840s.[10] By the 1860s, all major High Anglican churches included heft organs, with the surprising effect that the plainsong revival of the late 1840s – spearheaded by influential figures including William Dyce and John Mason Neale – morphed into a very different kind of sound and liturgical experience. In 1843, Dyce had published the *Book of Common Prayer Noted* and *The Order of Daily Service with Plain Tune* between 1842 and 1844, which provided plainsong notation for Book of Common Prayer services including morning and evening prayer, the Litany and the Communion service and the psalter, drawing on revived interest in John Merbecke's settings. It was both a practical object along avant-garde Gothic Revival lines and a work of art in itself. Writing in the *British Critic*, the plainsong revivalist Frederick Oakeley remarked that 'sight of [Dyce's] book, with its vermilion rubrics, graceful borders, and exquisitely carved text, brings forcibly to one's mind the days of illuminated missals, and gold-encased pontifical, and jewel-studded chalices'.[11] Dyce combined his musical expertise

---

[9] J. E. Blanton, *The Revival of the Organ Case* (Albany, TX: Venture, 1965), 31.
[10] Bernarr Rainbow, *The Choral Revival in the Anglican Church, 1839–1872* (Oxford: Oxford University Press, 1970).
[11] Frederick Oakeley, *British Critic* 34 (October 1843), 294.

with his key role as an artist and arts administrator at the South Kensington Schools. Among his work was the east wall of William Butterfield's All Saints, Margaret Street, which was vigorously restored by Ninian Comper when the pigment had degraded in the early twentieth century.[12]

By the 1860s, change in choral singing and the application of medievalist traditions was rapid. As the musicologist Bernarr Rainbow explains:

> [As] the introduction of organs became more general, the restrained *a capella* repertoire originally recommended by the *Parish Choir*, a popular publication on church music that focused on plainsong adapted to modern Victorian congregations, appeared less relevant, and the movement to encourage the use of unisonous Gregorian tones was also weakened. In either case the use of an organ tended to encourage the use of prodigal harmonic resource imitating the chromatic idiom ... an idiom utterly at variance with the astringent modality of the Tractarian musical ideal.[13]

Rainbow goes on to pinpoint how a hybrid form of church music emerged: 'to the Victorian music-lover, the romantic antiquity of the Gregorian tones was more than outweighed by their emotional sterility. And in a misguided attempt to compensate for the "coldness" of the tones, many Victorian organists accompanied the psalms with harmonies of exuberant chromaticism'.[14] It was within this experimental and medievally modern hybrid context that the church music reformer and composer Henry Smart remarked that a search for accompaniment harmony in conjunction with plainsong-derived congregational singing was a search for 'the living kernel of the Gregorian without its husk'.[15]

Before Comper: Sutton and Victorian Gothic Revival organ cases

On 14 March 1888, the precentor of Lincoln Cathedral wrote in *The Guardian*, '[in] architecture, painting, sculpture, music, glass-painting, wood-carving, metalwork, organ-building, enamels, illuminations – in short, in everything

---

[12] Caroline Babington, *William Dyce and the Pre-Raphaelite Vision* (Aberdeen: Aberdeen City Council, 2006); Anthony Symondson and Stephen Bucknall, *Sir Ninian Comper* (Reading: Ecclesiological Society and Spire Books, 2006), 280.
[13] Rainbow, *Choral Revival*, 270.
[14] Rainbow, *Choral Revival*, 270.
[15] Smart, *Musical Times* 14: 556. Quoted in Rainbow, *Choral Revival*, 271.

in which art lends itself as a handmaid to religion, Mr Sutton's knowledge was as wide and accurate as his taste was refined and his judgement sound'.[16] Frederick Heathcote Sutton was a gentleman commoner at Magdalen College, Oxford. Ordained in the early 1860s, he used his significant inheritance to fund church restoration and ecclesiastical decorative projects throughout his life. He was rector at Brant Broughton, where he worked closely with his friend and colleague, the architect George Frederick Bodley, to renovate the interior. He designed the stained glass, most of the interior fittings and the organ case. Sutton was so central to Bodley and Thomas Garner's architectural practice as an organ case designer that he was practically a third partner in the firm.

His cases were often tall and integrated within chancels, designed in accordance with the *Werkprinzip* layout, in which the Swell is over the Great with pedal pipes at the sides, so the instrument 'speaks' directly into the church.[17] For one of his smaller organs, at his own church in Theddingworth, Hilary Davidson suggests that Frederick Sutton looked to Pugin's painted organ case at Jesus College, Cambridge for inspiration in decorating the shutters with images of musical angels (Figure 8.2). Though the form of these two organs is very different, this connection between the instruments is especially significant as the Pugin organ case at Jesus College, Cambridge was the direct result of the friendship and patronage of John Sutton, a Fellow at Jesus and an elder brother of Frederick Heathcote Sutton. Therefore for one of F. H. Sutton's first painted organ projects, he was following directly in his brother's footsteps, looking to the organ he and Pugin produced for Jesus College in 1849.[18]

Organs designed by Sutton, Bodley and Garner working in partnership include the organ at Hoar Cross, Staffordshire; St German's in Cardiff and numerous others. Later organs in Bodley churches after Sutton's death in 1888, such as the church of St John the Evangelist for the Society of St John the Evangelist in Oxford – which was completed at the turn of the twentieth century – are deeply influenced by Sutton's theories and case designs. Sutton's organ at Bilton, near Rugby, was an important response to his study of the early organ at Old Radnor in Wales. One of Sutton's most important contributions to organ design was his transformation

---

[16] *Guardian* (14 March 1888), quoted in Hilary Davidson, 'Introduction' to Frederick Heathcote Sutton, *Church Organs: Their Position and Construction, with an Appendix Containing Some Account of the Medieval Organ Case Still Existing at Old Radnor, South Wales* (Oxford: Positif Press, 1998), 7.
[17] Davidson, introduction to Sutton, *Organ Cases*, 13.
[18] http://www.jesus.cam.ac.uk/about-jesus-college/history/pen-portraits/sir-john-sutton/. See also E. H. Davidson, *Sir John Sutton: A Study in the True Principles* (Oxford: Positif Press, 1992). See also Davidson introduction to Sutton, *Organ Cases*, 39.

Figure 8.2 A. W. N. Pugin, organ case, Jesus College Chapel, Cambridge, 1849. © Jesus College Cambridge, with kind permission of the Master and Fellows of Jesus College, Cambridge.

of earlier instruments into more evidently theological visual objects. This was particularly the case at Theddingworth, where an eighteenth-century domestic organ was transformed through Gothic motifs into an object more conducive to church aesthetics and emergent ecclesiological design concerns.[19] Sutton painted the wings not with large-scale figurative scenes as Comper did, however, but with patterned vegetal motifs, cresting, inscription and angels playing instruments. Comper took this form and pushed it further towards a particular medieval precedent that linked organ case and altarpiece more explicitly.

As a pupil in Bodley and Garner's offices in the early 1880s, Comper worked on plans for Holy Angels, Hoar Cross in Staffordshire, which houses one of Sutton's most complex organ cases. Comper recalled Sutton's work with his architectural mentors, and noted that at Sutton's own parish of Brant Broughton, where he stayed from 1874 until his death in 1888, priesthood and the arts were remarkably integrated. In designing the sanctuary and high altar together with Bodley, Sutton donated one of his own paintings, a Northern Renaissance depiction of the Annunciation. At the rectory, Comper recalled, 'Frederick Sutton painted glass, his butler embroidered and he started the village blacksmith in iron-work which gained a deserved reputation. . . . He was a frequent visitor [to Bodley and Garner's office] and I may add a peace-maker amongst us pupils.'[20]

---

[19] I am grateful to John Harper for this insight regarding Sutton at Theddingworth.

[20] Comper quoted in Davison, introduction to Sutton, *Organ Cases*, 39–40. The organ case at Brant Broughton was not inserted until c. 1903. Research has yet to reveal images of the interior's organ during Sutton's time.

When Comper began to design his own organ cases in the 1890s, a decade after his Hoar Cross work in Bodley and Garner's offices, he took his lessons from Sutton with him, but ultimately ended up creating instruments with a very different visual and theological impact.

The St Sepulchre Chapel at St Mary Magdalene, Paddington

In 1893, Ninian Comper designed the memorial brass for the Rev. Temple West, the first vicar of St Mary Magdalene's in Paddington. This project led to a larger commission in 1895–6, Temple West's chantry chapel of St Sepulchre in the church's undercroft. The small organ at the west end responds to the sumptuous gilded altarpiece and tester in the sanctuary. Each of the tracery panels is painted with delicate strips of colour and floral motifs. The blue ceiling, restored in the 1960s by Ninian Comper's son Sebastian Comper, now in a damp state of disrepair and neglect, is punctuated by stars and angels executed with an elaborate Gothic intricacy. The stained glass windows on the south side of the chapel, also designed by Comper, depict souls entering heaven and hell, based closely on Comper's study of Rogier Van der Weyden. Each section of the chapel's walls – a holy place within a holy place – is decorated with a scroll (Figure 8.3). Each scroll offers a fragment of plainsong. They are sequential – it is possible to sing the chapel by being attentive to its perimeter and the holy verses it declares. The chapel itself is a text, a hymn, a song of praise. Its jewel-like quality and subterranean location create a sense of profound intimacy, and Comper intensified worshippers' experience of closeness and preciousness not only through the controlled colour scheme of blues and golds, but also through the manipulation of light. He revived a medieval East Anglian technique of using mirrored curved metal in the central star elements fixed to the ceiling to ensure that what light was available in the room would glint and sparkle across the blue sky of heavenly vaulting. Church historian Peter Anson described it as 'a sumptuous late-medieval dream world, where the wealth of gilded decoration is almost overpowering'.[21]

An amplification of any Lady Chapel's qualities of holiness nested within holiness, the St Sepulchre Chapel within St Mary Magdalene's is a manifestation of a wider interest for Comper. Comper was fascinated by microarchitecture,

---

[21] Peter F. Anson, *Fashions in Church Furnishing, 1840–1940* (London: Faith Press, 1960), 280–1.

Figure 8.3 Ninian Comper, plainsong scroll, St Sepulchre Chapel, 1895. Photo: author.

and designed pyxes, windows and microarchitectural objects including the hanging pyx he designed for Egmanton in Nottinghamshire in 1898, which is now in the Victoria and Albert Museum. Indeed, Comper was responsible for the first pyx in the Church of England since the Reformation, for the upper chapel at St Matthew's Westminster in 1893.[22] The organ Comper designed is, arguably, a holy sight/site within a holy site, within a holy site. It performs its devotional imagery and summarizes the promises of the resurrection whether it is being played or not, and its microarchitectural status is a core element of the St Sepulchre Chapel's aesthetic and liturgical impact.

St Sepulchre's chapel was one of Comper's most important projects despite the fact that he himself was embarrassed by it years later. Many recognized the particular appeal of this small glowing sacred space, and none more than the poet and architectural writer John Betjeman. Betjeman championed Comper's work from the 1930s onwards, despite having an ambiguous and sometimes

---

[22] Anson, *Fashions*, 286.

barbed professional relationship with him.[23] In the early 1940s, Betjeman wrote to Comper,

> I saw for the first time the other day your crypt at St Mary Mag, Paddington. My! It is a gleaming vision of perp [Perpendicular Gothic] resplendence. I have already taken the following people to see it: H. de C. Hastings, Editor of the Architectural Review, Dr N. Pevsner, John Piper, Osbert Lancaster, T. D. Kendrick, Keeper of Brit and Medieval Antiquities at the BM and I have recommended it to Sir Kenneth Clark. All are stupefied to silence by its magnificence.[24]

He later wrote regarding the dominance of modernist architecture that Comper's Gothic Revival could be a kind of architectural tonic: 'I am continually demolishing high-brow functionalists by giving them my London course on Comper.'[25] Whether designing in a primarily Gothic idiom or in a blend of Gothic and Classical motifs in a method that Comper described as 'unity by inclusion', the primary goal was the pursuit of a particular kind of beauty. Its features – a great deal of gold, heroic and indeed homoerotic images of triumphant saints and figures of Christ and the preference for painted decoration over structural polychromy – are all subordinated to one deceptively simple theme in their arrangement within architectural interiors: the Eucharist. In an account of Comper's characteristics, a writer for the *Times Literary Supplement* stated, in

> all of his works the altar is his chief concern – how best to show the altar, how to lead the eye to it through colour and light, how to bend the knee to it through scale, how to humble the heart to it. . . . His work is simple in its elaboration, because wholly subordinated to the purpose of a Catholic church – the worship of the Incarnate Son of God in the Sacraments.[26]

Anthony Symondson has suggested that the precedent for Comper's St Sepulchre Chapel is the chapel of St Mary Undercroft in Canterbury Cathedral, with additional details inspired by Pugin's drawings for church furnishings.[27] The chapel's sumptuousness was used by a small group of Anglican nuns, as well as hallowing the memory of Temple West, the first vicar of the parish. West's heraldry and imagery of penitence, devotion and heavenly reward are key features of the chapel interior, and West himself is depicted in the southernmost

---

[23] Symondson and Bucknall, *Ninian Comper*, 220; see also John Betjeman, 'A Note on J. N. Comper, Heir to Butterfield and Bodley', *Architectural Review* 85 (1939): 70–82.
[24] Betjeman to Comper, 17 October 1943, quoted in Symondson and Bucknall, *Ninian Comper*, 220.
[25] Betjeman to Comper, 23 December 1948, quoted in Symondson and Bucknall, *Ninian Comper*, 222.
[26] *TLS*, 27 April 1951, quoted in Anson, *Fashions*, 287.
[27] Symondson and Bucknall, *Ninian Comper*, 60.

stained glass window. The altarpiece is richly polychromed and marked by as much gilding as possible. The altar and principal parts of the reredos are stone, with plaster detail.[28] The chapel's sanctuary is bounded by a rood screen, and it features stalls, a piscina and sedilia. Originally Comper designed a pyx for the chapel, evident in an early drawing for the project, which was removed most likely in the first few years of the chapel's life. This was possibly due to controversy regarding reservation of the Blessed Sacrament, which erupted into all-out protest, most notably by John Kensit at another London Anglo-Catholic church, St Cuthbert's Philbeach Gardens, in the late 1890s. These skirmishes continued towards the turn of the twentieth century,[29] but the pyx's removal at St Sepulchre was not the end of reservation in the chapel. Rather, Comper devised a tabernacle within the altarpiece itself. The central image of the rood directly above the altar is itself a small door, which can be opened by gently inserting a finger around the arm of Christ's crucifix. Physical contact with the suffering body of Jesus reveals the consecrated host within the altarpiece, which was understood by this community of High Anglicans to controversially and truly be the True Presence of Christ in the Sacrament.

The canopy above the altar, projecting from the east wall, combines IHS monograms on shields with images of the instruments of the Passion on its underside (Figure 8.4). The inscription along the westernmost surface of the canopy, beckoning worshippers to the altar, is *Delicie meae esse cum filiis hominum* ('my delights were to be with the children of men'), a scriptural quote from Prov. 8.31 and an unusual choice. Indeed, earlier sketches of the altar plan suggest a different inscription may have been initially preferred and the reasons for selecting this one are unclear. It is likely that if the commission proceeded similarly to contemporary chapels designed by Bodley and others, the choice was Comper's own. It is an apt inscription in a chantry chapel dedicated to the memory of the first vicar of the parish who tirelessly campaigned to bring the gospel to what was then a very deprived area of London, as well as a chapel so filled with images of the Blessed Virgin Mary, Mary Magdalene and Christ's resurrection. It is more than this, however. First, the biblical inscription indicates the presence of the Blessed Sacrament within the tabernacle and by extension the altar and altarpiece as a whole. Additionally, this chapel's position within the Anglo-Catholic socio-religious aspect of the Church of England and the sumptuousness

---

[28] Alan Baxter Associates Report, St Mary Magdalene, 2015.
[29] 'The Ritual Controversy', *Tablet*, 30 July 1898, http://archive.thetablet.co.uk/article/30th-july-1898/23/the-ritual-controversy.

Figure 8.4 Ninian Comper, altar canopy, St Sepulchre Chapel, 1895. Photo: author.

of its treatment mean that this room, what it contains, and how it represents the resurrection, can be likened to a deviant jewel, glistening underground and awaiting discovery. The space, indeed, delights through Gothic ornament and musical symbolism, in the Eucharist and in the presence of God among humanity. Moreover, there is an Aesthetic Movement quality embedded within this biblical choice too. In 1882, Comper was introduced to Alfred Gurney, parish priest of St Barnabas, Pimlico. He offered Comper one of his earliest commissions, to insert a rood and produce interior decoration for the crypt chapel.[30] Gurney was well connected in artistic circles and in 1893 reviewed Edward Burne-Jones' retrospective exhibition for the *Newberry House Magazine*.[31] Through Gurney and his connections, Comper's world as an emergent architect and designer was shaped by Aesthetic encounter, in which the 'cult of beauty' was a core theme in shaping a new medievalist and devout Anglican beauty of holiness.[32] Reflecting on his early career in the offices of George Frederick Bodley and Thomas Garner, Ninian Comper believed that in 'the writings of Bodley and still more in his work

---

[30] Symondson and Bucknall, *Ninian Comper*, 75.
[31] Colette Crossman, 'Seeing the Sacred: Burne-Jones's Reception as a "Great Religious Painter"', *Nineteenth-Century Art Worldwide* 14, no. 2 (summer 2015), http://www.19thc-artworldwide.org/summer15/crossman-on-burne-jones-s-reception-as-a-great-religious-painter.
[32] Hall, *George Frederick Bodley*, 150–5.

there is trace of slight preciousness, an affinity perhaps with Pater, or a more delicate expression of the Aesthetic side of William Morris'.[33] Comper would very likely have known Pater's essay on William Morris' poetry, first published in *The Renaissance* and re-issued in 1889 as 'Aesthetic Poetry'. Here, Pater traces the intertwining relationships between Greek and Gothic influence in relation to a new flowering in late Victorian poetics. In 1895, the same year that Comper devised his designs for the St Sepulchre Chapel at St Mary Magdalene, Pater's *Greek Studies* was published.[34] This collection of essays traversed the Hellenic arts and did so through characteristically sophisticated cultural references. When it came to church architecture, Pater was an active critic. Indeed, in 1894, he wrote to the incumbent at Holy Redeemer, Clerkenwell, a Classical building recently completed by the architect John Dando Sedding. While remarking on its successful and appealing design, Pater admitted, 'I am one of those who think that when Gothic may perhaps have fallen into disuse again everywhere else, it will still continue to be our sacred style of architecture.'[35] Pater's investment in poetic beauty, Aestheticism and religion would have made him a key figure for the young Anglo-Catholic London-based Comper. In 1894, the same year he visited Clerkenwell to comment on the architecture (and while Comper was building his London profession as Anglo-Catholic Aesthete), Pater wrote 'The Age of Athletic Prizemen: A Chapter in Greek Art'. In the conclusion of this essay, Pater turns to scripture to account for Greek ideal masculine beauty in athletic action.

> He had been faithful, we cannot help saying, as we pass from that youthful company, in what comparatively is perhaps little – in the culture, the administration, of the visible world; and he merited, so we might go on to say – he merited Revelation, something which should solace his heart in the inevitable fading of that.

Moving swiftly forward from the notion of revelation, Pater seizes on the vitalizing force of the Logos:

---

[33] Ninian Comper, 'Architects: Bodley', c. 1944 (private collection), quoted in Hall, *Bodley*, 281.
[34] Lene Ostermark-Johansen, 'Enshrined in a Library Edition, and an Incubus to Get Rid of: Walter Pater's *Renaissance* around 1910', *Nineteenth-Century Art Worldwide* 14, no. 2 (summer 2015), http://www.19thc-artworldwide.org/index.php/summer15/ostermark-johansen-on-walter-pater-s-renaissance-around-1910.
[35] Walter Pater to Edward Vincent Eyre, 1 July 1894. Lawrence Evans, ed., *The Letters of Walter Pater* (Oxford: Clarendon Press, 1970), 141.

We are reminded of those strange prophetic words of the Wisdom, the Logos, by whom God made the world, in one of the sapiential, half-Platonic books of the Hebrew Scriptures:– 'I was by him, as one brought up with him; rejoicing in the habitable parts of the earth. My delights were with the sons of men.'[36]

Pater ends his essay on Greek ideal beauty with Prov. 8.31, the same unexpected scriptural quotation that Comper chose – as a revised idea in 1895 – for the canopy over the altar within which the True Body of Christ, perfect man, was reserved for the worship of all.

In the Incarnation, to dwell with humanity – to be made human and to be the Word made flesh – was to save humanity. Comper also designed an altar frontal for the chapel featuring the initials M.M for Mary Magdalene and many-winged seraphim standing on cruciform wheel-like sprays. The chapel's walls are adorned with plainsong Introits and the Easter Sequence from the Sarum Missal and the Antiphoner.[37] The organ's painted surfaces and the canvas scrolls around the chapel interior both relate to Easter themes and Christ's resurrection appearances delineated in the *Victimae Paschali Laudes* sequence. These design strategies were in keeping with the interests of the Plainsong and Medieval Music Society, which was seeking to revive pre-Reformation music in Church liturgical contexts. By 1906, they had published *Hymn-Melodies for the Whole Year from the Sarum Service-Books*, offering plainsong square notation for liturgical use.[38] Its form and aesthetic are remarkably similar to the painted canvas sequences Comper produced for the St Sepulchre Chapel.

In order to understand the small, richly decorated organ case designed by Comper in the mid-1890s from both a theological and an art historical perspective in conjunction with its implications for church plainsong revival in late Victorian Britain, it is useful to investigate Comper's approach as a visual theologian, informed by scriptural accounts of Christ's resurrection appearance to Mary Magdalene:

> But Mary stood without at the sepulchre weeping: and as she wept, she stooped down, and looked into the sepulchre, and seeth two angels in white sitting, the one at the head, and the other at the feet, where the body of Jesus had lain. And they say unto her, Woman, why weepest thou? She saith unto them, Because they have taken away my Lord, and I know not where they have laid him. And

---

[36] Walter Pater, 'The Age of Athletic Prizemen: A Chapter in Greek Art' (1895) in Pater, *Greek Studies: A Series of Essays* (London: Macmillan, 1922), 269–74.
[37] Symondson and Bucknall, *Ninian Comper*, 62.
[38] I am grateful to John Harper for this reference.

when she had thus said, she turned herself back, and saw Jesus standing, and knew not that it was Jesus. Jesus saith unto her, Woman, why weepest thou? whom seekest thou? She, supposing him to be the gardener, saith unto him, Sir, if thou have borne him hence, tell me where thou hast laid him, and I will take him away. Jesus saith unto her, Mary. She turned herself, and saith unto him, Rabboni; which is to say, Master. Jesus saith unto her, Touch me not; for I am not yet ascended to my Father: but go to my brethren, and say unto them, I ascend unto my Father, and your Father; and to my God, and your God. Mary Magdalene came and told the disciples that she had seen the Lord, and that he had spoken these things unto her.[39]

Comper's organ is an off-the-peg Casson Positive organ readily and relatively inexpensively available in London.[40] He then went about building and painting the case around it, transforming it markedly from its form as-sold. The organ's left wing depicts the three Marys at the empty tomb, confronted by an angel who both comforts and bewilders with the news that their beloved Jesus is absent. The right wing of the triptych-like organ depicts the *noli me tangere*, Christ's dialogue with Mary Magdalene in the garden after his resurrection when, filled with grief, she does not recognize him and mistakes him for a gardener. In all depictions of the Magdalene – both on the organ's wings and within the niches of the altarpiece, her alabaster jar – a traditional association between the Magdalene and the woman who anoints Jesus, weeps with the strength of her faith and worship, and wipes his feet with her hair – accompanies the figure of Mary. This is done both as a simple process of symbolic identification and to bring the earlier phases of the gospel narrative to bear within these powerful gold-backed images of resurrection. If the organ's surfaces when the wings are open can be interpreted as a triptych – a direct response to the imagery of the gilded altarpiece it faces – then the organ itself, the source of music and the call to worship in harmony and in plainchant, is an image of resurrection through sound and through praise.

The organ is an encapsulation not just of the key passage of the Gospel of John ('Do not touch me for I have not yet ascended'). Its inscription along the bottom of the pipes is the conclusion of that passage – when Mary meets the disciples and they ask her what she has seen; and the left-hand wing is *not* the version of the finding of the empty tomb from John's gospel, but from the Gospel of Mark. Thus, a more polyvalent and fuller account of Christ's

---

[39] John 20.11-18 (KJV).
[40] National Pipe Organ Register, http://www.npor.org.uk/NPORView.html?RI=D04959.

resurrection narratives from across the gospels is implied in the trio of Marys meeting a single angel as depicted on the left-hand wing of the organ. In both, Mary Magdalene is the prominent figure, present at the encounter with the hopeful void of the tomb and the shocking presence of Christ himself, not yet ascended. In both cases, Mary Magdalene is denied the desire to touch Jesus. In the Eucharist, as Comper and his network would have understood it, all may touch Jesus through the True Presence in the consecrated bread and wine. Notably, St Sepulchre's was designed both as a chantry and as a chapel for the reserved sacrament, a controversial aspect of High Anglican theology and practice in the 1890s.

This interpretation of the three-fold organ-triptych with the central zone of the pipes themselves carrying significance, rather than double image of the hope of the resurrection in the paintings alone, is affirmed by the presence of two angels above the instrument in the centre of the organ case holding a scroll. The angels are flanked by two saints: Cecilia patron saint of music, and Gregory the Great, who is strongly associated with this hymn. The scroll contains plainsong: the first verse of the Chorus Novae Jerusalem attributed to Gregory the Great. This plainsong inscription is bounded on the other side of the organ pipes by a painted inscription that does not feature notation but is from a sung section of the Easter liturgy, the *Victimae Paschali Laudes*. The inscription reads, *Dic nobis Maria, quod viditi in via? Sepulchrum Christi viventis* ('Tell us Mary, what did you see on your way?' Mary replies: 'The tomb of the living Christ'). On one side of Comper's St Mary Magdalene organ lies the curious void of the open tomb. On the other its former occupant in triumphant gold, red and white, the living Christ appearing and yet resisting touch. Both are images of resurrection, both are images of confusion and shock and both are images of hope and the certainty of Christ's triumph over death. The organ is an image of resurrection as revealed to Mary Magdalene, and as revealed to all Christians. It is a visual, musical and textual summary of the biblical narratives of Christ's dying and rising.

Comper's organ at St Mary Magdalene, Paddington is also an outworking – albeit on a smaller scale – of Comper's earliest ideas about organ design. These were, though Gothic in a manner similar to the late Victorian cases by Sutton, Bodley and their circle, distinguished by the radical extent to which they are vehicles for representational art and an echo or reflection of an altarpiece. The most striking example in Comper's 1890s output is All Saints, St Ives in Huntingdonshire, a monumental instrument perched on the centre of a rood loft

Figure 8.5 Ninian Comper, organ case, All Saints, St Ives, Cambridgeshire, 1894–9. Photo: author.

where the organ encompasses and contains – indeed, glorifies – the image of the rood, with Christ crucified flanked by the Virgin Mary and St John (Figure 8.5).

By the time the New Palace of Westminster was essentially complete in the 1860s, Pugin himself had been dead for a decade, but the organ designer and Gothic Revivalist Frederick Sutton had yet to write his influential book on organ cases. It took more than a generation for the phenomenon of the painted organ case to come back into its own as part of a coherent Gothic Revival interior in British sacred spaces. Even then, it never fully took hold as the ideal kind of Victorian and Edwardian organ experience was far louder and broader than what would be suitable for the slimmer sounds of a small organ like the type that Comper chose for his St Mary Magdalene chapel beneath George Edmund Street's High Victorian vigorous Gothic Revival church in Paddington. In the Anglican context in particular, organ cases were an experimental fusion of microarchitecture, altarpiece, the musical tradition of complex artificial voice through the powerful aspirant pipes in conjunction with multiple layers of keyboards and stops – a full-body experience both to play and to hear in a manner unique among musical instruments. The relationship between the instrument's centrality to the continuity and the reframing and reviving of church musical styles allowed for its aesthetic to be flexible in some cases and fixed in others. In every instance, the organ case is always a response to the historicist environment which surrounds it, the resonating chamber of stone, glass and indeed worshippers and musicians themselves surrounding and housing the visual as well as the aural content of the case and its internal components.

9

Secularizing the Sacred, Sanctifying the Commercial

Tonic Sol-fa and the Professionalization of Evangelical Hymnody

Erin Johnson-Williams

At a packed public event on 30 December 1874 inside London's grand Exeter Hall, the Nonconformist minister and self-avowed musical amateur John Curwen (1816–1880) was publicly honoured for his lifetime contribution to the growth of the tonic sol-fa singing movement.[1] The Tonic Sol-fa Association presented Curwen with a life-sized oil portrait of himself (an artwork for which he had intensely disliked sitting)[2] and an award of £200, which he immediately dedicated towards the founding of the new Tonic Sol-fa College.[3] Contrary to his usual practice of extemporizing, such was the significance of the occasion that Curwen had written out his speech.[4] Opening with a rhetorical flair, Curwen described the 'thirty years struggle' of tonic sol-fa singing in the face of persistent 'professional prejudice, against the stern weight of government repression'[5] – a reference to the struggles he had consistently undergone with Her Majesty's Inspectors of Music and the London School Boards in accepting the singing practices of a hymn-based, non-hierarchical and Nonconformist

---

[1] For a biography of Curwen, see Bernarr Rainbow, *John Curwen: A Short Critical Biography* (Sevenoaks: Novello, 1980).
[2] See John Spencer Curwen, *Memorials of John Curwen, Compiled by His Son J. S. Curwen. With a Chapter on His Home Life, by his Daughter, Mrs. Banks* (London: Curwen & Sons, 1882), 205.
[3] The Tonic Sol-fa College lasted officially from 1879 to 1916 and has now been renamed the Curwen College of Music. The portrait in question was immediately donated to the college, according to Curwen, *Memorials of Curwen*, 205.
[4] Curwen, *Memorials of Curwen*, 206.
[5] As quoted in Curwen, *Memorials of Curwen*, 206.

vocal system.[6] But now that the success of the movement was indisputable – tonic sol-fa manuals were continuing to sell rapidly for school and church use, despite the government's preference for the alternative methods of his rival John Hullah – Curwen was optimistic about a future of 'new enterprises'.[7] By selling hymns and songs cheaply, Curwen reminded the Exeter Hall audience, their collective 'music mission' had reached (and, he insisted, morally improved) the lives of millions of working-class Christians in Britain and the colonial world.

The commercial success of the Tonic Sol-fa Association as constructed in Curwen's speech cannot be easily separated from his evangelical, missionary-like zeal for the singing system.[8] As he saw the growth and success of tonic sol-fa to be a logical extension of his religious work as a congregational minister, Curwen made no apologies for having left his official duties in the clergy to manage the spread of tonic sol-fa as his full-time occupation: '[t]here are many ways of serving the holy and the true beside that of the pulpit', he explained later in the speech.[9] These alternative religious 'callings' would, for Curwen, include the world of commercial music notation – so long as what was being promoted was an accessible, evangelical singing system that also carried moralizing undertones. Moreover, Curwen justified his work through constant reminders about the voluntary, philanthropic social cultures that upheld the tonic sol-fa movement: 'more hopeful far than any amount of money or personal responsibility', he concluded, 'is this other fact that our method is rooted in the great voluntary movements of our kingdom'.[10]

Utopian visions aside, Curwen ran the tonic sol-fa movement like a business operation. At the end of his speech this is exposed with an extensive analogy between the spread of tonic sol-fa singing classes and the running of the industrial Victorian factory:

---

[6] On the type of speeches occurring at Exeter Hall in particular, see Diarmid A. Finnegan, 'Exeter-Hall Science and Evangelical Rhetoric in Mid-Victorian Britain', *Journal of Victorian Culture* 16, no. 1 (2011): 46–64.

[7] The transcript of this speech is found in Curwen, *Memorials of Curwen*, 206–19. The phrase 'new enterprises' appears on p. 206.

[8] I have taken my use of the word 'evangelicalism' from David W. Bebbington's historical work, where he specifies that the history of British evangelicalism 'is not to be equated with any single Christian denomination, for it influenced existing churches' across the eighteenth and nineteenth centuries. See David W. Bebbington, *Evangelicalism in Modern Britain: A History from the 1730s to the 1980s* (London: Routledge, 1989), 1. While Bebbington does not comment on the tonic sol-fa movement, he does reference the centrality of the evangelical Nonconformist hymn-singing movements such as Moody and Sankey (whose hymns were certainly adapted to tonic sol-fa notation in their own day) as being central to acts of conversion and the attainment of 'holiness'. Bebbington, *Evangelicalism in Modern Britain*, 173–5.

[9] Curwen, *Memorials of Curwen*, 211.

[10] Curwen, *Memorials of Curwen*, 218.

My brother-in-law, who had a cotton factory, long ago taught me that it always answered to use the best machinery. When a better loom was invented he turned the old ones out and installed the new. I should never have won your fellowship in labour – the personal affection which you show to-day – if the Tonic Sol-fa method merely, or the sale of Tonic Sol-fa books had been the object of my life. My object is to make the people of this country and their children sing, and to make them sing for noble ends.[11]

In this comparison, the 'machinery' of the tonic sol-fa enterprise is justified by an impulse to sing for nobler ends; the commercial, while transparently important, is rationalized by an overarching imperative for democratic, moral singing. This use of the emerging systems of late Victorian capitalism as a means of promoting religious singing on a global scale was reflected in many Victorian missionary schemes. The optimism behind such projects, and the vision of Zion with its marginalized people struggling under oppression in order to sing together, was employed as a justification for the necessity of cultivating a new, imperial marketplace for cheaply produced hymns. In the case of Curwen's speech, the mercantile aims of the institution were clothed in rhetoric that praised the civilizing and moralizing aspects of nondenominational mass singing.[12] However, like many forms of Victorian 'rational recreation', the growth of the tonic sol-fa movement also exhibited many of the tensions between the commercialization of theological merchandise and the propagation of socially conservative moral claims.[13]

As this chapter investigates, the late Victorian perception of the new social practice of evangelical and working-class singing, as systematically managed through the examination and accreditation of tonic sol-fa teachers and the mass marketing of printed materials, outlines a unique intersection between the British commercial media and the popular spread of Victorian evangelical hymnody. While the idea of nondenominational and so-called classless hymn-singing resonated with contemporary ideas about universalism and British

---

[11] As quoted in Curwen, *Memorials of Curwen*, 219.
[12] On the tensions between ideals of Victorian liberal reform and wider issues of 'controlling' the masses through music education for the lower classes, see the essays in Sarah Collins, ed., *Music and Victorian Liberalism: Composing the Liberal Subject* (Cambridge: Cambridge University Press, 2019), especially Erin Johnson-Williams, 'Musical Discipline and Liberal Reform', 15–36 and Rosemary Golding, 'Music and Mass Education: Cultivation or Control', 60–80.
[13] On Victorian rational recreation, see Peter Bailey, *Leisure and Class in Victorian England: Rational Recreation and the Contest for Control, 1830–1885* (London: Methuen, 1987).

social progress,[14] the persistent links of tonic sol-fa to a growing industry of domestic and international mission kept the movement largely separate from more elite strands of Victorian music education, such as the foundation, over the course of the nineteenth century, of conservatoires like the Royal Academy of Music, the Guildhall, Trinity College of Music and the Royal College of Music.[15] Focusing more specifically, for this chapter, on the broader cultural reception of tonic sol-fa in the late nineteenth century, I suggest that while the tonic sol-fa movement reappropriated its interests from the theological to the commercial, it also, perhaps paradoxically, garnered unique public attention to populist discourses about a Nonconformist evangelical mode of respectability across a wide variety of secular musical contexts.

Secularizing the sacred

Curwen's 1874 speech provides a rich starting point for discussing the unique intersections between hymn-singing, social class and commerce in late nineteenth-century Britain. The Exeter Hall event was not simply an occasion to praise the spread of hymnody alone – even the physical presence of Exeter Hall in this period was redolent of very specific theological and political convictions.[16] Like many examples of the spread of nineteenth-century hymnody, the Tonic Sol-fa Association used music as a means of enacting social change.[17] By 1875,

---

[14] I have based my understanding of Victorian 'universalism' on Michael Strand, who holds that what emerged over the course of the Victorian period was the 'development of moral principles expressing a distinct imperative to reorder social relations according to *universalistic* standards', where 'Universalism refers to an elementary demand for the impartiality of moral claims, not reflecting contextual determinants like class, culture, gender, race or nationality'. This definition works well with Curwen's claims for the tonic sol-fa movement as being for 'all people'. See Michael Strand, 'The Genesis and Structure of Moral Universalism: Social Justice in Victorian Britain, 1834–1901', *Theory and Society* 44 (2015): 538. For a historiographical survey of how theories of universalism impacted British political imperial thinking, see Duncan S. A. Bell, 'Empire and International Relations in Victorian Political Thought', *Historical Journal* 49, no. 1 (2006): 281–98.

[15] In an excellent recent book, critical sociologist Anna Bull has pinpointed the elitist hierarchies of these Victorian conservatoires as issuing a long-lasting dividing line during the nineteenth century between 'high' art education and the tonic sol-fa movement, which 'sought to foster social equality through [a] collectivist aesthetic ideal', that, although less prevalent in mainstream British education of the twentieth and twenty-first centuries, was nonetheless a very popular alternative to 'elite' musical education at the time. See Anna Bull, *Class, Control, & Classical Music* (New York: Oxford University Press, 2019), 35.

[16] On Exeter Hall, see David W. Bebbington, *The Dominance of Evangelicalism: The Age of Spurgeon and Moody* (Leicester: Inter-Varsity Press, 2005) and Chapter 7 of the present volume by James Grande.

[17] Studies about and relating to the broader culture Victorian hymnody and missions include: Charles Edward McGuire, *Music and Victorian Philanthropy: The Tonic Sol-fa System* (Cambridge:

the notational practice had spread far beyond the Sunday School (the context in which it was first invented by Sarah Glover)[18] and into secular performance contexts such as Exeter Hall, the Crystal Palace and beyond.[19]

Bernarr Rainbow's histories of British music were some of the first academic writings to take on the movement in its historical context.[20] More recent studies of the history of tonic sol-fa by Charles McGuire, Grant Olwage and Rosemary Golding have further explored how the growth of this movement was intertwined with social class, morality and a utopian vision of the organization of the 'gathered masses'.[21] Most scholarship on the tonic sol-fa system has come from within music studies, rather than from theology and religion, and, as such, the biblical and Nonconformist implications of the singing movement have been somewhat sidelined in favour of explanations of its accessible, if now outmoded, musical features.[22] As tonic sol-fa has emerged as an unequivocally powerful societal force in Victorian Britain, however, music scholars have demonstrated its significance as a movement that ultimately promoted the kind of social and moral obedience that would be useful for disciplining the labouring classes, if not

---

Cambridge University Press, 2009); Ian Bradley, *Abide With Me: The World of Victorian Hymns* (London: SCM Press, 1997); Brian Stanley, *The Bible and the Flag: Protestant Missions and British Imperialism in the Nineteenth and Twentieth Centuries* (Leicester: Apollos, 1990) and Alisa Clapp-Itnyre, *British Hymn Books for Children, 1800–1900: Re-Tuning the History of Childhood* (Farnham: Ashgate, 2016).

[18] Sarah Glover (1786–1867) first invented the tonic sol-fa system as a pedagogical tool for her Norwich Sunday School classes, but did not express interest in marketing it, a decision that would later cause potential friction between her and John Curwen, who regularly corresponded with her and tried to give her due credit for the system, dedicating a testimonial to her at the Tonic Sol-fa College. On Sarah Glover, see Peggy D. Bennett, 'Sarah Glover: A Forgotten Pioneer in Music Education', *International Journal of Music Education* 4, no. 27 (1984): 27–35 and Jane Southcott, *Sarah Anna Glover: Nineteenth-Century Music Education Pioneer* (Lanham, MD: Lexington Books, 2020).

[19] As is well documented by Musgrave in his history of the Crystal Palace concerts, tonic sol-fa notation played a vital, if now somewhat downplayed, role in the musical concerts at Sydenham. See, for example, Michael Musgrave, *The Musical Life of the Crystal Palace* (Cambridge: Cambridge University Press, 1995), 186.

[20] See Dickinson, *Bernarr Rainbow on Music: Memoirs and Selected Writings* (Woodbridge: Boydell, 2010); and Rainbow, *John Curwen: A Short Critical Biography*; 'The Age of Rival Systems', in *Music in Educational Thought and Practice*, vol. 23, *Classic Texts in Music Education*, ed. Peter Dickinson (Woodbridge: Boydell, 2006), 198–222 and *The Land Without Music: Musical Education in England 1800–1860 and its Continental Antecedents* (London: Novello, 1967).

[21] See McGuire, *Music and Victorian Philanthropy*; Bernarr Rainbow and Charles McGuire, 'Tonic Sol-fa', in *Grove Music Online; Oxford Music Online*, http://oxfordmusiconline.com/public/, accessed 11 December 2020; Charles McGuire, 'Music and Morality: John Curwen's Tonic Sol-fa, the Temperance Movement, and the Oratorios of Edward Elgar', in *Chorus and Community*, ed. Karen Ahlquist (Urbana, IL: University of Illinois Press, 2006), 111–38 and Grant Olwage, 'Singing in the Victorian World: Tonic Sol-fa and Discourses of Religion, Science and Empire in the Cape Colony', *Muziki: Journal of Music Research in Africa* 7, no. 2 (2010): 192–215.

[22] See, for example, the essays in Martin Clarke, ed., *Music and Theology in Nineteenth-Century Britain* (London and New York: Routledge, 2016).

the future military.²³ As Arthur Somervell's 1902 publication *Music Education in British Schools* claimed:

> [The] singing class may be made the microcosm of [the] noblest aspect of national life. In the singing lesson, where each child may be encouraged to feel as though he alone were singing his song to the teacher, knowing at the same time that he is only a small part of the whole, it is possible for us to have focused the great principles of liberty acquiescing in control, of independence recognizing powers outside of and more important than itself, and of self-expression subservient to the general good; and by means of absolute freedom under communal control, we have a great opportunity to evoke in the children whom we teach the germ of the feeling for the need of rhythmic order in life and conduct, in voluntary surrender for the good of others, of their naturally too-outspoken individuality, the delight of co-operation, and through these awakened feelings to lay the foundation of the highest (or as I prefer to put it, the truly musical) social and communal life.²⁴

Somervell also implies here that acts of communal singing had emerged as a beacon of both individual and national progress in many areas of nineteenth-century British culture, not just in churches but also as a means of pedagogical discipline.²⁵ As H. R. Haweis had detailed in his highly celebrated *Music and Morals* (1871), while congregational singing was highly desirable, it would require disciplined organization to bring about:

> In all times men and women have shown a strong disposition to express their praises and lamentations by what for some better term may be called a kind of howling or wailing. This method may not be thought very musical or hymn-like. Nevertheless, all such vocal expressions are actually attempts to utter deep feeling through appropriate channels of sound. When properly disciplined and elaborated, that mode of utterance becomes congregational singing.²⁶

---

[23] See Johnson-Williams, 'Musical Discipline and Liberal Reform', 15–36.

[24] Arthur Somervell, quoted in Gordon Cox, ed., *Sir Arthur Somervell on Music Education: His Writings, Speeches and Letters* (Woodbridge: Boydell Press, 2003), 65.

[25] There are numerous examples of tonic sol-fa publications that were disseminated widely for state school use. See, for example, T. M. Hunter, *School Songs for Junior Classes: Tonic Sol-fa Edition* (Edinburgh: T. M. Hunter, 1873); T. M. Hunter, *School Songs for Advanced Classes: Tonic Sol-fa Edition* (Edinburgh: T. M. Hunter, 1874); Thomas Crampton, *School Songs: Tonic Sol-fa Edition* (London: no publisher, 1882) and Thomas Pattison, *School Life: Tonic Sol-fa Edition* (London: Curwen & Sons, 1887).

[26] Hugh Reginald Haweis, *Music and Morals* (London: no publisher, 1871; New York: Harper and Brothers, 1889), 117.

By extension, enterprises such as the London Missionary Society saw group singing as a vital component of colonial conversion and discipline.[27] For most nineteenth-century British missionaries, music was employed as what McGuire has termed a 'tool of control for evangelism and civilization'.[28] Indeed, the use of hymn-singing as a medium for communal bonding, and as a means of enhancing if not accelerating conversion to Christianity, has been well established by theologians and musicologists alike.[29] But the highly successful spread of music as a tool of conversion by British missionaries within and beyond Britain did not come about until the missionaries had a notational tool that could simply and accessibly appeal to the untrained musician and even, perhaps, to the illiterate convert.

First invented by Sarah Glover (1785–1867) and transformed into an unprecedentedly lucrative 'publicity machine'[30] in the later nineteenth century by John Curwen and his son, John Spencer Curwen (1847–1916) (hereafter Spencer Curwen), the tonic sol-fa system resonated in particular with Nonconformist ministers and missionaries.[31] The growth of tonic sol-fa was so successful in part because the Curwen enterprise emphasized its accessibility by replacing standard staff notation with simple alphabetical letters and hand signals representing solfege scale degrees (d, r, m, f, s, l, symbolizing doh, re, mi, fa, sol, lah, etc.). Additionally, the low reproduction costs of a visually simpler notation system enabled the cheap mass production of hymnals. Tonic sol-fa was thus synonymous with industry, empire and a new kind of religious expression that was upheld as inherently non-hierarchical while at the same time financially benefitted from the new culture industries that thrived on intersections between 'rational' recreation and mass cheap printing.[32]

As the gulf in the marketplace between elite and popular genres grew wider during the second half of the nineteenth century, then, the supporters of tonic

---

[27] See John Mackenzie, *The London Missionary Society in South Africa: A Retrospective Sketch* (London: London Missionary Society, 1888) and Richard Lovett, *History of the London Missionary Society, 1795–1895* (London: London Missionary Society, 1899).
[28] McGuire, *Music and Victorian Philanthropy*, 114.
[29] See Bradley, *Abide With Me*; and *Lost Chords and Christian Soldiers: The Sacred Music of Sir Arthur Sullivan* (London: SCM Press, 2013); Kirstie Blair, *Form and Faith in Victorian Poetry and Religion* (Oxford: Oxford University Press, 2012) and J. R. Watson, *The English Hymn: A Critical and Historical Study* (Oxford: Clarendon Press, 1997).
[30] The phrase 'publicity machine' is used by McGuire, *Music and Victorian Philanthropy*, 115.
[31] See Robin Stevens, 'Missionaries, Music and Method: Dissemination of Tonic Sol-fa in Asia-Pacific Countries During the Nineteenth Century', in *APSMER 2005: 5th Asia Pacific Symposium on Music Education Research Proceedings* (Seattle: APSMER, 2005), 1–19.
[32] See Bailey, *Leisure and Class*, especially chapter 8, 'Dispensing Recreation to the Masses in the New Leisure World', 80–105.

sol-fa speculated that their movement might even supersede older forms of musical notation, such as the 'staff' notation that is now still dominant for elite forms of music education and musicological study today. Various opponents of the system in the nineteenth century were, indeed, irritated by the wide attractiveness of cheap tonic sol-fa publications, particularly when tonic sol-faists referred to their system as the 'new' notation, and staff notation as the 'old'.[33] Taking over his father's business in the 1880s, Spencer Curwen attempted to nuance this binary, describing the 'new' notation as a crucial stepping stone to the 'old', and ironing out such objections with claims to widening access to the universal art of music itself, regardless of its visual appearance in notation.[34] Spencer Curwen was, after all, a graduate and associate of the Royal Academy of Music and worked strategically towards the end of his life to become the bridge between the two systems that his father could never be.

Over the course of the second half of the nineteenth century, nonetheless, arguably far more people sang from tonic sol-fa notation in Britain and the Colonies than from staff notation. By 1889, the *Musical Times* noted that nearly every major British musical festival choir consisted of singers of tonic sol-fa.[35] As early as 1869, two years before the opening of the Royal Albert Hall, what later officially became the Tonic Sol-fa College had been informally established,[36] and the Curwen Press signed a contract with Novello, opening publishing

---

[33] 'It is only by the help of the new notation, we think, that this fund of information could have been made available, as now it is to the mass of the people.' John Curwen, *Singing for Schools and Congregations: A Course of Instruction in Vocal Music* (London: Thomas Ward & Co., 1843), 26.

[34] 'Tonic Sol-faists, it may be thought, will be completely at sea with a notation so different from their own. All the time they have spent in learning the new notation will, it may be supposed, be thrown away when they come to study the Staff. On the contrary, experience shows that all the knowledge they have gained will be of use; it will render their progress quicker, and make them more certain readers of Staff Notation. They have not a new language to learn, but a new set of characters for the language with which they are already familiar. Music is music, in whatever way it may be written.' John Spencer Curwen, *A Staff Primer for Tonic Sol-fa Pupils* (London: Tonic Sol-fa Agency, 1883), 2. Spencer Curwen also ensured, when he took it over, that the Curwen Press could publish both in tonic sol-fa and in staff notation: see Herbert Simon, *Song and Words: A History of the Curwen Press* (London: George Allen & Unwin Ltd, 1973), 42.

[35] Rainbow and McGuire, 'Tonic Sol-fa', http://oxfordmusiconline.com/public/, accessed 11 December 2020.

[36] The London Tonic Sol-fa College was prolific in publishing educational materials: see, for example, *Calendar for 1871* (London: Tonic Sol-fa College, 1871); *Specimen Tunes for Memory Tests, for Pupils Preparing for the Junior, Elementary, and Intermediate Certificates of the Tonic Sol-fa College* (London: Tonic Sol-fa College, 1883); *Intermediate Class Book for Pupils Preparing for the Intermediate Certificate of the Tonic Sol-fa College* (London: Tonic Sol-fa College, 1884); *Matriculation Memory Tests: Suggested for Use by Pupils Preparing for the Matriculation Certificate of the Tonic Sol-fa College* (London: Tonic Sol-fa College, 1886) and *The School Music Teacher: A Text-Book for the School Teacher's Music Certificate Examination of the Tonic Sol-fa College* (London: Curwen & Sons, 1889). The journal of the college was entitled *The Tonic Sol-fa (College) Record: The Official Organ of the Tonic Sol-fa College* and was published between 1904 and 1906.

offices in the United States, and disseminating sheet music to Australia, New Zealand, South Africa, Canada, the United States, India, China, Japan and across the Pacific Islands.[37] Many churches in the Pacific Islands and southern Africa continue to sing from tonic sol-fa hymnals in the twenty-first century, a legacy noted by recent scholars.[38] Within Britain, tonic sol-fa is still taught in church singing schools in rural, working-class Wales (particularly in old mining towns) and in various rural parts of Scotland and Ireland. In the former imperial metropole tonic sol-fa has, like Exeter Hall itself, been largely pushed into archives, but it is worth remembering that the December 1874 speech geographically situated the movement as being centralized within urban London.

Certainly, the ideological seeds of singing as a means of British temperate, working-class control had long been fermenting by the mid-nineteenth century, a time when London was teeming with seemingly uncontrollable masses of migrant workers.[39] Certain music educationists had already begun to propose that the answer to the unification (and moral control) of the classes in Britain was group singing. For example, Joseph Mainzer (1801–1851), a music teacher who had left Germany for England in the 1830s, published two socialist monographs, *Singing for the Million* (1841) and *Music and Education* (1848) – the latter was the first published volume specifically calling for non-elite music education in British state schools.[40] In 1842, Mainzer had prophesied in an article entitled 'Congregational Singing' that the future of British national progress lay in the communal, congregational singing of the masses, declaring that '[t]he time is hastening when the soldier and the sailor, the plodding labourer and the dusky artisan, will forsake the pot-house and the gin-palace for the singing-school, and so become raised in the scale of civilisation – raised in the scale of humanity'.[41] In this mid-century prediction, communal singing would thus discipline

---

[37] See articles by Robin S. Stevens, 'Emily Patton: An Australian Pioneer of Tonic Sol-fa in Japan', *Research Studies in Music Education* 14 (2000): 40–9; 'Samuel McBurney: Australian Advocate of Tonic Sol-fa', *Journal of Research in Music Education* 34, no. 2 (1986): 77–87 and 'Samuel McBurney: "The Stanley of Sol-fa"', *Unicorn: The Journal of the Australian College of Education* 18, no. 3 (1992): 68–72.

[38] See Stevens, 'Missionaries, Music and Method', 1–19.

[39] For a contemporary account, see Henry Mayhew, *London Labour and the London Poor* (London: Wordsworth, 1850–1852) and *The Criminal Prisons of London and Scenes of Prison Life: With Numerous Illustrations* (London: T. Harold & Sons, 1862), 62.

[40] See Joseph Mainzer, *Singing for the Million: A Practical Course of Musical Instruction* (London: The Author, 1842) and *Music and Education* (London: Longman, Brown, Green, and Longmans, 1848). Mainzer also founded one of the first explicitly populist British music periodicals, *Mainzer's Musical Times*, in 1842, which later became the *Musical Times and Singing Class Circular* and, eventually, the *Musical Times*.

[41] Joseph Mainzer, 'Congregational Singing', *Mainzer's Musical Times* 18 (1842), as cited in Weliver, 'On Tonic Sol-fa', www.branchcollective.org, accessed 8 January 2015.

and moralize the masses and raise a new sober population 'in the scale of civilisation'.[42] Mainzer's argument was that, since Britain had no 'great' tradition of its own orchestral music – especially in comparison to Germany – singing as a means of national, communal pride was the best way forward for a specifically British form of music-making.

By the middle of the nineteenth century, then, two new themes had emerged: first, the conscious desire to moralize a new global mass populace, from the imperial centre of London out to the peripheries of empire; and, second, the idea that working-class communal singing could be a way to effect such social control. To frame this another way, the disciplining of the body through congregational singing rendered all converted bodies as one controlled (or, 'converted') communal voice. As Weliver has claimed, working-class and colonial hymn-singing became an efficacious method for 'achieving that imagined state of individual and national harmony'.[43] Therefore, once the Curwen Press increasingly branched out into more secular publication ventures, the possibilities of imagining British social harmony through tonic sol-fa practice expanded greatly. Such transcendence of musical genre – where the secular can still retain the disciplining and moralizing implications of a democratizing notational system even through commercial use – also enabled the Nonconformist origins of the sol-fa system to even surpass denominational affiliations.

Curwen's starting point was cheap and accessible musical literacy. For those who could not read, whether very young children starting school or illiterate lower-class workers, Curwen introduced from 1870 onwards a visual system of hand signs, which were later, and now more famously, reappropriated in the twentieth century by Zoltán Kodály.[44] As an analogue to 'mental effects', these hand signs envisaged the character of each solfege note: the strong major tonic note 'doh' was visualized as a firmly closed fist; the weak minor tonic note 'lah' was pictured as a limp dangling wrist. Interpreting the hand signs, young children and illiterate adults (and, by extension, international converts who did not speak English) could mimic scale degrees and physically internalize the

---

[42] On the strong links between tonic sol-fa and the Victorian temperance movement, see McGuire, *Music and Victorian Philanthropy*, 'Temperance and Sol-fa', 68–112 and Annemarie McAllister, 'Temperance Battle Songs: The Musical War Against Alcohol', *Popular Music* 35, no. 2 (2016): 191–206.

[43] Weliver, 'On Tonic Sol-fa'.

[44] These were often included or issued in conjunction with Curwen's *Standard Course of Lessons and Exercises in the Tonic Sol-fa Method of Teaching Music* published by the Curwen Press after 1870.

social, moralizing connotations associated with Western scales. Moreover, the conception of tonic sol-fa as more visually accessible than staff notation allied the latter with abstract education, and tonic sol-fa as a very physical symbolization of the working classes, who used their hands for manual labour.[45]

Expanding the visual analogue of the hand signs to theological imagery, Curwen took explicit pains to draw a parallel between the firm fist of 'doh' in the scale and the natural pull of the Divine: God's invincible hold over creation could be denoted in the strength of the Western major scale tonic note. Drawing on notions of biblical infallibility, tonic sol-fa therefore enabled the truth of 'the THING – music' to become visible and accessible to the singer, in the same way that the 'WORD' of God became accessible to the new convert to Christianity, particularly the child.[46] The distance of this pedagogical system from standard histories of music education was of no interest to Curwen; as his son was to later recall, '[a]t every point he took the view of an educationist. Musical tradition was of no account; everything was weighed, and nothing that could confuse a beginner was accepted'.[47]

The international success of the simple notation system as a tool of moral Christian work continued undisputed in the second half of the nineteenth century. Despite the omission of this recognition in many standard histories of nineteenth-century music, Curwen's position as leader of the international singing masses was secure. As Spencer Curwen reminisced,

> The friendships which Mr. Curwen's work led him to form amongst all classes were to him very gratifying. Now and then came tokens of regard which pleased him greatly, as, for instance, a walking stick made by a working man Sol-faist in Scotland, a barrel of tamarinds from some coloured disciples of the system in Jamaica. There was a nobleman in the troublous times of [18]'48 who said that for his own part he did not care what happened in the way of revolutions, for he had a valet in every capital in Europe. The Tonic Sol-fa system put Mr. Curwen in a more enviable position than even this nobleman, for it gave him a friend in every village, and in distant colonies and mission stations. Often in his journeys, giving his name at a shop, a railway station, or a post office, he would be greeted

---

[45] I have further discussed the visuality of the tonic sol-fa hand signals, and their role in colonial conversion, in Erin Johnson-Williams, 'The Examiner and the Evangelist: Authorities of Music and Empire, c.1894', *Journal of the Royal Musical Association* 145, no. 2 (2020): 344–6. See also Olwage, 'Singing in the Victorian World', 192–215.

[46] See Curwen, *Memorials of Curwen*, 38. Curwen, speaking of what attracted him to Glover's system, criticized the 'old' staff notation as being antithetical to 'the thing – music', which tonic sol-fa notation rendered accessible.

[47] Curwen, *Memorials of Curwen*, 43–4.

with a glow of pleasure, and a deference that sometimes amused him, by some humble adherent of the Tonic Sol-fa movement. He had indeed been the means of putting a new pleasure into thousands of lives.[48]

Curwen's tonic sol-fa work in this recollection had thus enabled him to transcend class, denomination and colony, for he had gone beyond the nobleman who needs a valet in every capital to inhabit a *more enviable* position of being hosted by fellow singers as equals. Thus, although he never travelled abroad himself, the image of Curwen as an international champion of 'true' British singing values was complete. However, because of the movement's working-class associations it was not generally seen by music professionals as a valid option for the future of British music, at least when compared with the work being achieved by the London conservatoires. This was persistently the case despite the fact that the tonic sol-fa movement arguably influenced the composers of the 'English Musical Renaissance' far more than we might suspect.[49]

Sanctifying the commercial

The potential of the tonic sol-fa movement to transcend the genre of nondenominational hymnody became evident after the passing of the 1870 Education Act, despite the fact that the British Government did not favour the musical system.[50] But the reality of the growth of free state education at the moment that the sol-fa system took off was that Curwen was able to capitalize on a culture of education for 'all people', with the even more compelling theological inference that the musical system itself could do the work of spreading 'The Word' more subtly than explicit acts of conversion. One account of Curwen

---

[48] Spencer Curwen, as quoted in Curwen, *Memorials of Curwen*, 75.
[49] See McGuire, 'Music and Morality', 111–38.
[50] Following the passage of the Education Act of 1870 (commonly known as Forster's Education Act, described by British Parliament today as 'the very first piece of legislation to deal specifically with the provision of education in Britain'), a framework was established for all children between the ages of five and thirteen to attend government-funded schools in England and Wales. In a series of further Education Acts to 1893, state-funded instruction, state school inspections and national examining as an integral part of British education became standardized on an unprecedented scale. This also provided a bureaucratic model of initiating mass educational improvement for the British Empire. See 'Overview: 1870 Education Act', http://www.parliament.uk/about /living-heritage/ transforming society/livinglearning/school /overview/1870educationact/, accessed 28 September 2015. A separate act extended similar provisions to Scotland in 1872. See also Cox, *Somervell on Music Education*, 3.

hearing tonic sol-fa sung in a London Jewish school, complete with a Hebrew rendition of the *Hallelujah Chorus*, for example, is particularly notable.[51]

In this vein, the Curwen Press successively published a tract entitled *The Tonic Sol-fa Method in the Church of England* between 1870 and the late 1890s, a document which makes the case for the system's applicability to all Christian denominations. This publication contained numerous testimonies from Anglican priests and bishops, as well as recommendations from esteemed musical figures such as composer Sir John Stainer, who concluded that the tonic sol-fa system was 'invaluable as a logical and philosophical method of teaching singing'.[52] More specifically, the testimonials by Anglican clergy, such as the Rev. William Pheasant, assistant curate of Newbury, praised the system for being inclusive to average singers who might otherwise be intimidated by staff notation:

> On an ordinary staff it is not at once apparent to the eye whether a perfect or augmented fourth, for instance is being sung, and the first rendering of the interval very often suffers terribly in consequence. I know something of the rapid progress made by members of a certain Temperance Choral Society, and I am sure that their progress was due more to the simplicity of the Tonic Sol-fa system than to the special musical talent of the members.[53]

The tonic sol-fa system itself, then, promoted the entry-level participation of the new convert (musical or otherwise) rather than prior musical training. What leads to the idea of 'sanctifying the commercial' is where the very existence of tonic sol-fa *notation itself* began to imply this religious fervour regardless of whether the text or genre of the notated music was religious or secular. An interview with Spencer Curwen in 1895, for example, revealed that the growing numbers of children singing tonic sol-fa were beginning to be statistically measurable in working-class schools that issued formal group lessons, implying moralizing discipline whether or not the music sung was sacred:

> The figures relating to the [use of tonic sol-fa within] elementary schools are the most reliable we have, because they are taken from the Blue Books. Summarizing these, I may say that in the quarter of a century which has elapsed since the passing of the Education Act, five million children have left the schools with

---

[51] 'It was marvellous to me, when I remembered that only about a year ago there was no singing taught in the [Jewish] school. These Hebrews must indeed be a grand old musical race.' John Curwen, quoted in Curwen, *Memorials of Curwen*, 200–1.

[52] John Stainer, quoted in *The Tonic Sol-fa Method in the Church of England*, 7th edn (London: J. Curwen & Sons, 1890), 16.

[53] Rev. William Pheasant, quoted in *Tonic Sol-fa Method*, 3.

a knowledge of Tonic sol-fa, and at the present time three and a half million children are learning it in the schools. If you add the number of Sol-faists in America and the Colonies and include those who learnt the system before 1870, it would be a modest estimate to fix the number of pupils at ten millions.[54]

If an estimated ten million people were singing tonic sol-fa globally by this time, and if choral societies were promoting the system, then inevitably – particularly once the publishing enterprise was in the hands of the well-connected Spencer Curwen – the music printed in this notation would become rapidly more diverse than simple four-part Protestant hymnody.

Figures 9.1–9.4 provide a minuscule sample of this enormous variety. Whereas Curwen's first publications focused on nondenominational hymnody, the later ventures of the tonic sol-fa publishing 'machine' spread beyond the Curwen Press to other offices across the world. Curwen did not mind, in any case, that several colonial publishing companies, such as Lovedale in South Africa, among others, were using tonic sol-fa notation; what he wanted was for the system to replicate itself across the globe, as this would only make his press, journal and training college in London successful. Figures 9.1–9.4, in turn, provide examples of sacred hymnody printed in Xhosa from a Scottish Mission Station in Lovedale, South Africa (1894);[55] a schoolboy's school song page from the *Tonic Sol-fa School Song Wreath* (1877); an 1896 tonic sol-fa edition of Mozart's *Requiem*; and finally, an excerpt from an 1899 tonic sol-fa opera by Arthur Roby, entitled *At Home Aboard*.[56]

These four examples afford only a small glimpse of the vast variety of music published in a notation that was originally used for Nonconformist Sunday School classes. Indeed, many cursory explanations of the tonic sol-fa movement still simply position the notation in relation to Nonconformist hymnody, often because it is mostly in Nonconformist chapels in which the notation still persists.[57] A much larger study might examine the complexities of the various subsets of the genre in most tonic sol-fa publications, which I have broadly divided into: English-language Protestant hymnody, foreign-language Protestant hymnody, school songbooks, oratorio-style arrangements of larger works for massed choirs (specifically in the Handelian tradition)

---

[54] 'Mr. J. Spencer Curwen on the Tonic Sol-fa Notation', *Strand Musical Magazine* (1895): 254–5.
[55] For further discussion of *Lovedale Music*, see Johnson-Williams, 'The Examiner and the Evangelist', 344–6.
[56] It is worth noting that this entry incorrectly appears in the British Library catalogue as *At Home Abroad*, but, as Figure 9.4 demonstrates, the opera is actually entitled *At Home Aboard*.
[57] For example, Stevens, 'Missionaries, Music and Method', 1–19.

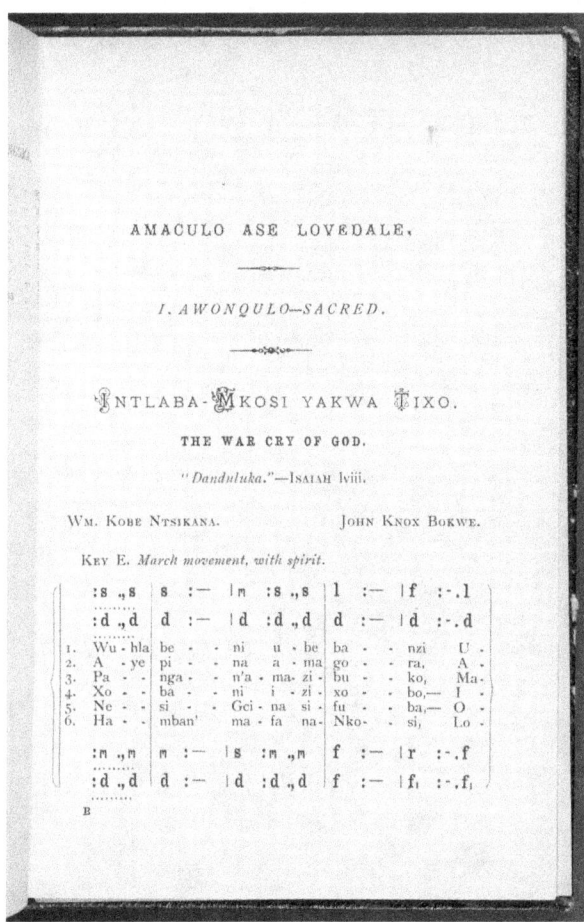

Figure 9.1 John Knox Bokwe, *Amaculo Ase Lovedale*, 2nd edn (Lovedale: Lovedale Mission Station, 1894), 1. British Library System number 004227689.

and miscellaneous theatre works such as in Figure 9.4. The last of these categories is the least common and was marketed to musicians undertaking amateur productions of works in settings where the performers would likely have known tonic sol-fa from their local choral society. The largest publishing categories were hymn books for missionary use and school songbooks, offering up children and colonial converts as the chief targeted demographic. However, scores like *At Home Aboard* and the technically demanding solfege notation of the Mozart *Requiem* are often at odds with the original outlook of simple hymnody, as their avenues of performance diverge from the humble school or church singing class.

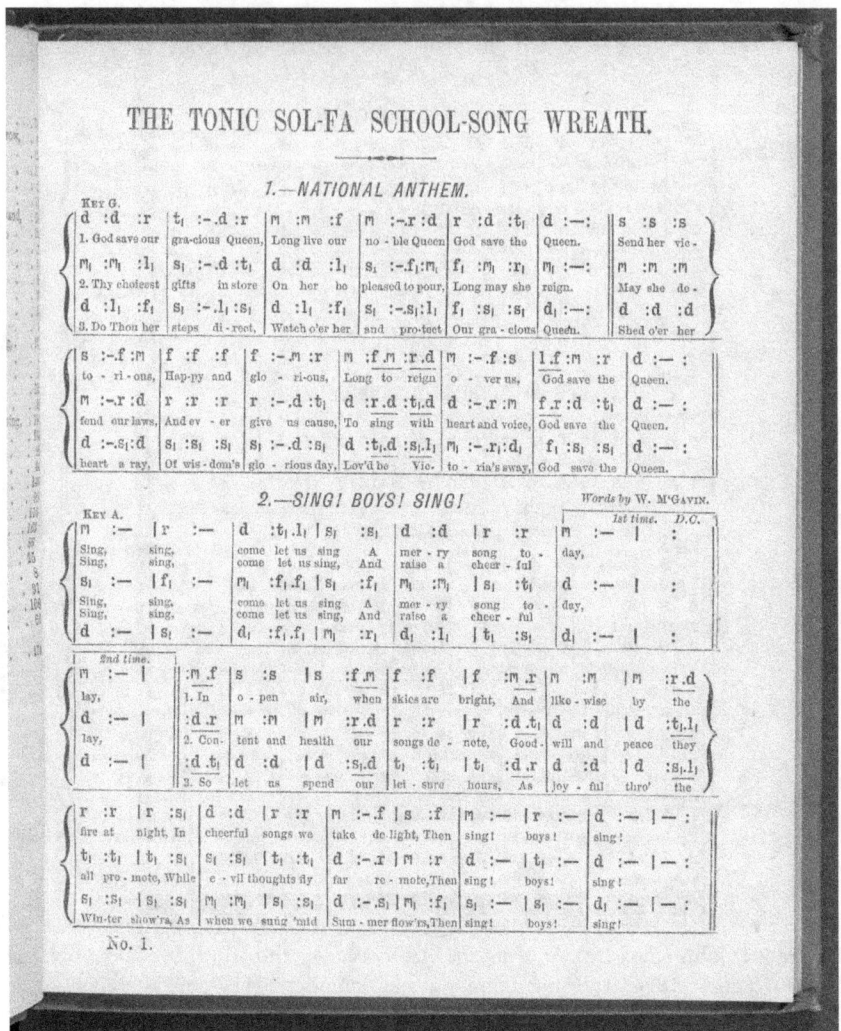

Figure 9.2 William Macgavin, *The Tonic Sol-fa School Song Wreath: A Collection of Songs Arranged for Two Trebles and Bass* (Edinburgh: Gall & Inglis, 1877), 1. British Library System number 004500402.

In a framework of 'sanctifying the commercial', however, technical virtuosity beyond the scope of a standard Protestant hymn, or even music hall secularism, does not matter; for the connotations of tonic sol-fa notation being there at all would centre the performance back to a universalist vision of humble religiosity. This begs the question of whether it was possible for a nondenominational British churchgoer who sang from tonic sol-fa by the

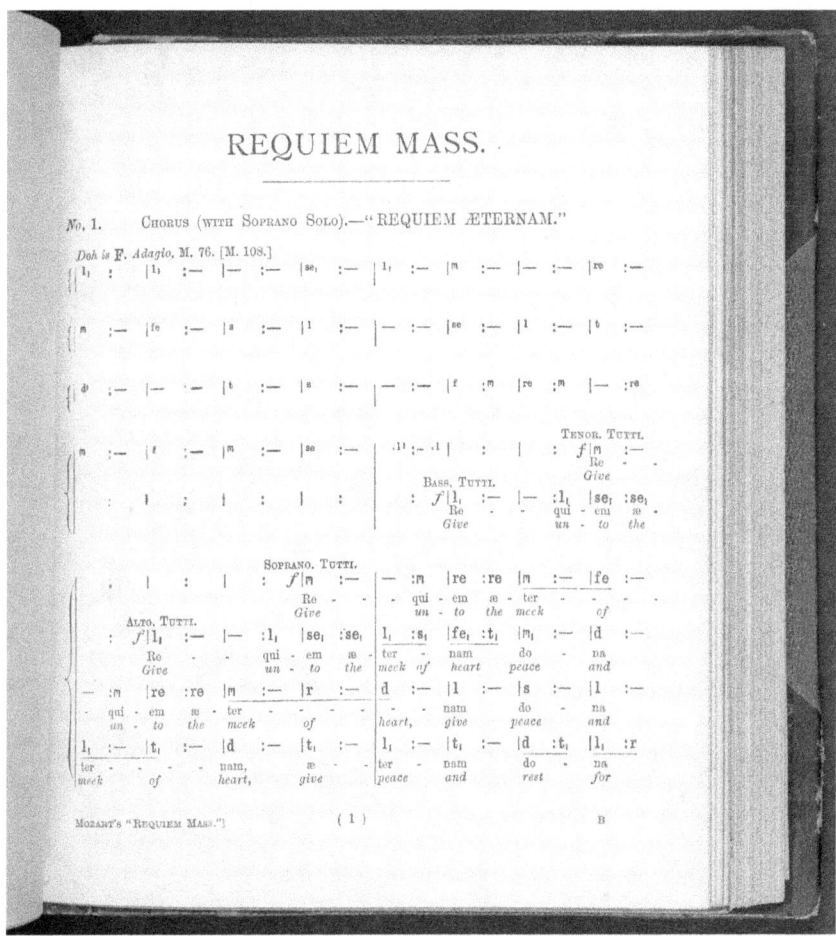

Figure 9.3 Wolfgang Amadeus Mozart, ed. W. G. McNaught, *The Requiem Mass: Translated into Tonic Sol-fa Notation* (London: Novello, Ewer and Co., 1896), 3. British Library System number 004542625.

late nineteenth century to conceive of the permeable boundaries of a system that had now perhaps also entered their local amateur operatic theatre. Put more practically, if the notation of music hall operas like *At Home Aboard* in tonic sol-fa could attract otherwise musically 'illiterate' singers, then not only was tonic sol-fa notation reaching beyond church doors, but the commercial sphere of the music hall was now also effectively 'sanctified' by the publication of cheap, accessible musical notation that upheld a working-class, evangelical respectability.

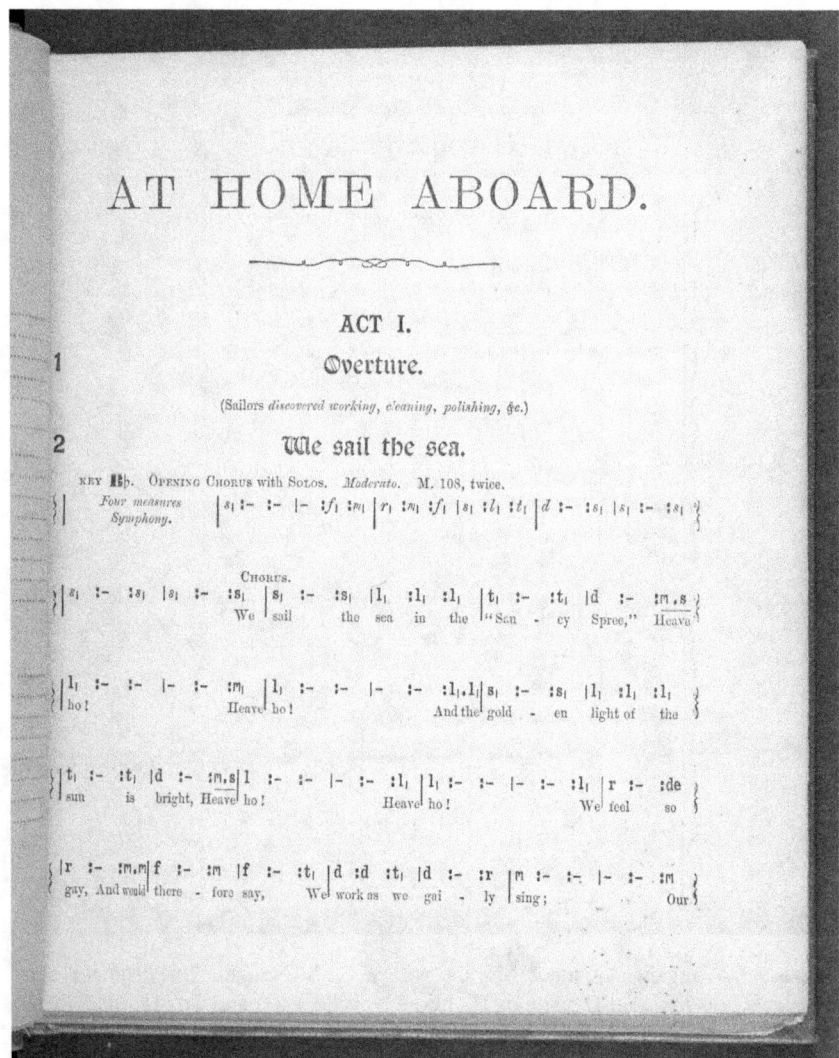

Figure 9.4 Arthur Roby, *At Home Aboard: A Comic Opera in Two Acts* (London: J. Curwen & Sons, 1899), 1. British Library System number 004614824.

Consequently, the perceived differences between the 'new' and 'old' forms of notation, as mentioned previously, were not merely discrepancies between solfege versus staff notation, but, more broadly, between evangelical movements about British national strength versus broader fears of the cultural degeneracy of imported elite traditions. 'Healthy', populous spaces for Victorian music-making like choral societies and community brass bands did not reflect the elite affectations associated with imported operatic effeminacies,[58] but instead with the respectable homosociality of working-men's societies, even if – or, especially if – the notation in which the music was printed transcended the boundaries of church, school and community hall. The success of this so-called democratic, but also capitalistically shrewd, movement was of course threatening if not offensive to the secular London conservatoires that used staff notation to focus on advanced concert repertoires.[59] As Olwage's work has acknowledged, the omission of tonic sol-fa from elite Victorian narratives about British music, particularly those set up by George Grove, reflects a historiographic bias about the grassroots nature of the movement:

> As with most nationalist narratives, this celebratory account of national musical awakening harboured a lack: the tonic sol-fa movement, a popular Victorian grassroots music education initiative, had been written out of the story. *The Musical Herald*, the mouthpiece of the tonic sol-fa movement, claimed that Grove's exscription of the tonic sol-fa story entailed an act of intentional amnesia, an 'omission' that could 'scarcely be accidental'. For, as secretary of the Crystal Palace Company, which hosted tonic sol-fa events for several decades, Grove 'had the best possible opportunity of observing year by year, from 1857 to 1880, the quality and extent of Tonic Sol-fa work'.[60]

Spencer Curwen openly protested the conspicuous omission of his father's biography from Grove's *Dictionary of Music and Musicians* (the first volumes of which were published between 1879 and 1889), noting that

> the inference from Sir George Grove's argument is that, given the backward condition of music which he describes, the way of national musical advance is to be found in establishing and endowing a college. We have, however, pointed out that a wide-spread popular cultivation of music must go hand in hand with such work as is done at the R.C.M. [Royal College of Music] if any effect is to be produced. It is this work, the foundations of which are now almost entirely laid in this country by Tonic Sol-fa teachers, that the late director of the R.C.M. ignores.[61]

---

[58] On the long-held associations in London of opera as an elite, imported and (to British men at the time) sometimes controversially effeminate art, see Christina Fuhrmann, *Foreign Opera at the London Playhouses: From Mozart to Bellini* (Cambridge: Cambridge University Press, 2015), especially 7–24.

[59] On the strong links between London's Royal College of Music and the model of the Leipzig Conservatoire in particular, see the section on British musicians in Phillips, 'The Leipzig Conservatory', 26–34.

[60] Olwage, 'Singing in the Victorian World', 193.

[61] J. S. Curwen in 1892; cited in Olwage, 'Singing in the Victorian World', 193.

Today, the *Grove Music Online* article on tonic sol-fa recognizes that the nineteenth-century 'rebukes by Macfarren, Stanford and others, as well as the failure of some of the more radical adherents to the notation to integrate the learning of Tonic Sol-fa with an understanding of staff notation, led to the perception by professional music educators that many of Curwen's British followers were in a musical cul-de-sac', and that these opponents to the movement 'also incidentally brought tonic sol-fa itself into disrepute in the United Kingdom'.[62] This was the story as Spencer Curwen advertised it: that Grove as director of the Royal College of Music consciously omitted the tonic sol-fa movement from the history of musical progress in Britain because of the connotations of lower social class and cheap commercialism. What is important to remember, however, is that Spencer Curwen himself went to one of London's elite conservatoires and knew the members of this musical world very well.[63] Therefore, the struggles of the tonic sol-fa movement against mainstream musical education were well known within the 'establishment'.

Yet perhaps it was also the complex intersection of Nonconformist religion and imperial commercialism that has contributed to the historiographic silences about tonic sol-fa. Another difference between the Curwens and Grove was not only one of music and class but also of denomination. Grove was a devout member of the Church of England and a supporter of Her Majesty's Government's decision to support Hullah's state school music educational practices, a direct rival to Curwen's.[64] Indeed, debates in the Victorian press itself about the spread of tonic sol-fa from the 1870s onwards often centred more around governmental support for standardized music education, rather than denominational differences. Yet one of the most contentious pedagogical issues leading up to this time was the debate over whether British schools should be operated by the Church of England, other denominations or the state, within which school singing had traditionally been restricted to the practice of Church of England hymns. What Her Majesty's government had not bargained for was

---

[62] Rainbow and McGuire, 'Tonic Sol-fa', http://oxfordmusiconline.com/public/, accessed 11 December 2020.
[63] Spencer Curwen would use the leverage of his Royal Academy training to then advertise tonic sol-fa materials; this accreditation is sometimes even written into the title page of various tonic sol-fa publications that he issued when he took over from his father. See, for example, *A Staff Notation Primer, for Tonic Solfa Pupils* (London: Tonic Sol-fa Agency, 1883), which is listed as being 'By J. Spencer Curwen, *Associate of the Royal Academy of Music, and President of the Tonic Sol-fa College*'.
[64] See Michael Musgrave, 'Themes of a Lifetime: The Many Interests of a Great Victorian', in *George Grove: Music and Victorian Culture*, ed. Michael Musgrave (London: Palgrave Macmillan, 2003), 3–22.

the ease of tonic sol-fa notation for young children, thus sparking a notorious rivalry between Curwen's nondenominational and 'universalist' system, and that of Hullah's, who was the first person to inhabit the role of Her Majesty's Inspector of Music in Schools from 1872.[65] Hullah's own system of sight-singing was based upon a 'fixed doh' idea, where 'doh' was always middle C, and students were encouraged to transpose solfege. Hullah's system required that the student have a much stronger grasp of music theory, and also eschewed the idea that each note of the scale had a fixed 'character' that could be visualized, as in the tonic sol-fa hand signs.

Notably, Hullah's alternative sight-singing system never really took off, despite the fact that it was given governmental support that was never afforded to the tonic sol-fa system. Yet Hullah upheld more 'straightforward' forms of bureaucratic musical standardization through professional accreditation than did Curwen, and for this reason his singing movement also lacked the backbone of religious fervour that the tonic sol-fa system offered. Hullah's position as HM Inspector of Music was thus antithetical to Curwen's grassroots ideals of social reform, temperance and accessible singing for all people, and ultimately, in all musical genres. Moreover, the civic attention given to tonic sol-fa singing as a symbol of national unification was always greater than any notice that was given to Hullah's system. For example, the performance of Handel's *Messiah* on 2 September 1858 that was sung by three thousand children from tonic sol-fa notation was widely hailed as one of the largest gatherings of people for a concert on record at the time.[66] Curwen said of the event that 'every newspaper in the Country' commented on the concert – a moment of unifying all of Britain to a common moralizing cause.[67] One newspaper remarked that '[i]t was left for an almost unknown institution to draw a larger concourse of persons than has ever been attracted in this country to listen to a musical performance'.[68] Eyewitness accounts from the time are evocative of the experience of London's pilgrim-like attention to the concert, mentioning the crush of several injured passengers trying to board trains from London Bridge to Sydenham.[69]

---

[65] Cox, *Somervell on Music Education*, 3.
[66] On the history of Handel oratorios and massed children's choirs in London, see Paul Henry Lang, *George Frederick Handel* (London: Dover, 2012), 334 and William Weber, 'Handel's London: Social, Political and Intellectual Contexts', in *The Cambridge Companion to Handel*, ed. Donald Burrows (Cambridge: Cambridge University Press, 1997), 45–54.
[67] Quoted in Curwen, *Memorials of John Curwen*, 140; and Musgrave, *Musical Life of the Crystal Palace*, 187.
[68] Curwen, *Memorials of John Curwen*, 140.
[69] Curwen, *Memorials of John Curwen*, 140.

After this 1858 spectacle, tonic sol-fa was embedded within popular memory as a practice that was intrinsically British (hence, being unconcerned with Hullah's Continental models), and inherently moral, a nondenominational practice that could bridge gaps of class, religion and (with the growing empire) race. This eventually led to the growth of not only publishing but also to a rise of public events, such as tonic sol-fa choir competitions, and to secular institutions adopting the system.[70] By 1870, several operettas were printed in tonic sol-fa,[71] and by 1889 it was claimed that 'nearly every major British musical festival choir consisted of a mixture of singers of tonic sol-fa'.[72] There were even news reports that in Australia fund-raising 'tonic sol-fa balls' were being held, which caused an amount of righteous consternation in the *Tonic Sol-fa Reporter*, although, as the journal took no pains to hide the existence of such colonial events, perhaps even acts that distorted the system's core values of temperance could be somewhat sanctified within a broader narrative about the movement's international success.[73]

Conclusion

Social and moral reform was to remain the strongest association of the tonic sol-fa movement, reaching beyond specific denominational or geographical boundaries. In this way, the sacred could be secularized for public outreach, and the commercial, in turn, could be sanctified by association with such a moralizing musical system. The fact that Curwen continually placed a greater emphasis on universal moral improvement than on musical prowess is also telling.[74] As his son recalled, '[h]is connection with the subject was not artistic

---

[70] As Musgrave notes, the 'competitive aspect of the sol fa method was quickly grasped and its progressive dimension emphasized by its adoption by the adult choral community, the numbers of which would rival those of children and juveniles in later massed meetings. The first Crystal Palace Sol Fa Competition took place in October 1860 and involved five choirs, from Staffordshire, Finsbury, West Riding, Brighton and Edinburgh, with West Riding as winners'. Musgrave, *Musical Life of the Crystal Palace*, 187.

[71] Musgrave, *Musical Life of the Crystal Palace*, 116.

[72] Rainbow and McGuire, 'Tonic Sol-fa', http://oxfordmusiconline.com/public/, accessed 11 December 2020.

[73] See *Tonic Sol-fa Reporter* (1865); and Curwen, *Memorials of Curwen*, 93.

[74] Curwen, *Memorials of John Curwen*, 20. Curwen never failed to publicly reiterate that the art of music was unintelligible to him until he learned Sarah Glover's first formulation of the tonic sol-fa system, a process through which music was rendered intelligible to this devout working-class man who was to become more a campaigner for the moralizing use of community singing than a proficient musician himself. As his son remembered of him, '[he] passed through life a methodiser, a graduator, an educationist, having no special skill in any one subject, but maintaining the attitude of the learner, and pointing the way'. Curwen, *Memorials of Curwen*, 25.

but moral and religious'.[75] Here, the fact that music was unintelligible to Curwen prior to his discovery of tonic sol-fa was precisely his point of mass marketing: always refusing to be labelled a 'musician', he was proud to play no instrument and reiterated that, even once he started singing, his voice was unremarkable. As Spencer Curwen reminisced, '[o]ften he remarked that if he had been quick at music he would not have been able to sympathise with beginners and those possessing no natural advantages'; and, indeed, this approach was integral to the accessibility and conceptual groundwork of the musical system itself.[76]

In short, what was more important than performance or musicianship in the tonic sol-fa mindset – and, arguably, why it sold so well – was the view that tonic sol-fa gave regular citizens access to a moralizing, disciplining, yet also universalizing, communal activity.[77] As Curwen himself wrote in a letter to a friend:

> I saw yesterday 420 young thieves, who are in a reformatory, with kind teachers to teach and help them. Mrs. McCallum, the governor's wife, has a prayer meeting with them once a week, and the boys conduct it themselves. Two hundred of them often come to it – all of their own accord, and they pray very earnestly. Most of them become good boys through the kindness that is shown them. They forget all their bad street songs, and learn to love Sol-fa songs. One boy was put in prison yesterday for bad behaviour, and he was Sol-faing all the time. The boys sang to me, and I told them the story of ragged Tom. I daresay you can imagine what parts of it they were most interested in. I made them chant a text. I was very glad that Sol-faing was doing so much good.[78]

The ease of Curwen's methods for the criminal, child or amateur learner thus offered direct access to a kind of porous musical truth. If an entire nation, or even empire, of children could grow up accessing musical truth in this way, then the future of music education was accessible and promising, and religious evangelism could even influence secular musical genres.

Curwen's many years of work were to produce significant achievements: annual tonic sol-fa conventions and festivals at the Crystal Palace; a Tonic Sol-fa Composition Club (1867); increased funds for the tonic sol-fa publishing company; contractual connections with the publisher Novello and the Tonic

---

[75] Curwen, *Memorials of Curwen*, 38.
[76] Curwen, *Memorials of Curwen*, 43–4.
[77] McGuire has commented on Curwen's opposition to 'mere performance'. McGuire, 'Music and Morality', 126.
[78] Curwen, *Memorials of Curwen*, 76.

Sol-fa College (which issued thousands of proficiency certificates, many of them widely accessible correspondence qualifications 'by post'). The Tonic Sol-fa College continued to train teachers in the system until after the First World War. By the beginning of the twentieth century, the *Tonic Sol-fa Record* boasted that there was a formal list of sixty-four different musical institutions in Britain that officially recognized the system.[79] Fuelled by this creed of accessibility, the *Times* noted by the 1891 tonic sol-fa jubilee that sight-singing had become 'a mighty force, which has almost attained the position of a religious doctrine'.[80]

Finally, Curwen's persistent analogy of the pull of various notes of the scale to the biblical truth of the Scripture was a vivid reminder that just as the Christian message permeates the convert's life, and all things encountered through life, so the tonic sol-fa method possessed an internal validity, spread evangelistically through homes and schools by teachers and missionaries – even on a subconscious level. As the *Tonic Sol-fa Record* noted, by the end of the century: '[tonic sol-fa's] distinctive principles were being taught – oftentimes unconsciously – by the leaders of all systems of musical training. Perhaps it would not be too much to say that more tonic sol-fa was being taught outside of our classes than within them'.[81] An unwitting and permeable propagation of a system that continually replicates itself through and beyond church walls: was this not, after all, the ultimate missionary success?

Concluding his Exeter Hall speech in December 1874, Curwen triumphed that his movement had thus transcended the 'stern weight of government repression', and that it would continue to do so, because the boundaries of the movement were not based on political party, institutionalized state church or other restrictions on the movement of 'free' people.[82] Instead, in offering up the utopian vision for the new Tonic Sol-fa College, Curwen excused the necessary presence of musical capitalism and fund-raising through an appeal to a transcendent vision of musical democracy:

> And now by your bounty, and by your campaign for five thousand pounds, we hope soon to rear a People's College for Music; a College to which the friends of every good movement that can be promoted by music shall come and learn to

---

[79] *Tonic Sol-fa Record* (1904), 119.
[80] 'The Press on the Jubilee', *The Times* (1891): 243. This is also quoted in Olwage, 'Singing in the Victorian World', 194.
[81] *Tonic Sol-fa Record* (1904), 142.
[82] See Curwen, *Memorials of Curwen*, 206.

teach; a College from which a new Musical Profession shall go forth, a profession of music teachers for the people.[83]

In this vision, tonic sol-fa was a movement for and by 'the people', justified and professionalized through a religious moralism, and brought into being through commercial successes that took the system far beyond its origins in the congregational hymn.

Curwen's singing movement is thus a fascinating example of how the moral marketplace of Victorian hymnic notation would bring about enormous financial capital clothed in, and justified by, the language of democratic, universalizing salvation. Yet perhaps because the exact practices that upheld the tonic sol-fa system were founded on a populist evangelism that defined itself so strongly against the grand narratives of the elite conservatoires, the importance of the tonic sol-fa movement to British and British-imperial music history has often been downplayed. It is thus revealing to consider how integral nineteenth-century Nonconformist and evangelical movements were to the history of a musical system that still has significant repercussions on cultures of music education in the postcolonial world.[84] Even in its heyday, as we saw with Curwen's Exeter Hall speech in 1874, the tonic sol-fa movement directly challenged more teleological and elitist narratives about what could and should be included as important in the national recognition of Britain's musical developments. This demonstrates, in turn, the historiographic significance of recognizing that the boundaries between the secular and the sacred were not only porous but were evolving in direct relation to a changing industrial and imperial world.

---

[83] Curwen, *Memorials of Curwen*, 219.
[84] The place of tonic sol-fa in colonial and postcolonial contexts is a growing area of scholarship. In addition to the works by McGuire, Olwage and Stevens cited above, see also Jane Southcott, 'The First Tonic Sol-fa Missionary: Reverend Robert Toy in Madagascar', *Research Studies in Music Education* 23, no. 1 (2004): 3–17 and Andrew-John Bethke, '*Ingoma* and *St Matthew's Tune Book*: Two South African Missionary Tonic Sol-fa Hymn-Tune Collections', *Journal of the Musical Arts in Africa* 16, nos. 1–2 (2019): 1–27.

10

Antisemitism and Hebrew Music in Carl Engel's *The Music of the Most Ancient Nations* (1864)

Bennett Zon

Ethnomusicologist Carl Engel (1818–1882)[1] was the first person in Britain to publish systematically on ancient and national music, his publications comprising some of the most seminal writings of the Victorian period, including *The Music of the Most Ancient Nations* (1864), *Introduction to the Study of National Music* (1866) and *A Descriptive Catalogue of the Musical Instruments in the South Kensington Museum* (1870), *The Literature of National Music* (1879) and his entry on music for the first edition of *Notes and Queries on Anthropology* (1874). Like much ethnological writing of the period *The Music of the Most Ancient Nations* probes the past for answers in the present, and to do that Engel turned to music of the Assyrians, Egyptians and Hebrews. Engel found the music of the Hebrews to be especially problematic, however, and for two particular reasons: firstly, he, like so many contemporary and more recent writers, considers ancient Hebrews to be a fundamentally nationless nation – what Eric Gans forcefully describes more politically as 'the archetypal stateless nation';[2] and secondly, he identifies modern Jews as their descendants. *The Music of the Most Ancient Nations* wrestles with these concerns in a typically Victorian fashion by relying upon evolutionary theories which contest a relationship between historical Hebrews and modern Jews and modern Jews and contemporary Judaism. Perhaps inadvertently Engel also applies to musicology a Victorian antisemitic commonplace – a Christian history purged of any noticeable Jewish

---

[1] This essay is a revised and extended version of Bennett Zon, 'Carl Engel and the Non-Darwinian Revolution', in Carl Engel, *The Music of the Most Ancient Nations* (Commented Reprint), ed. Arnd Adje Both (Berlin: Ekho Verlag, 2014), xxv–xxxii.
[2] Eric Gans, 'Who are We Now?', *Chronicles of Love and Resentment* 265 (20 July 2002). http://anthropoetics.ucla.edu/views/vw265/, accessed 20 July 2022.

ancestral taint, despite manifest similarities between Hebraic cantillation and Gregorian chant,[3] and not unrelatedly the wide-ranging and abiding significance of its influence in psalm-based Christian repertoire, including psalms, chants, hymns and the other types of sacred music St Paul would call 'spiritual songs' (Eph. 5.19). This chapter tests Engel's credentials as representative of Victorian culture's complex antisemitic mores. To do that it examines *The Music of the Most Ancient Nations* as a representatively self-conflicted antisemitic tract and digs beneath the surface to explore its relationship to Victorian evolutionary science – and more particularly to what historian of science Peter Bowler calls the 'non-Darwinian revolution'. Together, antisemitism and non-Darwinian evolutionism meet in Engel to produce what I argue is an anthropological paradox – a grudging recognition of Jews as 'unfittest survivors'. The chapter divides into four main sections. The first section, 'Non-Darwinian evolutionism', provides key background information on Bowler's concept, including important scientific ideas (progress, the Great Chain of Being, recapitulation and development from simplicity to complexity) through a number of non-Darwinian writers including Spencer, Darwin, Haeckel and von Baer. The second section, 'Music of the most ancient non-Darwinian nations', explores how *The Music of the Most Ancient Nations* typifies non-Darwinism thought by examining correspondence between the ideas of Spencer and Engel. The third section, 'Music of the most ancient *non-Darwinian* Hebrews', focuses in on Engel's attitude towards the Hebrews, probing his language for hints of antisemitism, and the last section, 'Music of the most ancient *Tylorian* nations', contextualizes *The Music of the Most Ancient Nations* through E. B. Tylor's concept of 'survivals'. A conclusion summarizes key points and offers further insights into Engel's not-untroubled legacy and rehabilitation.

Non-Darwinian evolutionism

'Like all aspects of Victorian culture, musical culture absorbed and reflected prevailing currents in evolutionary thought',[4] and so it comes as no surprise

---

[3] See Bennett Zon, 'Victorian Anti-Semitism and the Origin of Gregorian Chant', in *Renewal and Resistance: Catholic Church Music from the 1850s to Vatican II*, ed. Paul Collins (Oxford: Peter Lang, 2010), 99–120.

[4] Bennett Zon, 'The "non-Darwinian" Revolution and the Great Chain of Musical Being', in *Evolution and Victorian Culture*, ed. Bernard Lightman and Bennett Zon (Cambridge: Cambridge University Press, 2014), 196.

that work of Carl Engel should mirror contemporary Victorian scientific knowledge. Organologist, ethnomusicologist and music archaeologist Carl Engel (1818–1882) published extensively on ancient and national music and musical instruments, and all of his publications are steeped in the latest thought in evolutionism. It is perhaps more than coincidental, therefore, that *The Music of the Most Ancient Nations* (1864) was published by John Murray, the same firm which some five years earlier had published Darwin's *On the Origin of Species* (1859). Murray had a sixth sense for popularizing scientific literature,[5] and Engel's book – covering music of the Assyrians, Egyptians and Hebrews – complemented his publications list very well. Coming, as it did, only five years after Darwin's, one might expect *The Music of the Most Ancient Nations* to reflect Darwinian thought, and in some ways it is to Victorian musicology what the *Origin* was to evolutionary thought – broadly speaking, a book designed to explore descent. But beyond this shallow comparison the analogy ceases to be relevant, because methodologically the two books have almost nothing in common. In fact, *The Music of the Most Ancient Nations*, like Engel's work as a whole, is not only not Darwinian, it is positively *non-Darwinian*.

As Peter Bowler has argued, Darwinian theory was slow to gather followers among Victorians starved for evolutionary choice. Indeed, according to Bowler so myriad and heterodox were prevailing evolutionary theories that the *Origin* did nothing more than spark further debate about evolution. The Darwinian revolution is misunderstood; properly conceived, it was not Darwinian, but 'non-Darwinian': 'Darwin converted the scientific world to evolutionism, but not to Darwinian evolutionism.'[6] Darwin's 'mistake' – if one can call it that – was to develop an evolutionary theory which undermined Victorian confidence in Britain's irrepressible sense of progress; indeed, to Victorians like Engel progress was a byword for evolution. According to one of his most pervasive influences, Victorian social theorist Herbert Spencer:

> Whether it be in the development of the Earth, in the development of Life upon its surface, the development of Society, of Government, of Manufactures, of Commerce, of Language, Literature, Science, Art, this same evolution of the simple into the complex, through a process of continuous differentiation, holds throughout. From the earliest traceable cosmical changes down to the latest

---

[5] See Bernard Lightman, *Victorian Popularizers of Science: Designing Nature for New Audiences* (Chicago: University of Chicago Press, 2007).

[6] Peter J. Bowler, *The Non-Darwinian Revolution: Reinterpreting a Historical Myth* (Baltimore: Johns Hopkins University Press, 1988), 47.

results of civilization, we shall find that the transformation of the homogeneous into the heterogeneous, is that in which Progress essentially consists.⁷

Despite certain – and perhaps inevitable – contradictions within Darwin's own thinking (he writes unhelpfully in *On the Origin of Species*, for example, that 'all corporeal and mental endowments will tend to progress towards perfection'),⁸ his dangerous idea would itself evolve, and banish progress from evolutionary thought by substituting it with 'natural selection', a mechanism by which organisms better adapted to their environment tend to survive and reproduce – a mechanism which 'can only generate local adaptation to environments that change in a directionless way through time, thus imparting no goal or progressive vector to life's history'.⁹ No longer was evolution trapped as a function of improvement, and gone was belief in the ineluctable nature of progress.

Darwin captures evolutionary directionlessness – and his own uncertainty about it – in the chaotic branching of his first evolutionary tree. Found in his 1737 Beagle Notebook, and headed tentatively 'I think', the drawing is a tipping point in both Darwin's thinking and the history of science as a whole.¹⁰ By the time he published the first edition of *On the Origin of Species* in 1859, Darwin's certainty about evolutionary randomness had increased – the scrappy, earlier tree replaced by the conceptually confident and more visually orderly fold-out illustration in *On the Origin of Species* (1859). Darwin's ateleological universe attracted vociferous popular and academic criticism, especially among rearguard supporters of more teleological evolutionary theories like the Great Chain of Being. The Great Chain of Being appealed to non-Darwinian Victorian anthropologists like Engel for the same reason that Darwinian evolutionism did not – it guaranteed progress and allowed insecure people to feel confidence in their past, present and future. Tracing its origins as far back as Aristotle, by the Middle Ages the Great Chain of Being emerged as a comfortingly loaded ideological concept connecting man and heaven hierarchically, but by the eighteenth century God had been expectedly usurped by Enlightenment man. By the nineteenth century both man *and* God had been usurped, set adrift in a threateningly directionless, purposeless evolutionary sea. Edward Eichwald

---

⁷ Herbert Spencer, 'Progress: Its Law and Causes', *Westminster Review* 67 (April 1857): 445–7.
⁸ Charles Darwin, *On the Origin of Species by Means of Natural Selection, or the Preservation of Favoured Races in the Struggle for Life* (London: John Murray, 1859), 489.
⁹ Stephen Jay Gould, 'Introduction', in *Evolution: The Triumph of an Idea*, ed. Carl Zimmer (London: William Heinemann, 2002), xi–xiii.
¹⁰ Charles Darwin, Notebook B: Transmutation of Species (1837–38), 36, http://darwin-online.org.uk/content/frameset?pageseq=1&itemID=CUL-DAR121.-&viewtype=image, accessed 20 July 2022.

captures the ensuing chaos in 1829, in the very first evolutionary tree – pipping Darwin at the evolutionary post by some eight years. Unlike Darwin's scribble, however, Eichwald's tree is a beautifully aestheticized, theologically loaded, image with romantic shrivelight beams piercing the dark heavenly clouds.

While the Great Chain of Being would provide an ideological bomb shelter against Darwin's evolutionary explosion, it would also help consolidate another branch of developmental science depicting trees – embryology – and with it one of the nineteenth century's most culturally endemic and non-Darwinian evolutionary concepts: the concept of recapitulation. Born of German idealism, recapitulationism seeped into Victorian culture – and Engel's ethnomusicological frame of reference – largely through the ideological hegemony of Ernst Haeckel's iconic evolutionary treatise *Generelle Morphologie der Organismen* (1866); for Haeckel: '*Ontogenesis* [the growth of an individual embryo] *is a brief and rapid recapitulation of phylogenesis* [the evolution of species]'.[11] In simple terms this means that an individual human foetus passes in its development through *all* stages of human evolution, from protozoa to invertebrates, vertebrates and ultimately mammals; in other words, during gestation the foetus of a more developed animal therefore displays the individual adult form of lower animals. In 1866, Haeckel subsequently depicts this *scala natura* as a tree branching in a way not unlike Darwin's, but by 1874 he had characteristically retrenched into the Great Chain of Being, placing 'man' firmly at the top of a stoutly majestic oak.[12] Recapitulationism also had its opponents, Darwin not least among them. Anti-recapitulationism is found in its germinal form in the work of Haeckel's evolutionary predecessor, Ernst von Baer, whose widely read *Ueber der Verhältniss der Formen* (1828) set the pattern for years to come: 'the embryo of an animal', von Baer believed,

> exemplified from the beginning of its gestation only the archetype or Urform of that particular organism. . . . So a human fetus . . . would [only] move through stages in which it would take on the form of a generalized vertebrate, a generalized mammal, a generalized primate, and finally a particular human being. The form of the growing fetus moved from the general to the specific,[13]

---

[11] Ernst Haeckel (*Generelle Morphologie der Organismen*, 1866), cited in Ernst Haeckel and Joseph McCabe, trans., *Riddle of the Universe at the Close of the Nineteenth Century* (New York and London: Harper and Brothers, 1900), 81.
[12] Ernst Haeckel, *The Evolution of Man* (London: C. Kegan Paul & Co., 1879), vol. 2, 188–9. Originally from *Anthropogenie* (1874).
[13] Robert J. Richards, 'Karl Ernst von Baer', in *Evolution: The First Four Billion Years*, ed. Michael Ruse and Joseph Travis (Cambridge, MA: Harvard University Press, 2009), 441.

in other words, not from a lower to higher type of creature, but from a general to more highly specialized example of its species.

Music of the most ancient *non-Darwinian* nations

It was not, however, von Baer's militant anti-recapitulationism that caught the attention of non-Darwinians like Engel, but his more reassuring correlative message that embryos *progressed* from simplicity to complexity. And who should pick up on this evolutionary Achilles heel but none other than one of Engel's greatest influences, the previously mentioned Victorian celebrity, public intellectual, arch-anti-Darwinian progressivist, and, as it so happens, musical theorist Herbert Spencer. Spencer became acquainted with von Baer through reading W. B. Carpenter's *Principles of General and Comparative Physiology* (1841/1851), and subsequently used it to develop a systematic structuring of all organic and non-organic knowledge in his exhaustively comprehensive key to all mythologies, the *Synthetic Philosophy*. Given the intellectual reach of his synthetic project it was not long before Spencer turned his attention to musical subjects, and in 1857 he produced what is the first in a line of substantive essays on the origins of music, 'The Origin and Function of Music'. Here Spencer taps into the hierarchies of progress beloved of the Victorians, and argues that advanced modern music must have evolved from simpler, more primitive impassioned speech: 'music, adopting all these modifications [escalation of emotions], intensifies them more and more as it ascends to its higher and higher forms ... so there has little by little arisen a wide divergence between this idealized language of emotion and its natural language'.[14] By analogy the whole of musical development must follow the same process in one single Great Chain of Musical Being from primitive impassioned speech to civilized music:

> In music progressive integration is displayed in more numerous ways. The simple cadence embracing but a few notes, which in the chants of savages is monotonously repeated, becomes, among civilized races, a long series of different musical phrases combined into one whole; and so complete is the integration that the melody cannot be broken off in the middle nor shorn of its final note, without giving us a painful sense of incompleteness. When to the air,

---

[14] Herbert Spencer, 'The Origin and Function of Music', in *Literary Style and Music* (London: Watts, 1950), 69. Originally published in *Fraser's Magazine*, October 1857.

a bass, a tenor, and an alto are added; and when to the different voice-parts there is joined an accompaniment; we see integration of another order which grows naturally more elaborate. And the process is carried a stage higher when these complex solos, concerted pieces, choruses, and orchestral effects are combined into the vast ensemble of an oratorio or a musical drama.[15]

With his compelling theoretical bulwark firmly in place Spencer's influence was assured, amassing support and dividing opinion in turn among prominent Victorian intellectuals and musicians (Table 10.1).[16]

The composer, music historian and theoretical acolyte C. Hubert H. Parry is probably Spencer's most vocal advocate, paraphrasing him in numerous writings across his career, including *The Evolution of the Art of Music* (1893/6) and *Style in Musical Art* (1911). An earlier essay epitomizes his level of devotion:

> Yet in reality their work [the work of great composers] was only made possible by the work of those who went before them; and it will be impossible for us to understand its qualities and characteristics, or to realise justly the light it throws upon the state of music in our own time, without tracing the conditions which led to it, and following the steps from the small and insignificant beginnings to the masterpieces which we regard as triumphs of our art. . . . The study of the steps from elementary simplicity up to our complex condition of art shows how progression after progression became admissible by being made intelligible.[17]

Clearly, Engel's indebtedness to Spencer qualifies him as an honorary non-Darwinian. Compare Spencer's theory of impassioned speech to Engel's theory of national song:

> Susceptibility for music is, in a greater or less degree, natural to all men, and is not dependent on the state of civilization which has been attained. The savage thus gifted, however, little in some respects he may be elevated above the animals, is likely, when influenced by strong emotions, to be led by a natural impulse to give vent to his feelings in musical phrases improvised at the moment, without any external aid. If these phrases, or rather melodies, are particularly impressive and

---

[15] Herbert Spencer (*First Principles*, section 114, 324 f.), cited in John Offer, 'An Examination of Spencer's Sociology of Music and Its Impact on Music Historiography in Britain', *International Review of Aesthetics and the Sociology of Music* 14, no. 1 (1983): 44.

[16] For more information on Spencer's fraught relationship with other musicological thinkers, see Bennett Zon, *Representing Non-Western Music in Nineteenth-Century Britain* (Rochester, NY: University of Rochester Press, 2007), 145–56. A version of figure 10.1 appears in Zon, 'The "Non-Darwinian" Revolution', 203. Reprinted with permission.

[17] C. Hubert H. Parry, 'On Some Bearings of the Historical Method upon Music', *Proceedings of the Musical Association* 11 (1884–85): 3–4.

Table 10.1 Spencer's Great Chain of Musical Being

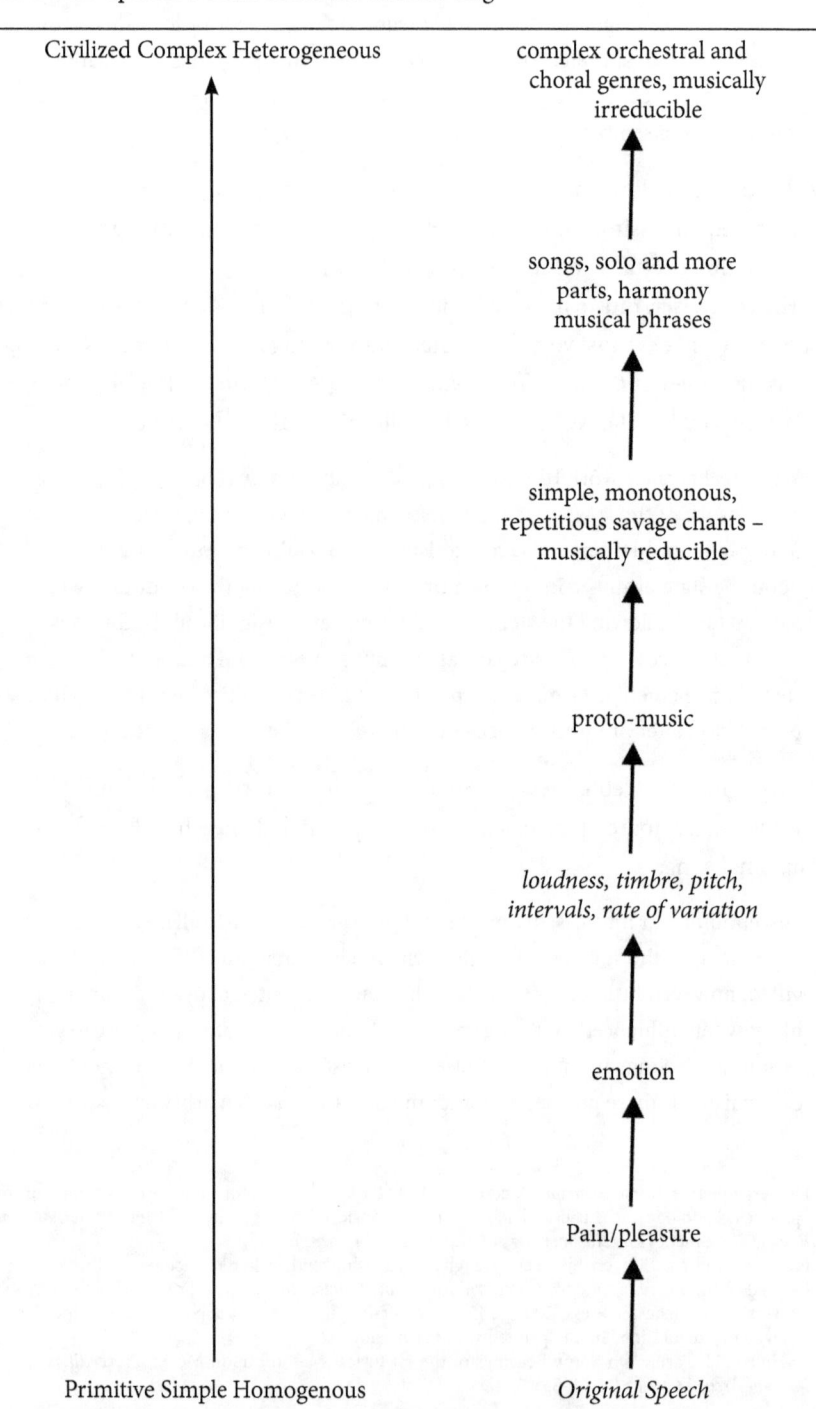

pleasing to others, they are soon caught and retained in the memory, and further circulated among the people. Such is usually the origin of national songs.[18]

Yet Engel was, arguably, also *non-Spencerian*, because he disputes his axiom 'That music is a product of civilization is manifest: for though some of the lowest savages have their dance-chants, these are of a kind scarcely to be signified by the title musical: at most they supply but the vaguest rudiment of music properly so called.'[19] For Engel, savages may have their dance chants, but dance chants are music too, no matter how rudimentary. Writing in *The Music of the Most Ancient Nations* he criticizes the opinion of those who would deprecate 'barbaric' music:

> Hitherto [the study of national music] has been almost entirely disregarded by musical *savants*. Sir John Hawkins, in the preface to his 'History of Music,' says: 'The best music of barbarians is said to be hideous and astonishing sounds. Of what importance then can it be to inquire into a practice that has not its foundation in science or system, or to know what are the sounds that most delight a Hottentot, a wild American, or even a more refined Chinese?' I have transcribed Hawkins's own words, because he precisely expresses the prevailing opinion, not only of his own day, but also of the present time. I think, however, a few moments' reflection will convince the reader of its fallacy.[20]

Spiritually, however, Engel commits to the teleological organization of Spencer's evolutionism. If for Spencer 'history confirms' the conclusion that all music progresses from the simple to the complex for Engel, as shown in Table 10.2, it progresses in microcosm from simple to complex intervals, from vocal to instrumental music and within instrumental music from the drum and pipe to lyre.[21]

Table 10.2 Correlation between Degrees of Civilization and Instrumental and Vocal Development in *The Music of the Most Ancient Nations* (1864)

Progress	Uncivilized ──────────────────────→ Civilized						
	['nations almost entirely unacquainted with instrumental music']						
Instrumental	Drum	Pipe	expanded drum	String	expanded pipe	expanded string
Vocal	third	second	sixth	octave	fourth	seventh

[18] Carl Engel, *The Music of the Most Ancient Nations* (London: John Murray, 1864), 21.
[19] Spencer, 'Origin and Function of Music', 68.
[20] Engel, *Ancient Nations*, 1.
[21] Spencer, 'Origin and Function of Music', 62.

Vocal music progresses from the unison, fifth, third, second, sixth, octave, fourth and seventh; and instruments appear afterwards to accompany song in the following evolutionary progression: nations almost entirely unacquainted with instrument music, to drum, pipe, expanded drum, string, expanded pipe and expanded string. According to Spencer, history confirms other evolutionary conclusions as well: 'The strong imitative tendency', he opines, 'notoriously displayed by the lowest human races, ensures among them a constant reproducing of likeness of things, forms, signs, sounds, actions and whatever else it imitable'.[22] Engel imitates this when suggesting that '[savages] are generally very imitative. Their dances are often representations of the peculiar motions and gambols of certain animals; and the *motivos* of their songs have not unfrequently been derived from a similar source, especially from the songs of birds'.[23]

Music of the most ancient *non-Darwinian* Hebrews

For all his advances in musical impartiality non-Darwinian Engel remains Spencerian in temperament, right down to his belief in the ultimate superiority of his own musical culture. Unable to explain the archaeologically incontestable perfection of Assyrian music, for example, he concludes that it did not develop, but must have been borrowed from another civilization:

> I shall only point out that the music of the Assyrians, though evidently greatly inferior to our own, yet appears to have attained a degree of perfection which it could have reached only after a long period of cultivation. It is not at all probable that music should have attained such a degree of perfection by cultivation during the existence of one nation, however extended the period of this existence may have been. We are therefore reasonably led to infer that the Assyrians derived their music in an already somewhat advanced state from some other nation or nations unknown to us, and that they only further developed what had been transmitted to them.[24]

Strangely, the same criticism does not apply to the music of the Hebrews; indeed, perhaps because Engel considered Hebrew music and literature to be so central to Christian tradition, the music of the Hebrews remains for him pure and

---

[22] Herbert Spencer, *Essays: Scientific, Political, and Speculative* (London: Longman, Brown, Green, Longmans, and Robert, 1858), 190.
[23] Engel, *Ancient Nations*, 20.
[24] Engel, *Ancient Nations*, 27.

unsullied by foreign contact, despite the egregious nature of their exile: 'During the Babylonian captivity, although the Hebrews adopted the Chaldæan language, their music does not appear to have undergone any important modification through foreign influence; so that, after their return to Jerusalem, about seventy years later, a fresh generation was enabled to re-establish at one in the temple the musical performances of their forefathers.'[25]

It remains uncertain why Engel claims that the Assyrians merely aped highly cultivated foreign music – and that Hebrew music does not evolve despite diasporic experience of foreign influence – but evolutionary stasis (through inherent inability to progress) and cultural cussedness are common features of the non-Darwinian revolution. As I argue in 'Victorian Anti-Semitism and the Origin of Gregorian Chant' (2010), Christian historians were conflicted over the origins of Western music and often appear to have omitted discussion of its Jewish synagogal (and heathen) origins to preserve the integrity of their own Christian lineage from what they deemed to be ascetic, non-progressive and monotonous properties and characteristics. Henry Wylde, for instance, extols Jewish worship for its purity and simplicity, but complains that it marked early Christian music with a 'lack of artistic feeling and the stern asceticism ... and antagonistic element to the progress of civilization'.[26] Writing in *The Music of the Bible* (1879) Parry's contemporary and Spencerian equal John Stainer encapsulates this view: 'That monotone, when used from century to century in the mouth of devout readers, will grow into a cantillation, or rude sort of chant, can be proved by the history of our early Church plain-song. Why should not the Hebrews have passed in their days through the same phase of musical development which other nations have done?'[27] The fact that certain musical cultures were omitted from evolution, because they were either insufficiently advanced and/or lacked the inherent capacity for advancement, points to the tenacious ideological shadow of the Great Chain of Musical Being.

Was non-Darwinian Engel a soft, passive musical antisemite, like Wylde and Stainer? Almost certainly not, but like so many Victorians the meaning of his language is frustratingly difficult to interpret. Note in the excerpt below Engel's choice of the evolutionarily loaded, Darwinian word 'modification' (Darwin calls evolution modification by descent). Does modification signal merely an

---

[25] Engel, *Ancient Nations*, 277–8.
[26] Henry Wylde, *Music in its Art-Mysteries* (London: L. Booth, 1867), 113.
[27] John Stainer, *The Music of the Bible, with an Account of the Development of Modern Musical Instruments* (London: Novello, Ewer & Co., 1879), 165.

evolutionary mechanism of change? Does modification preclude progress? Are modification and preservation mutually incompatible? Engel skirts the issues: 'I do not intend to imply', he maintains,

> that the music of the Hebrews has not, in the course of a thousand years, experienced considerable modifications ... there can scarcely be a doubt that, after the departure of the Hebrews from Egypt, their music acquired in the course of time certain characteristics which distinguished it from the Egyptian music, and which originated in the religious views and observances of the Jews, as well as from their intercourse with Asiatic nations, and from other circumstances.[28]

One aspect of 'Music of the Hebrews' which might, in the broadest sense, help answer some of these questions is the fact that Engel covers the full span of Jewish history, from the earliest period of the Bible up to the Victorian present. Integral to his coverage is a portrayal of Jews sedulously preserving tradition, with many tunes and instruments remaining notably similar across diasporic locations. Innocuous in itself, the language of preservation is, however, inflected by a vocabulary not dissimilar to that culminating in Matthew Arnold's *Culture and Anarchy* (lectures, 1867–8; published as book, 1869). Drawing upon contemporary antisemitic tropes, Arnold compares 'Hebraism' wantingly to 'Hellenism': 'The governing idea of Hellenism is *spontaneity of consciousness*'; he claims, 'that of Hebraism, *strictness of conscience*'.[29] Unsurprisingly, Arnold's dichotomous interpretation of culture has been roundly criticized by scholars of race and antisemitism. Jonathan Freedman characterizes Arnold's Hebrew as seizing 'upon certain plain, capital intimations of universal order, and ... [riveting] itself, one may say, with unequalled grandeur of earnestness and intensity on the study and observance of them'.[30] Robert Young is even more direct, echoing Freedman and railing against Arnold's contrast between Hellenism and Hebraism as 'antithetical, centripetal and centrifugal. . . . Hebraism involves a strict contraction of consciousness, while Hellenism produces its expansive free play, thus reproducing in subverting and containing, forward at work in society and history at large'.[31]

---

[28] Engel, *Ancient Nations*, 270, 280.
[29] Matthew Arnold, *Culture and Anarchy* (1869; New York: Macmillan, 1936), 128–9.
[30] Jonathan Freedman, *The Temple of Culture: Assimilation and Anti-Semitism in Literary Anglo-America* (New York: Oxford University Press, 2000), 18.
[31] Robert Young, *Colonial Desire: Hybridity in Theory, Culture and Race*, second edition (New York: Routledge, 2003), 61.

The concept of a Hellene/Hebrew antithesis was not new to Arnold of course. It is clear, for example, that he drew extensively upon neohumanist German philosophical antecedents which used philhellenism to smite Hebrew dualism between the spirit and body.[32] Thus, Heine remarks that the 'Jews looked on the body as a despicable thing [in contrast to the Greeks], as the pitiful envelope of the *Rouach hakodasch*, of the divine breath, the spirit; and to the latter only would they accord consideration, reverence, and worship.'[33] Hegel extends and applies this deprecation to Judaism as a whole: 'An essential of their religion [in contrast to that of the Greeks] was the performance of a countless mass of senseless and meaningless actions ... the holiest of things, namely, the service of God and virtue, was ordered and compressed in dead formulas.'[34] Engel never reaches these depths of virulent antisemitic philhellenism, but his language does reflect contemporary trends in Grecophilia: 'The Greeks were a remarkably enterprising and progressive nation; whatever they borrowed from other nations they soon further developed and expanded';[35] conversely,

> This [the retention of Eastern musical characteristics] would scarcely have been possible under the circumstances of their [the Jews] being so widely and thinly dispersed among other nations, were it not for the strictness with which they have always upheld their prescribed religious rites and ceremonies in which music is employed. They have, as we have seen, even preserved one of their old Hebrew musical instruments, the *shophar*.[36]

While there is nothing in *The Music of the Most Ancient Nations*, nor any of Engel's other writing, which can be branded categorically antisemitic, the language or even grammar of alterity[37] – 'a state of being other, or of not being of the self'[38] – is structurally embedded in the anthropological message of the book as a whole. Writing of 'Hebrew Music in the Present Day', for example, Engel consistently distinguishes between the object of Hebrew music as an archaeological or ethnomusicological artefact and the people (the Jews) who

[32] See Lionel Gossman, 'Philhellenism and Antisemitism: Matthew Arnold and His German Models', *Comparative Literature* 46, no. 1 (1994): 1–39.
[33] Heinrich Heine, *Religion and Philosophy in Germany: A Fragment*, trans. John Snodgrass (1835; Boston: Beacon Press, 1959), 74.
[34] Friedrich Hegel, 'On Christianity', in *Early Theological Writings of Friedrich Hegel*, trans. T. M. Knox and Richard Kroner (New York: Harper Torchbooks, 1961), 69.
[35] Engel, *Ancient Nations*, 202.
[36] Engel, *Ancient Nations*, 323–4.
[37] Andre Gingrich, 'Conceptualizing Identities: Anthropological Alternatives to Difference and Moralizing the Other', in *Grammars of Identity/Alterity: A Structural Approach*, ed. Gerd Baumann and Andre Gingrich (New York: Berghahn Books, 2006), 4.
[38] Clive Hazell, *Alterity: The Experience of Other* (Bloomington: AuthorHouse, 2009), xvii.

continue to perform it. The distinction between Hebrew (as object) and Jew (as subject) would seem merely semantic, but in fact it harkens back to much more deeply rooted antisemitic – frequently Christian – propaganda aiming to separate Semites from Jews, and Jews from Judaism. At its prejudicial worst, in ethically twisted books like Baden Powell's *Christianity without Judaism* (1857)[39] or Ernest Renan's *The Life of Jesus* (1863),[40] the distinction of Semite and Jew, Jew and Judaism produces the illusion of a Jew-less, Judaism-less Christianity. Steven Beller highlights these categorical distinctions in his opening definition of *Antisemitism: A Very Short Introduction* (2007):

> Antisemitism is a hatred of Jews that has stretched across millennia and across continents; or it is a relatively modern political movement and ideology that arose in Central Europe in the late 19th century and achieved its evil apogee in the Holocaust; or it is the irrational, psychologically pathological version of an ethnocentric and religiocentric anti-Judaism that originated in Christianity's conflict with its Jewish roots – and achieved its evil apogee in the Holocaust; or it is a combination of all of these.[41]

Antisemitism of the kind displayed by Engel – if indeed it can be called antisemitism – may be indicative of the more 'genteel', 'social' or 'polite' variety of the 'contained, temperate nature' of Victorian prejudice, but its more virulent counterpart circulated with all its anthropological and religious antipathies fully intact.[42] Indeed, the mutually parasitical enmities of antisemitism (against the Jews) and anti-Judaism (against the religion of the Jews) found their apogee in England in the pseudoscientific, paradigmatically racist ideologies of Houston Stewart Chamberlain.[43] Son-in-law of Richard Wagner and author of the toxically racializing project *Foundations of the Nineteenth Century* (1899), Chamberlain denigrates Jews (Semites) as degenerate spiritual backsliders and praises Christians (Aryans) as evolutionary religious progressivists. Engel does nothing of the kind, but his characteristically Victorian separation of Hebrew from Jew, object from subject, past from present locates the identity of the

---

[39] William Brustein, *Roots of Hate: Anti-Semitism in Europe Before the Holocaust* (Cambridge: Cambridge University Press, 2003), 88.
[40] Albert S. Lindemann, *Esau's Tears: Modern Anti-Semitism and the Rise of the Jews* (Cambridge: Cambridge University Press, 1997), 87–8.
[41] Steven Beller, *Antisemitism: A Very Short Introduction* (Oxford: Oxford University Press, 2007), Kindle loc. 254.
[42] Anthony Julius, *Trials of the Diaspora: A History of Anti-Semitism in England* (Oxford: Oxford University Press, 2010), Kindle loc. 623.
[43] Anne Harrington, *Reenchanted Science: Holism in German Culture from Wilhelm II to Hitler* (Princeton: Princeton University Press, 1996), 106–8.

Jew in a characteristically prejudicial anthropological time warp. Even in *An Introduction to the Study of National Music* (1866) Engel continues to deprive Jews of musical nationhood and define them in a largely perpetual present. Jews are, for example, the only living people, rather than nation, included in the book's 'Library of National Music'. And like many musicological works of the time *The Music of the Most Ancient Nations* compensates Jews for their lack of genuine development by indulging the transition myth, which redeems the stasis of Hebrew music by resolving its developmental dissonance into a larger transition towards Christian musical culture. 'In our Christian Church', he suggests,

> the intoning, chanting, and antiphonal singing are, in all probability are remains of the ancient Hebrew mode of performing in the Temple. The apostles were Hebrews, accustomed from their childhood to the usages of their nation, and must been practiced in the music which they have been in the habit of using in worship before they became Christians. And it is not likely that the primitive Christians would have adopted in their worship the musical performances of idolaters to which they were naturally averse.[44]

In microcosm the same redemptive progression occurs in relation to the music of Mendelssohn: 'Some of them [the Jews]', Engel proffers,

> exhibit in their compositions peculiarities which remind us of the synagogue. This is, in my opinion, also the case in the music of Mendelssohn, who, though a Christian, was of Hebrew origin. These peculiarities ... consist especially in the employment and frequent repetition of short melodious phrases, and passages of a peculiar rhythmical effect, frequently in the Minor, and of a certain monotony, which Mendelssohn, however, know how to render highly interesting by a skilful harmony.[45]

Here, like so many Victorian musicologists, Engel taps an antisemitic vein and portrays Mendelssohn as proof of model Christian redemption at work. Integral to this construction is the fact that Mendelssohn, like all Jews, remained congenitally Jewish despite his conversion: 'Jews remain Jews', Schumann proclaims, referring specifically to Mendelssohn.[46] Writing on the topic of Mendelssohn's Ps. 114 ('When Israel Went Out of Egypt') in the first edition of his famous dictionary George Grove reiterates this sentiment, opining that 'The

---

[44] Engel, *Ancient Nations*, 358–9.
[45] Engel, *Ancient Nations*, 348–9.
[46] Robert Schumann (marriage diary), cited in Peter Ostwald, *Schumann: The Inner Voices of a Musical Genius* (Athens, GA: Northeastern University Press, 1985), 119.

Jewish blood of Mendelssohn must surely for once have beaten fiercely over this picture of the great triumph of his forefathers'.[47] To both Engel on the 'benign' end of the antisemitic spectrum, and to other non-Darwinians on the opposite, malignant extreme of antisemitism (like Chamberlain), Jewishness is, in other words, inherited, and no act of cultural or religious assimilation can erase it.

Music of the most ancient *Tylorian* nations

In the non-Darwinian ferment of Victorian Britain, Jewish inheritance is a doubly troublesome term of reference, not only because of its inherently antisemitic properties but because the mechanism of inheritance – and its corollary, heredity – was not itself fully understood scientifically. At its most extreme, obsession with racial inheritance led to the Pandora's box of eugenics, a selective breeding programme founded by Darwin's first cousin Francis Galton and subsequently implicated in the ethnic cleansing of the Holocaust. Eugenics selects only what is 'good in stock, hereditarily endowed with noble qualities . . . [and which is] equally applicable to men, brutes, and plants'.[48] At its antisemitic (arguably) least severe, racial inheritance was a compulsory, yet perfectly ordinary part of the Victorian anthropological tool kit. Matthew Arnold speaks for a generality when on the one hand he gladly avows a historical and cultural continuity (and therefore resemblance) between Jews and Christians, but on the other eschews the idea of any quantifiable racial commonality.[49]

In their own way Arnold, Galton, Chamberlain, Grove, Schumann, Hegel, Heine, Parry, Wylde, Stainer and Engel all subscribe broadly to the Great Chain of Antisemitic Being – the concept of an immutable, if graded, ideological inheritance which selectively excludes (and therefore oppresses) Jews from the same inalienable right of progress leading Christians towards a more perfect future.[50] 'Nothing is more usual', Engel qualifies,

---

[47] George Grove, 'Mendelssohn', in *A Dictionary of Music and Musicians*, vol. 2 (London: Macmillan, 1880), 304, cited by Jeffrey S. Sposato, *The Price of Assimilation: Felix Mendelssohn and the Nineteenth-Century Anti-Semitic Tradition* (Oxford: Oxford University Press, 2006), Kindle loc. 209.
[48] Francis Galton, *Inquiries into Human Faculty and its Development* (London: J. M. Dent, 1883), 17.
[49] Vincent P. Pecora, 'Arnoldian Ethnology', *Victorian Studies* 41, no. 3 (1998): 375.
[50] Bruce Hawkins, 'Ideology, Metaphor and Iconographic Reference', in *Language and Ideology: Descriptive Cognitive Approaches*, Current Issues in Linguistic Theory, vol. 2, ed. René Dirven, Bruce Wayne Hawkins, Roslyn M. Frank, Esra Sandikcioglu, and Cornelia Ilie (Amsterdam: John Benjamins, 2001), 43.

than the notion that, in order to trace the art of music from its most primitive state and to observe its gradual development, we must commence our inquiries by penetrating the most remote periods . . . amongst the most ancient nations known to us – the Assyrians as well as the ancient Egyptians and Hebrews – music had already attained a degree of perfection considerably higher than we meet with in many nations of our own time.[51]

It behoves the musicologist, furthermore, to study 'the music of contemporary nations in different stages of civilisation' at the same time comparing 'the music of several nations standing at the same scale of civilisation'.[52] If, however, as these words suggest progress consists in an ineluctable force and evolutionary prerequisite driving improvement forward, how does Engel harmonize the historical stasis and modern development of Hebrew music? The answer lies in his friendship with anthropologist E. B. Tylor (1832–1917) and Tylor's controversial theory of 'survivals'.

E. B. Tylor is best known in the history of anthropology for his theory of 'survivals'; namely 'processes, customs, opinions, and so forth, which have been carried on by force of habit into a new state of society different from that in which they had their original home, and they thus remain as proofs and examples of an older condition of culture out of which a newer one has been evolved'.[53] Developed to an apogee in *Primitive Culture* (1871), Tylor's theory bequeathed to anthropology a temporal analogy representing Britain's imperial experience. The deep past became a foreign country ripe for metaphysical conquest, exploited to prove the evolutionary superiority of modern civilized (European/English) man. Tylor calls survivals 'mines of historic knowledge', and he believed that the presence of survivals was part of the evolutionary process itself.[54] This justified his belief that '[civilization], being a process of long and complex growth, can only be thoroughly understood when studied through its entire range; that the past is continually needed to explain the present, and the whole to explain the part'.[55] Here and elsewhere Tylor concludes that the

---

[51] Engel, *Ancient Nations*, 8.
[52] Engel, *Ancient Nations*, 9.
[53] E. B. Tylor, *Primitive Culture: Researches into the Development of Mythology, Philosophy, Religion, Language, Art and Custom*, 2 vols. (New York: Henry Holt, 1889), 16.
[54] Tylor, *Primitive Culture*, 71.
[55] E. B. Tylor, *Researches into the Early History of Mankind and the Development of Civilization* (London: John Murray, 1865), 2.

'civilization of any age is not a new creation to meet the wants of that age, but is a result of past times, modified to meet new conditions of life and knowledge'.[56]

For Engel the ethnographic and anthropological evidence of that process of modification proves that both the music of the Hebrews and the Jews themselves are Tylorian survivals. Survivals eschew modification, and so Tylor and Engel use the word 'modify' or 'modification' to heighten its developmental implications. As a function of modification Tylor insists that we study the 'lower tribes as related to the civilization of the higher nations';[57] for Engel, therefore, the music of uncivilized nations 'is capable of yielding important suggestions for the science and history of music, just as the languages of savage nations are useful in philological and ethnological inquires'.[58] Yet advances through modification do not prove the inferiority of earlier stages in a culture's history, and both condemn the denigration of primitive, savage peoples. Tylor insists that a belief in 'any known savage tribe' being 'improved by judicious civilizations, is a proposition which no moralist would dare to make';[59] Engel provides a modern example: 'It is remarkable that the great susceptibility and fondness for music which the ancient Hebrews evidently possessed have been preserved by their race until the present day. Many of our distinguished musicians, composers as well as *virtuosi*, are Jews, or of Jewish extraction.'[60]

Buoyed by their more ideologically modern stance, Engel and Tylor also created the very first British methodological desideratum for the study of non-Western and indigenous music, in essence the first British, professionally ratified, ethnomusicological framework for studying musical 'survivals' in the field. Engel's extensive contribution to *Notes and Queries on Anthropology, for the Use of Travellers and Residents in Uncivilized Lands* (1874), produced under the aegis of Tylor and reprinted in different editions until 1899, encapsulates Tylorian moral disinterest, focusing instead on the individual difference of national musical expression, and the importance, therefore, of absolutely faithful musical transcription:

> The music of every nation has certain characteristics of its own. The progression of intervals, the modulations, embellishments, rhythmical effects, &c. occurring in the music of extra-European nations are not unfrequently too peculiar to

---

[56] E. B. Tylor, 'On the Survival of Savage Thought in Modern Civilization', *Notices of the Proceedings at Meetings of the Members of the Royal Institution* 5 (1867): 533.
[57] Tylor, *Primitive Culture*, 1.
[58] Engel, *Ancient Nations*, v.
[59] Tylor, *Primitive Culture*, 31.
[60] Engel, *Ancient Nations*, 348.

be accurately indicated by means of our musical notation. Some additional explanation is therefore required with the notation. In writing down the popular tunes of foreign countries on hearing them sung or played by the natives, no attempt should be made to rectify any thing which may appear incorrect to the European ear. The more faithfully the apparent defects are preserved, the more valuable is the notation. Collections of popular tunes (with the words of the airs) are very desirable. Likewise drawings of musical instruments, with explanations respecting the constructions, dimensions, capabilities, and employment of the instruments represented.[61]

Engel's contribution to *Notes and Queries*, and his insistence on faithful transcription, brings to a conceptual head a Tylorian programme of musical survivals distinguishing culture (and its objects) from civilization (and its values). 'Survivals' problematize the relationship of culture and civilization. However, this is especially true in regard to music of the Hebrews because the vestigial nature of Hebrew culture forms no evolutionary function in the process of cultural modification towards civilization. That Tylor separates culture from civilization is strikingly obvious in the title of *Primitive Culture*; as George Stocking notes:

> [The] very idea is a contradiction in terms. To argue that culture actually existed among all men, in however 'crude' or 'primitive' a form, may be viewed as a major step toward the anthropological concept, especially insofar as it focused anthropological attention on manifestations of culture which on account of their 'crudity' were below the level of conscious cultivation where 'civilized' culture was to be found. Furthermore, the evolutionary approach contained at least the germ of an idea of cultural plurality.[62]

Yet paradoxically both Tylor and Engel continue subscribing to a belief in a Great Chain of Being unimpeded by historical atavisms (i.e. survivals): if Tylor saw 'cultural perfection only at the top of an endless evolutionary ladder, he was on the whole sure that each step up that ladder advanced us toward perfection. The cultural inferiority of those on lower rungs he never seriously doubted . . . European civilization was in this sense the goal of all cultural development'.[63] For Tylor and Engel, the goal of all cultural development may

---

[61] Carl Engel, 'Music', in *Notes and Queries on Anthropology, for the Use of Travellers and Residents in Uncivilized Lands. Drawn up by a Committee Appointed by the British Association for the Advancement of Science* (London: Edward Stanford, 1874), 110.

[62] George W. Stocking, Jr., 'Matthew Arnold, E. B. Tylor, and the Uses of Invention', *American Anthropologist*, New Series 65, no. 4 (1963): 794.

[63] Ibid., 79.

be the same, but according to Tylor, survivals have no ostensible goal other than perhaps their own inexplicable preservation; unlike their Darwinian evolutionary counterparts they are in many respects the truly *un*fittest non-Darwinian survivors.[64]

Conclusion

Is the music of the most ancient Hebrews an unfittest survivor? And what about other unfittest survivors, like folksong? Non-Darwinians would exploit the generic confusion between ancient and folk. Here, for example, is Engel struggling to explain primitive gradations in pitch:

> it must not be supposed that each interval is distinctly intoned: on the contrary, in the transition from one interval to another, all the intermediate intervals are slightly touched in a way somewhat similar to a violinist drawing his finger rapidly over the strong from one note to another to connect them; and [...] the intervals themselves are seldom clearly defined.[65]

And here is Spencer selectively paraphrasing Parry (*The Art of Music*, 1893; later retitled *The Evolution of the Art of Music*, 1896) selectively paraphrasing Engel:

> In those examples with which Sir Hubert Parry commences his chapter on 'Folk-Music', we have vocal utterances little above the howls and groans in which inarticulate feeling expresses itself. There is but an imperfect differentiation of the tones into notes properly so called. So that we see well exemplified that indefiniteness which characterizes incipient evolution in general; and already we have seen that indefiniteness continues to characterize the partially-differentiated tones of savage chants and songs.[66]

When it comes to ancient music, however – to the most ancient Assyrians and Hebrews – Engel is forced to acknowledge the attainment of an ancient historical pinnacle within an ancient historical pinnacle within a modern pinnacle – a Great Chain (Assyrians) within a Great Chain (Egyptians) within another Great Chain (Hebrews) of Being: there are nations, he proposes, 'which have not brought the cultivation of music to so high a degree of development as it

---

[64] George Stocking, *Race, Culture, and Evolution: Essays in the History of Anthropology* (Chicago: University of Chicago Press, 1968), 97.
[65] Engel, *Ancient Nations*, 20.
[66] Herbert Spencer, *Facts and Comments* (London: Williams and Norgate, 1902), 50.

has attained with us'.⁶⁷ And of course Engel is not alone: 'The educated world of Europe and America', Tylor suggests, 'practically settles a standard by simply placing its own nations at one end of the social series and savage tribes at the other, arranging the rest of mankind between these limits according as they correspond more closely to savage or to cultured life'.⁶⁸

Does this view make Engel a card-carrying non-Darwinian? Probably – almost certainly – not. The fact is that there was no such thing as a card-carrying non-Darwinian because the non-Darwinian revolution was an infinitely malleable broad church; in its ideological diversity it was the Anglican church of Victorian science. And like the church it promulgated a programme of redemption by resuscitating and spiritually 'saving' primitive and ancient cultures from their heathen ways; it is the Victorian anthropologist's burden. So how should Engel's work be remembered, if so ideologically layered? In an age of rampant prejudice, Engel was a stepping stone towards cultural equality, wrestling free from regressive anthropological straightjackets of the time. And although he would eventually be superseded, as Darwinian anthropological models proved their superior fitness, he initiated changes in scientific objectivity which would have considerable longevity in ethnomusicology and music history, especially in the pioneering ethnomusicological work of Charles Samuel Myers (1873–1946). Today Engel is largely forgotten, apart from neo-Marxist second folksong revivalists eager to criticize his ideological part in fashioning Cecil Sharp's high-minded, unreconstructedly bourgeois attitude towards his peasant informants.⁶⁹ But this is to misunderstand Engel (and Sharp's) agenda and to misread history for manifestly current ideological purposes. Read in his own time, by the standards of his day, Engel would have seemed a paragon of balanced musicological virtue, trampling on historical and contemporary injustices without upsetting the anthropological applecart. And perhaps this is how the *non-Darwinian revolution* should be remembered more broadly – as having your evolutionary cake and eating it too. But then this is the timeless paradox of scientific objectivity, whether Victorian, ancient or modern: different times produce different truths veiled as fact, and in the history of ancient music history, Engel is among the first to tell us so.

---

⁶⁷ Engel, *Ancient Nations*, 108.
⁶⁸ Tylor, *Primitive Culture*, 26.
⁶⁹ See, for example, Christopher James Bearman, 'The English Folk Music Movement 1898–1914' (PhD diss. University of Hull, 2001); Georgina Boyes, *The Imagined Village: Culture, Ideology and the English Folk Revival* (Manchester: Manchester University Press, 1993); David Harker, *Fakesong: The Manufacture of British 'Folksong': 1700 to the Present Day* (Milton Keynes: Open University Press, 1985) and A. L. Lloyd, *Folk Song in England* (London: Panther Arts, 1967).

Bibliography

Primary Works

The Baptist Hymnal: A Collection of Hymns and Spiritual Songs (London: Marlborough, 1879)

I. Braham, I. Nathan, and Lord Byron, *A Selection of Hebrew Melodies: Ancient and Modern* (London: I. Nathan, 1815)

Rabbi Francis L. Cohen and David M. Davis, *The Voice of Prayer and Praise: A Handbook of Synagogue Music for Congregational Singing* (1899; London: Office of the United Synagogue, 1933)

Josiah Conder (ed.), *The Congregational Hymn Book: A Supplement to Dr. Watt's Psalms and Hymns*. Revised Edition (1836; London: Jackson and Walford, 1844)

John Curwen, *Singing for Schools and Congregations: A Course of Instruction in Vocal Music* (London: Thomas Ward & Co., 1843)

George Eliot, 'O May I Join the Choir Invisible', in *The Legend of Jubal and Other Poems* (Edinburgh and London: Blackwood, 1874): 240–2

―――, *Daniel Deronda* [1876], ed. Graham Handley, with an introduction by K. M. Newton (Oxford: Oxford University Press, 2014)

Carl Engel, *The Music of the Most Ancient Nations* (London: John Murray, 1864)

―――, 'Music', in *Notes and Queries on Anthropology, for the Use of Travellers and Residents in Uncivilized Lands. Drawn up by a Committee appointed by the British Association for the Advancement of Science* (London: Edward Stanford, 1874)

W. H. Havergal, *A History of the Old Hundredth Psalm Tune, with Specimens* (New York: Mason Brothers, 1854)

Reginald Heber, *Hymns, Written and Adapted to the Weekly Church Service of the Year*, ed. Amelia Heber (London: John Murray, 1827)

―――, *Palestine, and Other Poems* (Philadelphia: Carey, Lea and Carey, 1828)

George Hogarth, *Musical History, Biography, and Criticism: Being a General Survey of Music, from the Earliest Period to the Present Time* (London: John W. Parker, 1835)

Enoch Hutchinson, *Music of the Bible, or Explanatory Notes Upon Those Passages in the Sacred Scriptures Which Relate to Music* (Boston: Gould and Lincoln, 1864)

Rudyard Kipling, 'The Man Who Would be King', in *The Phantom Rickshaw and Other Tales* (Allahabad: A.H. Wheeler, 1890): 70–114

Joseph Mainzer, *Singing for the Million: A Practical Course of Musical Instruction* (London: The Author, 1842)

James Martineau, *Hymns for the Christian Church and Home* (London: Longman, Brown, Green, Longmans and Roberts, 1859)

James Plumptre, *A Collection of Songs Moral, Sentimental, Instructive, and Amusing* (London: F.C. & J. Rivington, n.d.)

Ira D. Sankey, James McGranahan, and Geo. C. Stebbins, *Sacred Songs: Compiled and Arranged for Use in Gospel Meetings, Sunday Schools, Prayer Meetings, and Other Religious Services* (New York: Biglow and Main, 1873)

John Stainer, *The Music of the Bible, with an Account of the Development of Modern Musical Instruments* (London: Novello, Ewer & Co., 1879)

W. T. Stead, *Hymns That Have Helped* (New York: Doubleday, 1904)

Secondary Works

Chester Alwes, 'Choral Music in the Culture of the Nineteenth Century', in *The Cambridge Companion to Choral Music*, ed. André de Quadros (Cambridge: Cambridge University Press, 2012): 27–42

Misty G. Anderson, *Imagining Methodism in Eighteenth-Century Britain: Enthusiasm, Belief & the Borders of the Self* (Baltimore: Johns Hopkins University Press, 2012)

Thomas L. Ashton, *Byron's Hebrew Melodies* (London: Routledge & Kegan Paul, 1972)

Gareth Atkins, Shinjini Das, and Brian H. Murray (eds.), *Chosen Peoples: The Bible, Race and Empire in the Long Nineteenth Century* (Manchester: Manchester University Press, 2020)

Peter Bailey, *Leisure and Class in Victorian England: Rational Recreation and the Contest for Control, 1830–1885* (London: Methuen, 1987)

Jeremy Hugh Baron, 'Byron's Passovers and Nathan's Melodies', *Judaism* 51 (2002): 19–29

David W. Bebbington, *Evangelicalism in Modern Britain: A History from the 1730s to the 1980s* (London: Routledge, 1989)

———, *The Dominance of Evangelicalism: The Age of Spurgeon and Moody* (Leicester: Inter-Varsity Press, 2005)

John Betjeman, *Sweet Songs of Zion: Selected Radio Talks*, ed. Stephen Grimes (London: Hodder and Stoughton, 2007)

Kirstie Blair, *Form and Faith in Victorian Poetry and Religion* (Oxford: Oxford University Press, 2012)

Tim Blanning, *The Triumph of Music: Composers, Musicians and their Audiences, 1700 to Present* (London: Penguin, 2009)

Philip V. Bohlman, *Jewish Music and Modernity* (Oxford: Oxford University Press, 2008)

Mark Evan Bonds, *Absolute Music: The History of an Idea* (New York: Oxford University Press, 2014)

Kate Bowan and Paul Pickering, *Sounds of Liberty: Music, Radicalism and Reform in the Anglophone World, 1790–1914* (Manchester: Manchester University Press, 2017)

Ian Bradley, *Abide with Me: The World of Victorian Hymns* (London: SCM Press, 1997)

———, *Lost Chords and Christian Soldiers: The Sacred Music of Sir Arthur Sullivan* (London: SCM Press, 2013)

Callum Brown, *The Death of Christian Britain: Understanding Secularization, 1800–2000* (London: Routledge, 2001)

Anna Bull, *Class, Control, & Classical Music* (New York: Oxford University Press, 2019)

Daniel K. L. Chua, *Absolute Music and the Construction of Meaning* (Cambridge: Cambridge University Press, 1999)

Alisa Clapp-Itnyre, *British Hymn Books for Children, 1800–1900: Re-tuning the History of Childhood* (Farnham: Ashgate, 2016)

Martin V. Clarke (ed.), *Music and Theology in Nineteenth-Century Britain* (Farnham: Ashgate, 2012)

Paul Collins (ed.), *Renewal and Resistance: Catholic Church Music from the 1850s to Vatican II* (Oxford: Peter Lang, 2010)

Sarah Collins (ed.), *Music and Victorian Liberalism: Composing the Liberal Subject* (Cambridge: Cambridge University Press, 2019)

David Conway, *Jewry in Music: Entry to the Profession from the Enlightenment to Richard Wagner* (Cambridge: Cambridge University Press, 2011)

Delia da Sousa Correa, *George Eliot, Music and Victorian Culture* (Basingstoke: Palgrave Macmillan, 2003)

Carl Dahlhaus, trans. Roger Lustig, *The Idea of Absolute Music* (Chicago: University of Chicago Press, 1989)

Kieran Daly, *Catholic Church Music in Ireland 1878–1903: The Cecilian Reform Movement* (Dublin: Four Courts, 1995)

Kate Darian-Smith, Stuart Macintyre, and Patricia Grimshaw (eds.), *Britishness Abroad: Transnational Movements and Imperial Cultures* (Melbourne: Melbourne University Press, 2007)

James Q. Davies, '*Elijah*'s Nature', *19th-Century Music* 45.1 (2021): 49–64

Susan Drain, *The Anglican Church in Nineteenth-Century Britain: Hymns Ancient and Modern (1860–1875)* (Lewiston: Edwin Mellen, 1989)

J. Cheryl Exum, *Retellings: The Bible in Literature, Music, Art and Film: Reprinted from Biblical Interpretation* (Leiden: Brill, 2007)

Tina Frühauf, 'The Reform of Synagogue Music in the Nineteenth Century', in *The Cambridge Companion to Jewish Music*, ed. Joshua S. Walden (Cambridge: Cambridge University Press, 2015): 187–200

Vic Gammon, 'Problems in the Performance and Historiography of English Popular Church Music', *Radical Musicology* 1 (2006): n.p.

Lydia Goehr, *The Imaginary Museum of Musical Works: An Essay in the Philosophy of Music* (Oxford: Clarendon Press, 1992)

John M. Golby and A. W. Purdue, *The Civilisation of the Crowd: Popular Culture in England, 1750–1900* (London: Batsford, 1984)

Ruth HaCohen, *The Music Libel Against the Jews* (New Haven: Yale University Press, 2012)

Boyd Hilton, *The Age of Atonement: The Influence of Evangelicalism on Social and Economic Thought, 1785–1865* (Oxford: Clarendon Press, 1988)

Kate Horgan, *The Politics of Songs in Eighteenth-Century Britain, 1723–1795* (London: Pickering & Chatto, 2014)

Peter Horton and Bennett Zon (eds.), *Nineteenth-Century British Music Studies* (Farnham: Ashgate, 2003)

Abraham Zvi Idelsohn, *Jewish Music in Its Historical Development* (1929; New York: Schocken Books, 1972)

Monique Ingalls, Carolyn Landau, and Tom Wagner (eds.), *Christian Congregational Music: Performance, Identity and Experience* (Farnham: Ashgate, 2013)

Anders Jarlert (ed.), *Piety and Modernity. The Dynamics of Religious Reform in Northern Europe, 1780–1920* (Leuven: Leuven University Press, 2012)

Oskar Cox Jenesen, *The Ballad-Singer in Georgian and Victorian London* (Cambridge: Cambridge University Press, 2021)

David Kennerley, *Sounding Feminine: Women's Voices in British Musical Culture, 1780–1850* (Oxford: Oxford University Press, 2020)

Frances Knight, *Victorian Christianity at the Fin de Siècle: The Culture of English Religion in a Decadent Age* (London: I.B. Tauris, 2015)

Larry J. Kreitzer, '"The Son of God Goes Forth to War": Biblical Imagery in Rudyard Kipling's "The Man Who Would be King"', in *Borders, Boundaries and the Bible*, ed. Martin O'Kane (Sheffield: Sheffield University Press, 2002): 99–125

Charles LaPorte, *Victorian Poets and the Changing Bible* (Charlottesville: University of Virginia Press, 2011)

Timothy Larsen, *A People of One Book: The Bible and the Victorians* (Oxford: Oxford University Press, 2011)

Timothy Larsen and Michael Ledger-Lomas (eds.), *The Oxford History of Protestant Dissenting Traditions, Volume III: The Nineteenth Century* (Oxford: Oxford University Press, 2017)

Michael Ledger-Lomas and Scott Mandelbrote (eds.), *Dissent and the Bible in Britain, c. 1650–1950* (Oxford: Oxford University Press, 2013)

Alan Lomax, 'Song Structure and Social Structure', *Ethnology* 1.4 (1962): 425–51

Stephen A. Marini, *Sacred Song in America: Religion, Music, and Public Culture* (Champaign, IL: University of Illinois Press, 2003)

Nicholas Mathew, '"Achieved is the Glorious Work": *The Creation* and the Choral Work Concept', in *Engaging Haydn*, ed. Mary Hunter and Richard Will (Cambridge: Cambridge University Press, 2012)

Charles McGuire, 'Music and Morality: John Curwen's Tonic Sol-fa, the Temperance Movement, and the Oratorios of Edward Elgar', in *Chorus and Community*, ed. Karen Ahlquist (Urbana, IL: University of Illinois Press, 2006): 111–38

———, *Music and Victorian Philanthropy: The Tonic Sol-fa Movement* (Cambridge: Cambridge University Press, 2009)

Richard J. Mouw and Mark A. Noll (eds.), *Wonderful Words of Life: Hymns in American Protestant History and Theology* (Grand Rapids: Eerdmans, 2004)

Thomas E. Muir, *Roman Catholic Church Music in England, 1791–1914: A Handmaid of the Liturgy?* (Aldershot: Ashgate, 2008)

Michael Musgrave, *The Musical Life of the Crystal Palace* (Cambridge: Cambridge University Press, 1995)

——— (ed.), *George Grove: Music and Victorian Culture* (London: Palgrave Macmillan, 2003)

David W. Music and Paul Richardson (eds.), *'I Will Sing the Wondrous Story': A History of Baptist Hymnody in North America* (Macon: Mercer University Press, 2008)

Lynda Nead, *Victorian Babylon: People, Streets and Images in Nineteenth-Century London* (Yale: Yale University Press, 2000)

John Ogasapian and N. Lee Orr, *Music of the Gilded Age* (Westport, CT: Greenwood Press, 2007)

Grant Olwage, 'Singing in the Victorian World: Tonic Sol-fa and Discourses of Religion, Science and Empire in the Cape Colony', *Muziki: Journal of Music Research in Africa* 7.2 (2010): 192–215

M. Pauline Parker, 'The Hymn as a Literary Form', *Eighteenth-Century Studies* 8.4 (1975): 392–419

John M. Picker, *Victorian Soundscapes* (Oxford: Oxford University Press, 2003)

Stephen Prickett, *Origins of Narrative: The Romantic Appropriation of the Bible* (Cambridge: Cambridge University Press, 1996)

Bernarr Rainbow, *The Choral Revival in the Anglican Church, 1839–1872* (Oxford: Oxford University Press, 1970)

———, *John Curwen: A Short Critical Biography* (Sevenoaks: Novello, 1980)

Jeffrey Richards, *Imperialism and Music: Britain, 1876–1953* (Manchester: Manchester University Press, 2001)

Isabel Rivers and David Wykes (eds.), *Dissenting Praise: Religious Dissent and the Hymn in England and Wales* (Oxford: Oxford University Press, 2011)

Paul Rodmell (ed.), *Music and Institutions in Nineteenth-Century Britain* (Farnham: Ashgate, 2012)

Deborah Rohr, *The Careers of British Musicians, 1750–1850: A Profession of Artisans* (Cambridge: Cambridge University Press, 2001)

Doreen Rosman, *The Evolution of English Churches, 1500–2000* (Cambridge: Cambridge University Press, 2003)

Leigh Eric Schmidt, *Hearing Things: Religion, Illusion, and the American Enlightenment* (Cambridge, MA: Harvard University Press, 2000)

Howard E. Smither, *A History of the Oratorio, Volume 4: The Oratorio in the Nineteenth and Twentieth Centuries* (Chapel Hill: University of North Carolina Press, 2000)

Ruth A. Solie, *Music in Other Words* (Berkeley and Los Angeles: University of California Press, 2004)

Jane Southcott, *Sarah Anna Glover: Nineteenth-Century Music Education Pioneer* (Lanham, MD: Lexington Books, 2020)

Sheila A. Spector, 'The Liturgical Context of the Byron-Nathan "Hebrew Melodies"', *Studies in Romanticism* 47.3 (2008): 393–412

Jon Michael Spencer, *Black Hymnody: A Hymnological History of the African-American Church* (Knoxville: University of Tennessee Press, 1992)

Brian Stanley, *The Bible and the Flag: Protestant Missions and British Imperialism in the Nineteenth and Twentieth Centuries* (Leicester: Apollos, 1990)

W. H. Stevenson, 'The Sound of "Holy Thursday"', *Blake/An Illustrated Quarterly* 36.4 (2003): 137–40

Charles Taylor, *A Secular Age* (Cambridge, MA: Harvard University Press, 2007)

Nicholas Temperley, *Music of the English Parish Church*, 2 vols (Cambridge: Cambridge University Press, 1993)

Wiebke Thormählen, 'From Dissent to Community: The Sacred Harmonic Society and Amateur Choral Singing in London', in *London Voices, 1820–1840: Vocal Performers, Practices, Histories*, ed. Roger Parker and Susan Rutherford (Chicago: Chicago University Press, 2019): 159–78

Martha S. Vogeler, 'The Choir Invisible: The Poetics of Humanist Piety', in *George Eliot: A Centenary Tribute*, ed. Gordon S. Haight and Rosemary T. VanArsdel (London: Macmillan, 1982): 64–81

J. R. Watson, *The English Hymn: A Critical and Historical Study* (Oxford: Clarendon Press, 1997)

———, 'Ancient or Modern, "Ancient and Modern": The Victorian Hymn and the Nineteenth Century', *The Yearbook of English Studies* 36.2 (2006): 1–16

Michael R. Watts, *The Dissenters, Volume II: The Expansion of Evangelical Nonconformity* (Oxford: Clarendon Press, 1995)

William Weber, *Music and the Middle Class: The Social Structure of Concert Life in London, Paris and Vienna between 1830 and 1848* (Aldershot: Ashgate, 2004; first pub. 1975)

Phyllis Weliver (ed.), *The Figure of Music in Nineteenth-Century British Poetry* (Aldershot: Ashgate, 2005)

William Whyte, *Unlocking The Church: The Lost Secrets of Victorian Sacred Space* (Oxford: Oxford University Press, 2017)

John Wolffe, *God and Greater Britain: Religion and National Life in Britain and Ireland, 1843-1945* (London: Routledge, 1994)

———, '"Praise to the Holiest in the Height": Hymns and Church Music', *Religion in Victorian Britain*, vol. 5, ed. John Wolffe (Manchester: Manchester University Press, 1997): 59–99

Bennett Zon, *The English Plainchant Revival* (Oxford: Oxford University Press, 1999)

———, *Representing Non-Western Music in Nineteenth-Century Britain* (Rochester NY: University of Rochester Press, 2007)

——— (ed.), *Music and Performance Culture in Nineteenth-Century Britain* (London: Ashgate, 2012)

———, 'The "non-Darwinian" Revolution and the Great Chain of Musical Being', in *Evolution and Victorian Culture*, ed. Bernard Lightman and Bennett Zon (Cambridge: Cambridge University Press, 2014): 196–226

Index

Page numbers followed with "n" refer to footnotes.

Adler, Hermann   102, 112
Advent Songs: A Revision of Old Hymns to Meet Modern Needs (Patten)   91–2
Åhmansson, Josephine   121–2, 127
Ahnfelt, Oscar   128
'All Saints New' (Cutler)   86
Amaculo Ase Lovedale (Bokwe)   189
Anderson, Misty   6
Anglican (Church of England)   4, 7–9, 14, 25–6, 36, 41, 50, 54, 66, 73–8, 80, 82–4, 91, 94, 104, 110, 122, 135–6, 156, 164–7, 172, 187, 194. *See also* Anglo-Catholics; evangelicalism; Protestantism
   High-Church   25, 75, 77, 159, 166, 171
Anglo-Catholics   83, 84, 86, 166–8
Anglo-Jewish   10, 102–3, 108, 111, 114
anthems   9, 20, 41, 52, 54, 62, 63, 66, 88
anthropology   217–19, 221
anti-recapitulationism   205, 206
antisemitism   12, 18, 201–21. *See also* racism
Antisemitism: A Very Short Introduction (Beller)   214
Applegate, Celia   149
arias   17, 119, 123 n.31. *See also* opera
Armstrong, Isobel   17
Arne, Thomas   40–1
Arnold, Matthew   20, 212–13, 216
Assyrians   201, 203, 210–11, 217, 220
At Home Aboard (Roby)   188–9, 191–2
Attwater, Jane   5–6

Baer, Ernst von   202, 205, 206
ballad metre   32, 36, 80, 83
ballads   2–3, 6, 10, 12, 24, 29–47
Banfield, Stephen   63
Baptists   5, 85, 141

Bebbington, David   127, 128 n.51, 176 n.8
Beller, Steven   214
Benjamin, Walter   55–6
Berlioz, Hector   7
Betjeman, John   89, 164–5
Bezer, John James   44–5
biblical criticism   1, 3, 20
Bickersteth, Edward   84
Birch-Pfeiffer, Charlotte   123, 124
Blair, Kirstie   3, 77
Blake, William   7–8
Blessed Sacrament   155, 166
Bodley, George Frederick   155, 158, 161–3, 166, 167, 171
Bohlman, Philip   96, 113
Bowler, Peter   202, 203
Brady, Nicholas   12, 13, 50, 77
Brodie, Israel   112
Browning, Robert   91
Bulman, Joan   122
Burney, Charles   36
Butterfield, William   160
Byron, Lord George Gordon   9–14

Calvinism   6, 14–16, 49, 68, 140
Carlyle, Thomas   73, 144, 145
carols   37–8, 42
carol sheet   37
Catholicism   73–4, 80, 83–4, 165. *See also* Anglo-Catholics
   Roman Catholicism   4–5, 9, 10, 84, 85
Chamberlain, Houston Stewart   214, 216
Childe, C. F.   88
choirs   95–7, 109
   choral composition of Lewandowski   105–7, 113
   in Industrial Revolution age   101–4
   legacy of choral modernity   112–14

mixed-voice   110–12
Schir Zion (The Song of Zion, Sulzer)   104
synagogue choir   96–7, 99, 100, 103–5, 110, 112
tonic sol-fa notation   102–4
women in   110–12
choral. *See also* anthems; congregational singing; hymns
   music   101–2, 104, 114, 149
   singing   102, 109, 143, 160
   societies   135, 136, 138, 140–9, 151–3
Chorley, Henry   124
Chor-shuln (choral synagogues)   104
Christ (Jesus)   15, 64, 73, 76, 80–2, 84, 87, 90, 93, 127, 155–7, 165–6, 169–72, 214
Christ and His Soldiers (1878, Farmer)   87
Christian Psalmody (1834, Bickersteth)   84
Chrysal: Or, The Adventures of a Guinea (Johnstone)   31, 43
Church Missionary Society   63, 65 n.53, 88
Clarke, Martin   22–3
Cobbett, William   42
Cohen, Francis Lyon   23 n.75, 102
Comper, John Ninian   155–60, 162–72
Conder, Josiah   13, 84
Congregational Hymn Book (Conder)   84
congregational singing   5, 8–9, 23, 38, 40, 83, 109, 152, 160, 180, 183–4. *See also* choirs; choral; hymns
'Congregational Singing' (Mainzer)   183
Cook, Geoffrey   79
Cooper, Thomas   38–40
Cotterill, Thomas   9
The Creation (Haydn)   144, 153
Crystal Palace Handel Festival   133–5, 149, 153
Cunningham, Valentine   138
Curwen, John   102, 175–6, 178, 181, 184–6, 188, 194–9
Curwen, Spencer   181, 182, 185, 187, 188, 193, 194, 197, 198
Curwen Press   182, 184, 187
Cutler, Henry Stephen   86

Dale, Thomas Pelham   83–4
Daniel Deronda (Eliot)   16–19
Darwin, Charles. *See also* non-Darwinian
   evolution   203–5, 211–12
   natural selection   204
Davidson, Peter   59
Davidson, Hilary   161
Davies, Andrew   5
Davies, Llewellyn   20
Davis, David M.   102–3
Daye, John   83
Der Freischütz (Weber)   119
Dibdin, Charles the Elder   35, 41–2, 50, 53
Dickens, Charles   53, 137–8
Dissent   5, 7–9, 14–16, 24–6, 32, 37, 41, 76, 82, 135–8, 151, 152. *See also* Nonconformists; Protestantism; *individual denominations*
Dolin, Tim   16
Drain, Susan   75
Dyce, William   159–60

Edghill, John Cox   87
Education Act (1870)   186, 186 n.50, 187–8
Edwards, David   71–2
Eichwald, Edward   204–5
Elijah (Mendelssohn)   123 n.31, 131, 144 n.33, 149, 153
Eliot, George   14–20
emancipation, Jewish   96–8, 104, 113
Engel, Carl   201–5, 209, 217, 220–1
   antisemitism   214–16
   ethnomusicology   205
   non-Darwinian
      Hebrew music   210–16
      music of the most ancient nations   206–10
      theory of national song   207
      Tylorian survivals and   218–19
English Baptist Hymnal (1876)   85
Enlightenment
   Jewish   14, 97, 113
   secular European   97–8, 114, 204
ethnography   218
ethnomusicology   1, 26, 42, 201, 203, 205, 213, 218, 221

evangelicalism 13–16, 24, 25, 64, 74–7, 82–5, 102, 118–19, 121, 122, 125–8, 130, 131, 139–40, 142, 146, 152, 176–8, 191–3
evolution 20, 22, 26, 201–21. *See also* Darwin, Charles
Ewing, Juliana Horatia 87
Exeter Change 138–9
Exeter Hall 118, 138–49, 151–3, 175, 176, 178–9, 183, 198–9
Exeter Hall: A Theological Romance (McDonnell) 139
Exum, J. Cheryl 5

The Fall of Babylon (Spohr) 148
Farmer, John 87
Feiner, Shmuel 97
Feuerbach, Ludwig 16
Forster, Rumsey 120
Freedman, Jonathan 212
Frühauf, Tina 106, 107

Gandhi, Mohandas Karamchand 90
Gans, Eric 201
Garner, Thomas 161–3, 167
Gilbert, W. S. 68, 72
Glover, Sarah 102, 179 n.18, 181, 196 n.74
Golding, Rosemary 179
Goldschmidt, Otto 118, 129, 131
Gopinath, Sumanth 55–7
Gothic Revival organ cases
    Comper, John Ninian 155–9, 163–73
    St Sepulchre Chapel at St Mary Magdalene 155–7, 163–73
    Sutton, Frederick Heathcote 155, 160–3, 171, 172
Great Chain of Being 204–5, 211, 219, 220
Great Chain of Musical Being 206, 208, 211
Green, Rev. C. 66–7
Greenblatt, Stephen 61
Gregory the Great 171
Grote, Harriet 123, 125, 128
Grove, George 193, 194, 215
Günther, Julius 122, 124, 125
Gurney, Alfred 167

Haddon Hall (1892, Sullivan) 67
Haeckel, Ernst 202, 205
Handel, George Frideric 5–6, 11, 101, 133–5, 142–5, 147–8, 150–3, 188, 195
Handel Commemoration Festival of 1834 150–1
Harris, Claudius 118, 124–6, 131
Haweis, Hugh Reginald 180
Hawkins, John 209
Haydn, Joseph 7, 101, 144, 147, 151
hazzan 96, 98–100, 105–7, 112–13
Heber, Amelia 78, 80
Heber, Reginald
    death of 78–9, 82
    hymns 75–8, 80–1, 86–9
    legacy of 82–6, 90–4
    martyrdom 78–82
Heber's Hymns (Heber) 78
Heber's Hymns, Illustrated (Heber) 83
Hebraism 212
Hebrew. *See also* Judaism
    Bible 10–13, 19, 71, 95, 97, 105, 113, 169
    music 9–14, 18, 110–16, 95–115, 187, 201–3, 210–20
Hebrew Melodies (1815, Nathan) 9–14
    reviews and criticism 12–14
Hedstrom, Olof Gustaf 129, 130 n.58, 131
Hegel, Friedrich 213
Heine, Heinrich 213
Hellenism 212–13
Hill, Rowland 31–2, 40
Hoffmann, E. T. A. 21
Hogarth, George 151
Holland, Henry Scott 121–3, 125, 130
Hopkins, John 13, 32, 36, 83
Horgan, Kate 32, 41
Hosokawa, Shuhei 56–7
Howley, William 76–7
Hullah's system of music 195
Hutchinson, Enoch 2
hymns 1, 6–9, 13, 18, 20, 23–6, 33, 35–6, 38–45, 49–52, 54, 63–8, 74, 99, 102, 104, 109, 114, 128, 131, 152, 156, 163, 169, 171, 175–8, 180, 181, 183, 184, 186, 188–90,

194, 199. *See also* choirs; choral;
    congregational singing
Heber, Reginald   75–82, 86–94
    legacy of   82–6, 91
    High-Church   75–8
Hymns Ancient and Modern
    (Monk)   82, 83

Idelsohn, Abraham Zvi   99
Industrial Revolution, choirs in   101–4
instrumental music   20–1, 96, 104–10,
    113, 133 n.2, 149, 209–10
*An Introduction to the Study of National
    Music* (Engel)   215
Israel in Egypt (Handel)   133–4, 150

Jacobson, Israel   99–100
Jerrold, Douglas   37, 43
Jesus   15, 64, 73, 76, 80–2, 84, 87, 90, 93,
    127, 155–7, 165–6, 169–72, 214
John Flaxman, R. A.   29–30
Johnstone, Charles   31, 43
Judaism   10–14, 16–18, 23, 25, 69, 95–115,
    131, 187, 201–2, 211–16, 218. *See
    also* antisemitism; Hebrew
    Anglo-Jewish culture   10, 102–3, 108,
        111, 114
    conversion to Christianity   98
    emancipation   96, 98, 104, 113
    Enlightenment (*Haskalah*)   97, 113
    modernity   105–10
    orthodox   98, 103, 111–12
    reform   97–101, 103–5, 109–14

Kassabian, Anahid   55
Keble, John   3, 77, 78
Key, Emil   128
Kipling, Rudyard   92–4
Koch, Frances von   125, 128
Kol Rinnah u-T'fillah (1871,
    Lewandowski)   99, 106
Kol Rinnah V'Todah (The Voice of
    Prayer and Praise, Cohen and
    Davis)   102–3, 106

Langan, Celeste   10
Larsen, Timothy   3
Leavis, F. R.   16

Leneman, Helen   5
Lewandowski, Louis   95, 98, 99, 105–6, 113
Lind, Jenny   17, 117–32
    commitment to charity   126–7
    evangelicalism   121, 128, 130, 131
    involvement with the Pietist
        revival   127–8
    Methodism   118, 122, 123, 125–9, 131
    religious convictions   119, 121, 125, 130
    retirement   117–18, 121, 124
    tour of the United States   128–30
Livingstone, David   91
Lomax, Alan   42
London Missionary Society   41, 90, 91,
    139, 181
Love, David   46
Lumley, Benjamin   117–18, 119 n.8

McGuire, Charles   179, 181
Mackarness, John Fielder   83
Magdalene, Mary   169–71
Magee, John   46
Mah Tovu (Lewandowski)   95, 97,
    103, 106–7
Mainzer, Joseph   183–4
Manchester Reform Synagogue   108
Mandler, Peter   6
'The Man who would be King'
    (Kipling)   92–3
Marks, David Woolf   108
Marsden, Samuel   63–5
Marshall, Kimberley   158–9
martyrdom   73–4, 77–84, 87, 88, 91–4
maskilim   97
Mee, Jon   8
Mendelssohn, Felix   36, 54, 105–6, 122,
    123 n.31, 131, 149, 215–16
Messiah (Handel)   5–6, 117, 123 n.31,
    133, 134, 147, 153, 195
Methodism   6, 8, 9, 39, 40, 42, 46, 68, 85,
    118, 121–3, 125–9, 131, 140
Mills, John   68–72
Milman, Henry Hart   75, 77, 78, 82
missionaries   6, 24–6, 60, 63–6, 69, 72,
    79–80, 88–91, 93–4, 146, 177–8,
    188–9, 198
    Church Missionary Society   63,
        65 n.53, 88

London Missionary Society   41, 90, 91, 139, 181
mixed-voice choirs   110–12
mobile music   55–7
mobility   56, 57, 61
Mombach, Julius (Israel)   114
Monk, William Henry   82
Montgomery, James   9
Moore, Thomas   10
Moravians   6, 8, 85, 141
More, Hannah   33, 34
Morning Chronicle   136, 150
Morning Herald   143–4
Mozart, Wolfgang Amadeus   117–18, 121, 123, 147, 188, 189
Muir, Thomas   4
Murray, John   78, 203
The Musical Herald   193
Musical History (1835, Hogarth)   151
musical survivals   218–20
Musical Times   51, 134, 182, 183 n.40
Musical World   53, 143, 146, 151
musica mobilis, defined   56–7
The Music of the Most Ancient Nations (Engel)   201–3
   non-Darwinism   206–10
      Hebrews   210–16
      Tylorian survivals   217–20

Nathan, Isaac   10–13
nationalism   9, 10
national song   10, 14. *See also* anthems
   Engel's theory of   201, 207, 209, 215
natural selection   204. *See also* evolution; Darwin, Charles
Newman, John Henry   9 n.26, 85
Nonconformists   5, 7, 14–16, 44, 74, 76, 84–5, 104, 135, 152, 175–9, 181, 184, 188, 194, 199. *See also* Dissent; Protestantism; *individual denominations*
non-Darwinian   220–1
   evolutionism   202–6
   music of the most ancient
      Hebrew   210–16
      nations   206–10
   revolution   202, 211, 221

Notes and Queries on Anthropology, for the Use of Travellers and Residents in Uncivilized Lands (Engel)   201, 218, 219

Oakeley, Frederick   4, 159
'Old 81st'   82–3, 86
Old Hundredth   32, 36, 49–55, 57–8, 60–8, 71–2
Oliphant, Margaret   138
Olwage, Grant   179, 193
On the Origin of Species (Darwin)   203–4
opera   1, 5, 6, 15, 21, 25, 41, 57, 62, 67–8, 72, 117–32, 135, 146–7, 151–2, 188, 191–3. *See also* arias; oratorio
oratorio   6, 14, 25, 26, 87, 101, 102, 119, 123–4, 131–3, 136, 142, 144, 146–50, 152, 207
organ (music)   106–9
organ cases, Gothic Revival
   Comper, John Ninian   155–9, 163–73
   St Sepulchre Chapel at St Mary Magdalene   155–7, 163–73
'The Origin and Function of Music' (Spencer)   206
Orthodox Judaism   98, 103, 111–12

Parish Choir   160
Parry, C. Hubert H.   54, 207, 211, 220
Parry, William Edward   62, 63
Partridge, S. W.   80
Pater, Walter   21, 168–9
Patten, Simon Nelson   91–2
Pearsall, Ronald   150
Pheasant, William   187
plainsong   4, 155, 159–60, 163–4, 169–71, 211
Plumptre, James   31, 33–5
polyphony   4, 113
portability   55, 56
Presbyterian   50, 67
Primitive Culture (Tylor)   217, 219
Protestantism   5, 7, 16, 42–3, 51, 52, 73–4, 83, 84, 87, 91, 119, 152, 188. *See also* Dissent; Nonconformists; *individual denominations*

globalized   57–67
hymnody   188–90
Protestant martyrs   74, 80, 83
psalms   3, 6–10, 12–14, 18, 25, 31, 34–7, 40, 41, 76–7, 83, 86, 95, 97, 109, 113, 114, 125, 159, 140, 160, 202
   Old Hundredth   32, 36, 49–55, 57, 60–8, 71, 72
Pugin, A. W. N.   4, 161, 162, 165, 172

The Quiver   49, 53, 64, 65

race   1, 2, 10, 14, 19, 65, 74, 85, 196, 206, 210, 212, 216, 218
racism   23 n.75, 90. *See also* antisemitism
Rainbow, Bernarr   160, 179
recapitulationism   205
Reformation   74, 139, 156, 164, 169
Reform Judaism   97–114
Repeal of the Test and Corporation Acts (1828)   136–7, 151
The Requiem Mass: Translated into Tonic Sol-fa Notation (Mozart)   188, 189, 191
Richards, Jeffrey   87
Robinson, Thomas   79, 82
Roby, Arthur   192
Rockstro, W. S.   121–3, 125, 130
Roman Catholicism   4–5, 9, 10, 84, 85
Rosenius, Carl Olof   127–9
Rosman, Doreen   122
'Rule, Britannia' (Arne)   40–1

sacraments   155, 157, 165–6, 171
Sacred Harmonic Society   135, 136, 138, 140–9, 151–3
Sacred Songs (Sankey)   86
St Sepulchre Chapel at St Mary Magdalene   155–7, 163–73
Sala, George Augustus   39
Sankey, Ira   86, 176 n.8
Saxby, Mary   46
Schir Zion (The Song of Zion, Sulzer)   104
Schumann, Robert   215
Scott, Derek   54
Scott, George   127, 129
Scott, Walter   2–3, 11, 76–8

Senior, Nassau   121, 125
Shultz, Gladys   122
sight-singing   102, 133, 195, 198. *See also* tonic sol-fa
solfege   102, 181, 184, 189, 192, 195. *See also* tonic sol-fa
Solie, Ruth   18
Somervell, Arthur   180
Songs of Innocence and Experience (Blake)   7–8
'The Son of God goes forth to war' (Heber)   74, 80–2, 84–93
Southey, Robert   76, 79, 80
Spencer, Herbert   203, 206–10, 220
   Great Chain of Musical Being   206, 208
Spohr, Louis   147–9
staff notation   102, 103, 181–2, 182 n.34, 185, 187, 192–4
Stainer, John   187, 211, 216
Stanleys, Edward   121, 126
Stanyek, Jason   55–7
Stead, W. T.   74, 85, 90
Sternhold, Thomas   13, 32, 36, 83
Stocking, George   219
Stories of Famous Songs (Adair Fitz-Gerald)   67
Story of a Short Life (Ewing)   87
Sullivan, Arthur   67–8, 72
Sulzer, Salomon   98, 99, 104, 105
Supplement to the Congregational Hymn Book (1875)   85
Sutherland, Peter Cormack   58–63
Sutton, Frederick Heathcote   155, 158, 161–3, 171, 172
Symondson, Anthony   165
synagogue choir   95–7, 99, 100, 103–6, 109–15
Synthetic Philosophy (Spencer)   206

Tate, Nahum   12, 13, 50, 77
Temperley, Nicholas   6, 52
Thormählen, Wiebke   140
The Times   143, 145, 148, 152, 198
Todah W'Simrah (1876, Lewandowski)   106, 107
tonic sol-fa   102, 104, 175–9, 181, 183–6, 196. *See also* sight-singing; solfege
   accessibility   197

Association   175, 176, 178
Curwen, John   176, 184–6
Education Act (1870)   186, 186 n.50, 187–8
Grove Music Online article on   194
in *Kol Rinnah V'Todah*   102–3
movement   176–8, 178 n.15, 186, 188, 193, 194, 198, 199
musical institutions   198
notation   181–2, 184–5, 187, 188, 190, 191, 195
performance of Handel's *Messiah*   195
populist evangelism   199
publications   188–9
solfege   181, 184, 189, 192
staff notation   181–2, 182 n.34, 185, 187, 192–4
system   179, 179 n.18, 181, 182, 184–7, 195, 199
use in elementary schools   187–8
visual system of hand signs for children   184–5
Tonic Sol-fa College   198
Tonic Sol-fa Composition Club (1867)   197
The Tonic Sol-fa Method in the Church of England   187
Tonic Sol-fa School Song Wreath (1877, Macgavin)   188, 190
Tylor, E. B.   202, 217–21
'Tzaddik Katamar'   113

Unitarianism   15, 16, 85 n.47
Utopia, Limited; or, The Flowers of Progress (Sullivan)   68

Valéry, Paul   55–6
Verrinder, Charles Garland   110, 114
V'sham'ru prayer   113

Wagner, Richard   15, 17–18, 152
'The Walkman Effect' (Hosokawa)   56–7
Walsh, W. Pakenham   64–5
Watson, J. R.   23, 76, 77 n.17
Weber, Carl Maria von   41, 119–20
Weber, William   135, 136
Wesley, Charles   6, 76, 78, 82
Wesley, John   6
West London Synagogue   106, 108, 110
Whyman, Henry   129
Whyte, William   3–4
Williams, Henry   63
Williams, John   71
Williams, Peter   158
Wolffe, John   85
women in Reform choirs   110–12
The Work of the Church in the Army (Edghill)   87
Wright, David   102
Wylde, Henry   211

Young, Robert   212

www.ingramcontent.com/pod-product-compliance
Lightning Source LLC
Chambersburg PA
CBHW050326020526
44117CB00031B/1812